The Strengths Perspective in Social Work Practice

The Strengths Perspective in Social Work Practice

Second Edition

Edited by

Dennis Saleebey
University of Kansas

 LONGMAN

An imprint of Addison-Wesley Longman, Inc.

New York • Reading, Massachusetts • Menlo Park, California • Harlow, England
Don Mills, Ontario • Sydney • Mexico City • Madrid • Amsterdam

The Strengths Perspective in Social Work Practice, Second Edition

Longman, 10 Bank Street, White Plains, N.Y. 10606

Executive editor: Pamela A. Gordon
Associate editor: Hillary B. Henderson
Production editor: Linda Moser/Professional Book Center
Production supervisor: Edith Pullman
Cover design: Joseph DePinho
Compositor: Professional Book Center

Library of Congress Cataloging-in-Publication Data

The Strengths perspective in social work practice / edited by Dennis
   Saleebey.—2nd ed.
      p. cm.
  Includes bibliographical references and index.
  ISBN 0-8013-1745-2
    1. Social service—Psychological aspects. I. Saleebey, Dennis.
HV41.S827 1997
361.3'2'0973—dc20   96-25491
                                        CIP

1 2 3 4 5 6 7 8 9 10-MA-0099989796

To Ann, whose love is my strength, and to my children, Jennifer, David, John, and Meghan, who bring me increasing joy with each passing year.

In Memoriam: Bette A. Saleebey, Liane V. Davis

Their strengths live on in the lives of others.

Keep away from people who try to belittle your ambitions. Small people always do that, but the really great make you feel that you, too, can become great.
—*Mark Twain*

Sweet are the uses of adversity,
Which like the toad, ugly and venomous
Wears yet a precious jewel in his head . . .
—*William Shakespeare* (As You Like It)

Contents

PART II THE STRENGTHS APPROACH TO PRACTICE   37

PART III   USING THE STRENGTHS APPROACH WITH INDIVIDUALS 75

CHAPTER 9   HIDDEN TREASURES: UNLOCKING STRENGTHS IN THE PUBLIC SOCIAL SERVICES
Mary Bricker-Jenkins   **133**

CHAPTER 10   THE STRENGTHS PERSPECTIVE AND THE POLITICS OF CLIENTHOOD
Gary E. Holmes   **151**

Foreword

The mid-1990s have witnessed unprecedented attacks on human services, the social workers and other people who serve within them, and the clients who seek out their assistance. These salvos seem intellectually and spiritually detached from the human beings affected. It is dehumanizing to treat people infected with HIV, women and children on welfare, teenage parents, the elderly, and people with severe mental illness as "other" and to blame "them" for their plight. Oppressive and mean-spirited new policies coupled with reduced funding augur an era of challenge to humane social policy unprecedented since the Great Depression.

Within this dispiriting environment, the profession of social work continues to innovate with new ideas, methods, and perspectives. One of the most exciting of these may be the development of a strengths perspective and a strengths model of practice. This book is witness to the intellectual and practice energy devoted to this paradigm.

This book is also a celebration of the first decade of life of the strengths perspective. In just five years since the publication of the first edition of this volume, we have witnessed astounding developments. First, the strengths model, originally limited to work with people with severe and persistent mental illness has spread to work with the elderly in long-term care, emotionally disturbed youth and their families, employment assistance programs, people with substance abuse problems, protective services for adults, and even seen some initial forays into the field of corrections. Second, the strengths perspective is beginning to be applied in fields beyond direct practice including community organization and development, social administration, and policy analysis. The amount of scholarly activity around the strengths perspective is increasing rapidly and finding its way into course outlines and social work classes. Third, training manuals and curricula have been developed to teach strengths methods to practitioners working with welfare recipients, the elderly, and children and adults with severe mental illness. The first textbook on the strengths approach to case management is in preparation. Fourth, in the first six years of the strengths model, there were three published reports of research testing its efficacy in the field of mental health. In the last five years, there have been reports of research using experimental or quasi-experimental designs and some qualitative studies, all finding positive results in the lives of clients. An initial formulation of the theory of strengths has been developed. This theory-building has facilitated the integration of ideas, though not labeled strengths (for instance, empowerment, resilience, recovery, integration, community-building), that further enrich the perspective. Specificity and refinement of methods is proceeding.

This book, then, is a next step in theory-building, conceptualization, and practice of the strengths perspective. As you will see, the chapters in this volume attest to the promise of new possibilities. The strengths perspective allows us to see options where once we only saw constraints; wellness where we found sickness; and achievements where we perceived failure. New vistas for helping are uncovered once we break away from the current "conspiracy of understanding" centered on deficits. The essays in this book make a significant contribution to these new possibilities.

Charles A. Rapp, Ph.D.
Associate Dean and Professor
School of Social Welfare, University of Kansas

Preface

The interest in and work on the strengths approach to case management continues to flourish at the University of Kansas School of Social Welfare. The research, curriculum development, training, consultation, and practice done by faculty, staff, and doctoral students have all contributed to the continuing articulation of the strengths perspective in terms of theory, program, and practice. In this second edition of *The Strengths Perspective in Social Work Practice,* the authors bring you up to date on developments in strengths-based social work practice with a variety of populations. In addition, much more attention is paid in this volume to the articulation of strengths- and assets-oriented practice in the community.

In response to readers' reactions to the first edition as well as practitioners' responses to presentations of the strengths perspective in a variety of training environments, the authors have made a number of changes and additions. A much broader focus on community development, more attention to related literature and practice (resilience, assets-based approaches, health and wellness), more elaborate schemes for assessment and practice, more case examples all give this substantially revised edition a distinctively different flavor.

The authors acknowledge that work remains to be done in the continuing explication of strengths theory, program, and practice, but they are also convinced of the power of this approach in helping individuals, groups, and communities to successfully meet the challenges of their lives, and to move toward achieving their hopes and realizing their visions. We also believe that the chapters in this book can give the reader some ideas about how to use the strengths approach in practice with a variety of clients.

PLAN OF THE BOOK

The book is divided into three parts: Part I, "The Philosophy, Principles, and Language of the Strengths Perspective," introduces readers to some of the root assumptions of the strengths perspective, as well as guiding principles, and the basic lexicon of the perspective. In addition, Dennis Saleebey critiques the disease or deficit model of social work and contrasts it with the strengths approach. Howard Goldstein offers a trenchant analysis of the differing vocabularies and constructions of the strengths and pathology perspectives and provides moving examples of their differences from his interviews with now elderly survivors of an orphanage.

In part II, "The Strengths Approach to Practice," Ann Weick and Ronna Chamberlain, using some telling examples, show us what the problem is with the problem perspective. Then Dennis Saleebey provides a brief excursion into assessing and using client strengths in practice. Charles Cowger provides a more detailed assessment scheme in chapter 5 demonstrating how a strengths assessment can empower clients.

In part III, "Using the Strengths Approach with Individuals," the chapters' authors describe and analyze their experience in employing a strengths approach with a variety of populations. Richard Rapp discusses a very successful program that he and others at Wright State University have developed employing a strengths perspective in working with individuals who have substance abuse problems. In chapter 7, Walter Kisthardt brings us up to date on new developments in strengths-based case management with individuals with persistent and severe mental illness, providing principles and examples that highlight such an approach. In the next chapter, Becky Fast and Rosemary Chapin discuss and exemplify the critical practice components of case management grounded in a strengths orientation with elders. Mary Bricker-Jenkins, in chapter 9, discusses her research on effective social work practitioners in public social services, demonstrating with many examples and principles how their capabilities, beliefs, behaviors, and commitments can enhance the assets, resources, and strengths of clients. In chapter 10, Gary Holmes forcefully makes the case that turning people into clients sometimes has the unfortunate consequence of robbing them of power and dignity. Using examples of people with disabilities and people from different cultures, he demonstrates how we might empower "clients."

Part IV, "The Strengths Approach in the Environment: Groups and Community Development," brings together some of the exciting developments in community-based practice, much of which is now centered on discovering, promoting, and sharing the assets of members of a given community or organization.

Long an advocate for promoting the resilience of youth, Bonnie Benard shows us, using the school as a base, how we can advance the protective and strength-generating factors in families, schools, and communities to help children and youth at risk become competent and responsible citizens of their world. In chapter 12, W. Patrick Sullivan argues for, and demonstrates that, we can mobilize community resources—individuals, institutions, and organizations—and create restorative niches in helping people recover from serious and persistent mental illness. Dennis Saleebey, in chapter 13, reviews some successful community development programs that have implicitly and explicitly used a strengths approach, and he extracts some guiding principles for practice from these examples. In the final chapter in this section, James Taylor presents an intriguing theory of "niches," which has much promise in guiding our thinking about community development in terms of both practice and policy.

In the final part, "Conclusion," Dennis Saleebey takes a look at the possible developments that await the strengths perspective—the converging lines of research and practice that support the approach—and then attempts to respond to the most frequent critiques of the strengths perspective.

The authors of this volume hope that, at the least, it promotes some serious thinking about, and discussion of, the possibility of orienting your practice (or your teaching or research) around the idea that every individual, family, and community has assets, strengths, and resources that are the essential materials for building a better life, individually or collectively.

ACKNOWLEDGMENTS

The first declaration of my appreciation goes to the authors who have contributed to this book. I have learned from each of them and have benefited in my own teaching and practice from their ideas. I also understand and value the hard work that went into the preparation of these chapters. It should be clear to any reader that these individuals do not just preach the sermon, they live the message.

Joining the faculty of the School of Social Welfare at the University of Kansas in 1987 was a lucky break for me, turning me in a direction that I had not anticipated but now cherish. Besides getting tickets to Jayhawk basketball, I had the good fortune of being exposed to people like Charlie Rapp, Ann Weick, John Poertner, Pat Sullivan, Sue Pearlmutter, Ronna Chamberlain, Chris Petr, and Wally Kisthardt, all of whom were working to cultivate the strengths approach to practice, research, and teaching. Since that time, building on and believing in the strengths and capabilities of clients has become one of four defining themes in the curriculum of the school. I would also like to pay special thanks to contributors to the first edition who are not represented in this revised edition: John Poertner, John Ronnau, Eloise Rathbone-McCuan, and Julian Rappaport, all of whom continue to foster and nourish the strengths perspective in their work.

Hillary Henderson, associate editor at Longman, has been especially helpful. While guiding and helping to shape the evolution of this revision, she imparted not only a sense of direction but enthusiasm for the project. I do not think I would have considered doing it had she not believed so strongly in the project. Again, I thank Marian Abegg for her help in pulling the manuscript together. She has a perspective and intelligence about both the big and small issues in doing something like this that I prize.

I want to give a special acknowledgment to the residents of the public housing complexes who have welcomed KU Outreach into their communities over the past six years. Their courage, resilience, intelligence, and capability in the face of adversity has been an inspiration to our staff and our students, A special thanks to Diana Adorno-Boody, the KU Outreach Project Coordinator, who, in her practice and her daily life, is the embodiment of a strengths perspective.

The following individuals reviewed the manuscript and provided helpful suggestions:

Miriam Clubok, Ohio University

Katherine M. Dunlap, University of North Carolina, Chapel Hill

Sonja Matison, Eastern Washington University

Richard Stagliano, Rutgers University

Rebecca Van Voorhis, Indiana University

Yvonne B. Willis-Dulin, Eastern Michigan University

Martha K. Wilson, Boise State University

The Strengths
Perspective in
Social Work Practice

part I

The Philosophy, Principles, and Language of the Strengths Perspective

chapter **1**

Introduction: Power in the People[1]

Dennis Saleebey

The idea of building on clients' strengths has achieved the status of adage in the lore of professional social work. Authors of textbooks, educators, and practitioners all regularly acknowledge the importance of this principle. Many of these calls to attend to the capacities and competencies of clients are little more than professional cant. So let us be clear: The strengths perspective is a dramatic departure from conventional social work practice. Practicing from a strengths orientation means this— *everything* you do as a social worker will be predicated, in some way, on helping to discover and embellish, explore and exploit clients' strengths and resources in the service of assisting them to achieve their goals, realize their dreams, and shed the irons of their own inhibitions and misgivings. This is a versatile practice approach, relying heavily on the ingenuity and creativity, the courage and common sense, of both clients and their social workers. It is a collaborative process depending on clients and workers to be purposeful agents and not mere functionaries. It is an approach honoring the innate wisdom of the human spirit, the inherent capacity for transformation of even the most humbled and abused. When you adopt the strengths approach to practice, you can expect exciting changes in the character of your work and in the tenor of your relationships with your clients. Many of us believe (or have at one time believed) that we are building on client strengths. But many of us fall short. To really practice from a strengths perspective demands a different way of seeing clients, their environments, and their current situation. Rather than focusing on problems, your eye turns toward possibility. In the thicket of

---

[1] Part of this chapter is based on D. Saleebey, The strengths perspective in social work: Extensional cautions. *Social Work, 41*(3), 1996, 295–305. With permission of the National Association of Social Workers.

trauma, pain, and trouble you can see blooms of hope and transformation. The formula is simple: Mobilize clients' strengths (talents, knowledge, capacities, resources) in the service of achieving their goals and visions and the clients will have a better quality of life on their terms. Though the recipe is simple, as you will see, the work is hard. In the chapters that follow, you will encounter descriptions of the strengths approach used with a variety of populations, in a variety of circumstances. You will be exposed to schemes of assessment, methods of employment, examples of application, and discussions of issues related to moving from a concentration on problems to a fascination with strengths.

In the past few years, there has been an increasing interest in developing strengths-based approaches to practice, case management in particular, with a variety of client groups—the elderly, youth in trouble, people with addictions, people with chronic mental illness, even communities and schools (Benard, 1994; Chamberlain & Rapp, 1991; Kretzmann & McKnight, 1993; Miller & Berg, 1995; Parsons & Cox, 1994). In addition, rapidly developing literature, inquiry, and practice methods in a variety of fields bear a striking similarity to the strengths perspective—developmental resilience, healing and wellness, solution-focused therapy, assets-based community development, and narrative and story to name a few. The impetus for these elaborations comes from many sources, but of singular importance is a reaction to the fact that our culture is obsessed with, and fascinated by, psychopathology, victimization, abnormality, and moral and interpersonal aberrations. A swelling conglomerate of businesses and professions, institutions and agencies, from medicine to pharmaceuticals, from the insurance industry to the mass media turn handsome profits by assuring us that we are in the clutch (or soon will be) of any number of emotional, physical, or behavioral maladies. Each of us, it seems, is a reservoir of vulnerabilities and weaknesses usually born of toxic experiences in early life. The *Diagnostic and Statistical Manual of Mental Disorders IV* (American Psychiatric Association, 1994), has twice the volume of text on disorders as its predecessor, DSM IIIR, with only seven years between the publications. Not only are we mesmerized by disease and disorder, we have turned victimhood into a thriving and rapidly expanding business. Many of us, prodded by a variety of gurus, swamis, ministers, and therapists are in hot pursuit of our wounded inner children and find ourselves dripping with the residue of the poisons of our family background. If you listen carefully, you can hear the echoes of evangelism in some of these current cultural fixations.

To make these observations is not to callously disregard the real pains and trauma that individuals, families, and communities confront; nor is it to blithely turn away from the realities of abuse of all kinds inflicted on children; neither is it to deny the tenacious grip and beguiling thrall of addictions. It is, however, to foreswear the ascendancy of psychopathology as society's principal civic, moral, and medical categorical imperative. It is to denounce the idea that most people who experience hurt, trauma, and neglect inevitably suffer wounds and become less than they might be. It is to condemn the fact that the so-called recovery movement, now so beyond its original intents and boundaries, has "pumped out a host of illnesses and addictions that were by earlier standards, mere habits, some good, some bad.

Everywhere in public we find people talking freely, if not excitedly, even proudly, about their compulsions—whether it be gambling, sex, shopping, exercise, or the horrible desire to please other people. We are awash in a sea of codependency, wounded inner children, and intimacy crises" (Wolin & Wolin, 1993, p. 7).

Social work, like other helping professions, has not been immune to the contagion of disease- and disorder-based thinking. Social work has constructed much of its theory and practice around the supposition that clients become clients because they have deficits, problems, pathologies, and diseases; that they are, in some essential way, flawed or weak. This orientation leaps from a past where certitude and conception about the moral defects of the poor, the despised, and the deviant captivated us. More sophisticated terminology prevails today, but the metaphors and narratives that guide our thinking and acting, often papered over with more salutary language, are fundamentally negative constructions that are fateful for the future of those we help. The diction and symbolism of weakness, failure, and deficit shape how others regard clients, how clients regard themselves, and how resources are allocated to groups of clients. In the extreme, such designations may even invoke punitive sanctions.

The lexicon of pathology gives voice to a number of assumptions and these in turn have painted pictures of clients in vivid but not very flattering tones. Some of these assumptions and their consequences are summarized below.

The person is the problem or pathology named. Diagnostic labels of all kinds tend to become "master statuses" (Becker, 1963), designations and roles that subsume all others under their mantle. A person suffering from schizophrenia *becomes* a schizophrenic, a convention so common that we hardly give it a thought. Once a schizophrenic, other elements of the person's character, experiences, knowledge, aspirations, slowly recede into the background, replaced by the language of symptom and syndrome. Inevitably, conversation about the person becomes dominated by the imagery of disease and relationships with the ailing person re-form around such representations. To the extent that these labels take hold, the individual, through a process of surrender and increasing dependence, becomes the once alien identification (Goffman, 1961; Scheff, 1984).

The voice of the problem/deficit orientation speaks the language of "base rhetoric." Thomas Szasz (1978), citing the work of R. M. Weaver, suggests that base rhetoric is persuasive talk that debases, belittles, or discounts individuals or groups. The practitioner of base rhetoric is "always trying to keep individuals from the support which personal courage, noble associations, and divine philosophy provide . . ." (p. 20). Noble rhetoric, on the other hand, works to persuade individuals and groups that they have the tools to be their own masters. It animates self-esteem and moves people to honor themselves (Szasz, 1978). Much of the rhetoric of the helping professions, formal and informal, does not ennoble, and some of it is assertively base. Appellations like "chron," "perp," "schizo," "con," serve no purpose other than to debase and to distance the helper from the lifeworld of the client.

Accentuating the problems of clients creates a web of pessimistic expectations of, and predictions about, the client, the client's environment, and the client's capacity to cope with that environment. Furthermore, these labels have the insidious potential, repeated over time, to alter how individuals see themselves and how others see them. In the long run, these changes seep into the individual's identity. Freire (1973) has maintained for many years that the views and expectations of oppressors have an uncanny and implacable impact on the oppressed. Under the weight of these once-foreign views, the oppressed begin to subjugate their own knowledge and understanding to those of their tormentors.

Distance, power inequality, control, and manipulation mark the relationship between helper and helped. Goldstein (1992) puts it this way: The "posture of detached objectivity required to construct a 'case history' and diagnose another person's condition poses the risk of creating an aura of separateness. Such an approach becomes even more elitist should I intimate that I have the special knowledge of the professional which grants me the authority to define your problems and, out of this definition, determine the plan that should produce the desired results" (p. 32). The surest route to detachment is the building of a "case"—putting together a portfolio on the client created from the invalidating descriptions of, for example, DSM IV or the penal code. Furthermore, the legal and political mandates of many agencies, the elements of social control embodied in both the institution and ethos of the agency, may strike a further blow to the possibility of partnership and collaboration between client and helper.

Problem-based assessments encourage individualistic rather than ecological accounts of clients. When we transform persons into cases, we often see only them and how well they fit into a category. In this way, we miss important elements of the client's life: cultural, social, political, ethnic, spiritual, and economic. The irony here is that, in making a "case" we really do not individualize. Rather, we are in the act of finding an appropriate diagnostic niche for the individual, thus making the client one among many and not truly unique. All individuals suffering from bipolar disorder hence become more like each other and less distinctive. In doing this, we selectively destroy or ignore information that, although not salient to our assessment scheme, might well reveal to us the abiding distinction of the individual in this particular context.

The focus on what is wrong often reveals an egregious **cynicism** *about the ability of individuals to cope with life or to rehabilitate themselves.* Andrew Weil (1995) laments the profound pessimism and negativity in his own profession, medicine, about the body's innate inclination to transform, regenerate, and heal itself.

> I cannot help feeling embarrassed by my profession when I hear the myriad ways in which doctors convey their pessimism to patients. I . . . am working to require instruction in medical school about the power of words and the need for physicians to use extreme care in choosing the words they speak to patients. A larger subject is the problem of making doctors more conscious of the power projected on them by patients and the possibilities for reflecting that power back in ways that influence health for better rather than worse, that stimulate rather than retard spontaneous healing. (p. 64)

The situation is so bad that Weil refers to it as medical "hexing"—dire medical predictions and inimical attributions by physicians powerful enough to create anxiety, fear, depression, and resignation in patients. This is a common consequence of the biomedical model—a model that has profoundly influenced some fields of social work practice. The biomedical model, and its more widely influential kin in the human service professions, the "Technical/Rationalist" (Schön, 1983) model, are despairing of natural healing and people's capacity to know what is right. Extraordinarily materialistic, these models disregard the functional wholeness and fitness of any thing under their scrutiny—including human beings. Social work's continuing emphasis on problems and disorders and the profession's increasing commerce with theories that focus on deficits and pathologies tend to promote the portrayal of individuals as sites of specific problems and as medlies of singular deficiencies. Such an attitude takes the social work profession away from its avowed and historical interest in the person-in-context, the under-standing of the web of institutional and interpersonal relationships in which any person is enmeshed, and the possibility for rebirth and renewal even under dire circumstances.

The supposition of disease assumes a cause for the disorder and, thus, a solu-tion. Naming the poison leads to an antidote. But in the world of human relation-ships and experiences, the idea of a regression line between cause, disease, and cure ignores the steamy morass of uncertainty and complexity that is the human condition.

> In the varied topography of professional practice, there is a high hard ground where practitioners can make effective use of research-based the-ory and technique, and there is a swampy lowland where situations are confusing "messes" incapable of technical solution. The difficulty is that the problems of the high ground, however great their technical interest, are often relatively unimportant to clients or to the larger society, while in the swamp are the problems of greatest concern. (Schön, 1983, p. 42)

Remedies in the "lowland" usually begin with reinterpretations of the problem that come out of continuing dialogue with the situation and with clients. These ren-derings are mutually crafted constructs that may only be good for this client, at this time, under these conditions. Though they may have the power to transform clients' understandings, choices, and actions, these expositions are tentative and provi-sional. The capacity to devise such interpretations depends, not on a strict relation-ship between problem and solution but on intuition, tacit knowing, hunches, and conceptual risk taking (Saleebey, 1989). Schön (1983) has characterized the tension between the usual conception of professional knowing and doing and this more "reflective" one as that between rigor and relevance. Relevance asks these questions of us: To what extent are clients consulted about matters pertinent to them? What do they want? What do they need? How do they think they can get it? How do they see their situation—problems as well as possibilities? What values do they want to maximize? How have they managed to survive thus far? These and similar ques-tions, as answers draw near, move us a step toward a deeper appreciation of all cli-ents' distinctive attributes, abilities, and competencies.

THE STRENGTHS PERSPECTIVE:
CONCEPTS AND PRINCIPLES

We have seen that the obsession with problems and pathologies, while producing an impressive lode of technical and theoretical writing, may be less fruitful when it comes to actually helping clients grow, develop, change directions, realize their visions, or revise their personal meanings and narratives. What follows is a brief glossary of terms supporting an orientation to strengths as well as a statement of the principles of practice central to a strengths perspective. These are meant to give you a vital sense of what a frame of mind devoted to the strengths of individuals and groups requires.

The Lexicon of Strengths

"We can act," wrote William James (1902) in reflecting upon Immanuel Kant's notions about conceptions, "as *if* there were a God; feel as *if* we were free; consider nature as *if* she were full of special designs; lay plans as *if* we were to be immortal; and we find then that these words **do** [emphasis added] make a genuine difference in our moral life" (p. 55). Language and words have power. They can elevate and inspire or demoralize and destroy. Joseph Conrad (1900) knew the danger that words might harbor when he wrote, "There is a weird power in a spoken word. . . . And a word carries far—very far—and deals destruction through time as the bullets go flying through space" (p. 185). If words are a part of the nutriment that feeds one's sense of self, then we are compelled to examine our dictionary of helping to see what our words portend for clients. Any approach to practice speaks a language that, in the end, may have a pronounced effect on the way that clients think of themselves and how they act. In the strengths approach to practice, some words are primary as they direct us to an appreciation of the assets of individuals, families, and communities.

Empowerment.   Although rapidly becoming hackneyed, empowerment indicates the intent to, and the processes of, assisting individuals, groups, families, and communities to discover and expend the resources and tools within and around them. Julian Rappaport (1990) suggests that an empowerment agenda requires us to create opportunities for the alienated and distressed to seize some control over their lives and the decisions that are critical to their lives. To discover the power within people and communities, we must subvert and abjure pejorative labels; provide opportunities for connections to family, institutional, and communal resources; assail the victim mind-set; foreswear paternalism; trust people's intuitions, accounts, perspectives, and energies; and believe in people's dreams. Pursuing the empowerment agenda requires a deep conviction about the necessity of democracy. It requires us to address the tensions and conflicts, the institutions and people that subdue and limit those we help, and compels us to help people free themselves from these restraints (Pinderhughes, 1994). Too often, professions have thwarted this imperative by assuming a paternalistic posture, informing people about what is good for them, and exhorting people to do the right thing. The strengths approach imposes a different attitude and commitment.

> On the one hand it demands that we look to . . . settings where people are already handling their own problems in living, in order to learn more about how they do it. . . . On the other hand, it demands that we find ways to take what we learn from these diverse settings and solutions and make it more public, so as to help foster social policies and programs and make it more rather than less likely that others not now handling their own problems in living or shut out from current solutions, gain control over their lives. (Rappaport, 1981, p. 15)

The strengths of individuals and communities are renewable and expandable resources. Furthermore, the assets of individuals almost always lie embedded in a community of interest and involvement. Thus, the ideas of community and membership are central to the strengths approach.

Membership. To be without membership, writes Michael Walzer, is to be in a "condition of infinite danger" (1983, p. 32). To be without membership is to be alienated, to be at risk for marginalization and oppression. People need to be citizens, responsible and valued members of a community. To sever people from the roots of their "place" subverts, for all, civic and moral vigor. The strengths orientation proceeds from the recognition that all of those whom we serve are, like ourselves, members of a species, entitled to the dignity, respect, and responsibility that comes with such membership. But, too often, people we help have either no place to be (or to be comfortable) or no sense of belonging. The sigh of relief from those who come to be members and citizens and bask in the attendant rights and responsibilities, assurances and securities, is the first breath of empowerment.

Resilience. There is a growing body of inquiry and practice that makes it clear that the rule, not the exception, in human affairs is that people do rebound from serious trouble, that individuals and communities do surmount and overcome serious and troubling adversity. Much of this literature documents and demonstrates that particularly demanding and stressful experiences, even ongoing ones, *do not lead inevitably to vulnerability, failure to adapt, and psychopathology* (Benard, 1994; Werner & Smith, 1992; Wolin & Wolin, 1993). Resilience is not the cheerful disregard of one's difficult and traumatic life experiences; neither is it the naive discounting of life's pains. It is, rather, the ability to bear up in spite of these ordeals. Damage has been done. Emotional and physical scars bear witness to that. In spite of the wounds, however, for many the trials have been instructive and propitious. Resilience is the continuing growth and articulation of capacities, knowledge, insight, and virtues derived through meeting the demands and challenges of one's world, however chastening.

Healing and Wholeness. Healing implies both wholeness and the inborn facility of the body and the mind to regenerate and resist when faced with disorder, disease, and disruption. Healing also requires a beneficent relationship between the individual and the larger social and physical environment. The natural state of affairs for human beings, evolved over eons of time and at every level of organization from cell to self-image, is the repair of one's mind and body. Just as the resilience literature assures us that individuals have naturally occurring self-righting tendencies (Werner & Smith, 1992), it seems also the case that all human organisms have the inclination for healing. This evolutionary legacy, of course, can be compromised by trauma, by environmental toxins, by bodily disorganization, and, not the least, by some of our professional intervention philosophies and systems. But, the bottom line is this: If spontaneous healing occurs "miraculously" in one human being, you can expect it to occur in another and another. . . . Such organismic ingenuity only makes common sense. Otherwise, how could we have survived as a species for hundreds of thousands of years without hospitals, HMOs, physicians, psychiatrists, pharmacists, or talk show hosts? Healing occurs when the healer or the individual makes an alliance with, or instigates the power of, the organism to restore itself (Cousins, 1989; Gazzaniga, 1992; Weil, 1995). So healing and self-regeneration are intrinsic life support systems, always working and, for most of us, most of the time, on call. Such a reality has dramatic implications, not just for medicine but for all the helping professions. At the least, it challenges the assumption of the disease model that only experts know what is best for their clients and that curing, healing, or transformation comes exclusively from outside sources. At some level of consciousness, as Roger Mills (1995) reminds us, we have a native wisdom about what is right for us and what we should do when confronted with organismic or environmental challenges.

Dialogue and Collaboration.   Humans can only come into being through a creative and emergent relationship with others. Without such transactions, there can be no discovery and testing of one's powers, no knowledge, no heightening of one's awareness and internal strengths. In dialogue, we confirm the importance of others and begin to heal the rift between self, other, and institution.

Dialogue requires empathy, identification with, and the inclusion of other people. Paulo Freire (1973) is convinced, based on his years of work with oppressed peoples, that only humble and loving dialogue can surmount the barrier of mistrust built from years of paternalism and the rampant subjugation of the knowledge and wisdom of the oppressed. "Founding itself upon love, humility, and faith, dialogue becomes a horizontal relationship of which mutual trust between the dialoguers is the logical consequence" (pp. 79–80). A caring community is a community that confirms otherness; giving each person and group a ground of their own, affirmed through encounters that are egalitarian and dedicated to healing and empowerment.

The idea of collaboration has a more specific focus. When we work together with clients we become their agents, their consultants, stakeholders with them in mutually crafted projects. This requires us to be open to negotiation, to appreciate the authenticity of the views and aspirations of those with whom we collaborate. Our voices may have to be quieted so that we can give voice to our clients. Comfortably ensconced in the "expert" role, we may have great difficulty assuming such a conjoint posture.

Suspension of Disbelief. It would be hard to exaggerate the extent of disbelief of clients' words and stories in the culture of professionalism. While social work, because of its enduring values, may fancy itself less culpable in this regard than other professions, a little circumspection is warranted. As just one example (and probably somewhat unfair because this is a brief excerpt from a text on social work practice that generally assumes a positive view of clients), Hepworth and Larsen (1990) wrote:

> Though it is the primary source of information, verbal report is vulnerable to error because of possible faulty recall, distorted perceptions, biases, and limited self-awareness on the part of clients. It is thus vital to avoid the tendency to accept clients' views, descriptions, and reports as valid representations of reality. Similarly, it is important to recognize that feelings expressed by clients may emanate from faulty perceptions or may be altogether irrational. (p. 197)

Two observations: First, the idea that there are valid representations of reality is questionable. That is, there are many representations of the "real" world. Is, say, a Lakota understanding of fever any less relevant in context than a Manhattan internist's? Second, to begin work with clients in this frame of mind would seem to subvert the idea that clients often do know exactly what they are talking about and that they are "experts" on their own lives. Pessimism and cynicism may not be so uncommon among social workers. I see it frequently in training for, and supervision with, other social workers. Perhaps, the suspension of belief in clients' accounts comes from the radiation of scientific thinking throughout our culture and into the professions. The ideal of the scientific investigator as objective and dispassionate observer has been transfigured into a certain incredulity about, and distancing from, clients. If the rise of the professions (and the ideology of professionalism) was part of the extension and reinforcement of the institutions of socialization and social control during the Victorian era, then a certain detachment and restraint in accepting clients and their stories made sense (Bledstein, 1978).

Professionals have contained the affirmation of clients in a number of ways:

- by imposing their own theories over the theories and accounts of clients
- by using assessment in an interrogative style designed to ascertain certain diagnostic and largely preemptive hypotheses which, in the end, confirm suspicions about the client
- by engaging in self-protective maneuvers (like skepticism) designed to prevent the ultimate embarrassment for a professional—being fooled by, or lied to by a cunning client

The frequent talk about manipulative and resistant clients in many social agencies may stem from the fear of being made the fool. To protect self-esteem, non-normative lifestyles, self-interests, or benefits, clients may have a vested interest in not telling the truth. But we must consider the possibility that avoiding the truth may be a function of the manner in which the professional pursues and/or asserts the truth. The professional's knowledge, information, and perspective are privileged and carry institutional and legal weight. The client's do not.

In summary, the lexicon of strengths provides us with a vocabulary of appreciation and not aspersion about those with whom we work. In essence, the effort is to move away from defining professional work as the articulation of the power of expert knowledge toward collaboration with the power within the individual or community toward a life that is palpably better—and better on the clients' own terms.

Principles of the Strengths Perspective

The principles that follow are the guiding assumptions and regulating understandings of the strengths perspective. They are tentative, still maturing, and subject to revision and modulation. They do, however, give a flavor of what practicing from a strengths appreciation involves.

Every Individual, Group, Family and Community Has Strengths.   While it may be hard at times to invoke, it is essential to remind oneself that the person or family in front of you and the community around you possess assets, resources, wisdom, and knowledge that, at the outset, you probably know nothing about. First *and* foremost, the strengths perspective is about discerning those resources, and respecting them and the potential they may have for reversing misfortune, countering illness, easing pain, and reaching goals. To detect strengths, however, the social work practitioner must be genuinely interested in, and respectful of, clients' stories, narratives, and accounts—the interpretive slants they take on their own experiences. These are the most important "theories" that guide practice. The unearthing of clients' identities and realities does not come from a ritual litany of troubles, embarrassments, snares, foibles, and barriers. Rather, clients come into view when you assume that they know something, have learned lessons from experience, have hopes, have interests, and can do some things masterfully. These may be obscured by the stresses of the moment, submerged under the weight of crisis, oppression, or illness but, nonetheless, they abide.

In the end, clients want to know that you actually care about them, that how they fare makes a difference to you, that you will listen to them, that you will respect them no matter what their history, and that you believe that they can build something of value with the resources within and around them. But most of all, clients want to know that you believe they can surmount adversity and begin the climb toward transformation and growth.

Trauma and Abuse, Illness and Struggle May Be Injurious but They May Also Be Sources of Challenge and Opportunity. The Wolins (1993) point out that the "damage model" of development so prevalent in today's thinking only leads to discouragement, pessimism, and the victim mindset. It also foretells a continuing future of psychopathology and troubled relationships. Individuals exposed to a variety of abuses, especially in childhood, are thought always to be victims or to be damaged in ways that obscure or override any strengths or possibilities for redemption or rebound. In the Wolins' "challenge model," children are not seen as merely passive recipients of parental unpredictability, abuse, disappointment, or violence. Rather, children are seen as active and developing individuals who, through these trials, learn skills and develop personal attributes that stand them in good stead in adulthood. Not that they do not suffer. They do. Not that they do not bear scars. They do. But they also may acquire traits and capacities that are preservative and life affirming. There is dignity to be drawn from having prevailed over obstacles to one's growth and maturing. The Wolins (1993) refer to this as "survivor's pride." It is a deep-dwelling sense of accomplishment in having met life's challenges and walked away, not without fear, even terror, and certainly not without wounds. Often this pride is buried under embarrassment, confusion, distraction or self-doubt. But when it exists and is lit, it can ignite the engine of change.

Individuals, groups, and communities are more likely to continue development and growth when they are funded by the currency of capacities, knowledge, and skills (Kretzmann & McKnight, 1993). While the strengths perspective is powered by a similar belief, the observation of many who practice using a strengths approach is that many people who struggle to find their daily bread, a job, or shelter are already resilient, resourceful and, though in pain, motivated for achievement on their terms. Kaplan and Girard (1995) put it this way:

> People are more motivated to change when their strengths are supported. Instead of asking family members what their problems are, a worker can ask what strengths they bring to the family and what they think are the strengths of other family members. Through this process the worker helps the family discover its capabilities and formulate a new way to think about themselves. . . . The worker creates a language of strength, hope, and movement. . . . (p. 53)

Assume That You Do Not Know the Upper Limits of the Capacity to Grow and Change and Take Individual, Group, and Community Aspirations Seriously. Too often, professionals assume that a diagnosis, an assessment, or a profile sets the parameters of possibility for their clients. In our personal lives, looking back, we sometimes marvel at the road we traveled—a road that we, at the outset, might not have even considered taking—and the distance that we have come. For our clients, too often, we cannot imagine the prospect of similar dizzying and unanticipated destinations. The diagnosis or the assessment becomes a verdict and a sentence. Our clients will be better served when we make an overt pact with their promise and possibility. This means that we must hold high our expectations of clients and make allegiance with their hopes, visions, and values. In speaking of people struggling with serious addictions, Peele and Brodsky (1991) say,

> More often than not people rise to the occasion when they are given positive options. People typically strive to set their lives straight, and given time, usually succeed. Age tends to ameliorate or eliminate bad habits while bringing greater self-contentment and improved coping. Nearly all people have values that are incompatible with their addictions—the most remarkable cases of "instantaneous" cure occur when these values [and, I might add, visions] crystallize so that people reject the addiction. (pp. 162–163)

It is becoming increasingly clear that emotions have a profound effect on wellness and health. Emotions experienced as positive can activate the inner pharmacoepia, those chemicals that relax, help fight infection, and restore (Ornstein & Sobel, 1987). When people believe that they can recover, that they have prospects, that their hopes are palpable, their bodies often respond optimally. That does not mean that people do not get sick. It does mean that when people are sick, healers can make an alliance with the body's regenerative powers and augment them with real but nonetheless fortifying and uplifting expectations (Weil, 1995). Roger Mills's (1995) health realization/community empowerment projects (detailed in chapter 13) are based on similar principles. Mills's idea is that everyone has innate wisdom, intelligence, and motivating emotions and that these, even if muted by circumstance, are accessible through education, support, and encouragement. The goals of his projects are to "reconnect people to the [physical and mental] health in themselves and then direct them in ways to bring forth the health of others in their community. The result is a change in people and communities which builds up from within rather than [being] imposed from without" (Mills, 1993, cited in Benard, 1994, p. 22). So it is that individuals and communities have the capacity for restoration and rebound.

We Best Serve Clients by Collaboratoring with Them.   The role of "expert" or "professional" may not provide the best vantage point from which to appreciate clients' strengths and assets. A helper may best be defined as a collaborator or consultant: an individual clearly presumed, because of specialized education and experience, to know some things and to have some tools at the ready but definitely not the only one in the situation to have relevant, even esoteric, knowledge and understanding. Ms. Johnson knows more about thriving in a public housing project than anyone I can think of. Over the course of 35 years, she successfully raised 11 children. She maintained a demeanor of poise, and she demonstrated intelligence and vigor, even as her community underwent dramatic, often frightening changes. Her contributions to the community are, simply put, amazing. She has much to teach us and other residents of her community. I certainly would not presume to work on Ms. Johnson but would be privileged to work with her.

We make a serious error when we subjugate clients' wisdom and knowledge to official views. There is something liberating, for all parties involved, in connecting to clients' stories and narratives, their hopes and fears, their wherewithal and resources rather than trying to stuff them into the narrow confines of a diagnostic category or treatment protocol. Ultimately a collaborative stance may make us less vulnerable to some of the more political elements of helping: paternalism, victim-blaming (or, more currently, victim-creating), and preemption of client views. It is likewise important to get the stories and views of clients out to those who need to hear them—schools, agencies, employers, local governments, churches, and businesses. This is part of the role of advocacy. The policies and regulations that affect many of our clients are crafted in the halls of Congress and are often far removed from the daily reality of clients. Furthermore, these policies do not take advantage of the wisdom and resources of their intended beneficiaries and recipients.

Every Environment Is Full of Resources.   (See chapters 11, 12, 13, 14.) In communities that seem to amplify individual and group resilience, there is awareness, recognition, and use of the assets of most members of the community (Kretzmann & McKnight, 1993). Informal systems of individuals, families, and groups, social circuits of peers, and intergenerational mentoring work to assist, support, instruct, and include all members of a community (Benard, 1991). In inclusive communities, there are many opportunities for involvement, to make contributions to the moral and civic life of the whole; to become, in other words, a citizen in place. No matter how harsh an environment, how it may test the mettle of its inhabitants, it can also be understood as a potentially lush topography of resources and possibilities. Such an idea runs counter to conventional social work wisdom and public policy. However, in every environment, there are individuals, associations, groups, and institutions who have something to give, something that others may desperately need: knowledge, succor, an actual resource or talent, or simply time and place. Such resources usually exist outside the usual matrix of social and human service agencies. And, for the most part, they are unsolicited and untapped. Such a view of the environment, while seeming to comfort those who believe that people(s) should pull themselves up by their collective and individual bootstraps, *does not* abrogate the responsibility for working for social and economic justice. It does, however, recognize that while we await the Godot of political transformation, there are reservoirs of energy, ideas, talents, and tools out there on which to draw. To regard the environment as only inimical or toxic moves us to disregard these resources or mistakenly judge them as disreputable.

SOME PRELIMINARY THOUGHTS

Social work has had a kind of dissociative history with regard to building on client strengths. From its inception as a profession, the field has been exhorted to respect and energize client capacities. Bertha Capen Reynolds (1951) looked at the issue in terms of workers' obligations:

> The real choice before us as social workers is whether *we* are to be passive or active. . . . Shall we be content to give with one hand and withhold with the other, to build up or tear down at the same time the strength of a person's life? Or shall we become conscious of our own part in making a profession which will stand forthrightly for human well-being, *including the right to be an active citizen?* (p. 175, emphasis added)

The historical and continuing tension between the desire to become more professional, more technically adept, to focus on "function" rather than "cause" (Lee, 1929), to elevate social work to a new level of respect and comparability among the professions, and, on the other hand, to retain the interest in social action and the redress of social inequities seems to have been resolved recently in favor of the former. The writing, lexicon, and perspective of, say, clinical social work and those of social action or community development are quite different, maybe even at odds. While there is no implacable conflict between the interests of social work practice and social action, the infusion of psychodynamic thinking, the rise of private practice and vendorship, the mass appeal of DSM IV among other factors have driven social work toward a model of practice that is more heavily aligned with psychological thinking and psychopathology theories (Specht & Courtney, 1993). The theories that define such an alignment are typically oriented toward family and individual dysfunctions and disorders. While we must respect the impact of problems on the quality of life for our clients, we must also exercise extraordinary diligence to assure that the resources and positive attributes of clients draw our attention and define our efforts.

Today, social work practice texts, as we have said, typically nod in the direction of client strengths but provide little guidance to the student or worker about how to make an accounting of strengths and how to employ them in helping. Anthony Maluccio (1979) is one exception to this. In his study of the perceptions of workers and clients about the important elements of the helping process, he discovered that clients were closer to a strengths orientation than the workers.

> In general clients presented themselves as *pro-active*, autonomous human beings who are able to enhance their functioning and competence through the use of counseling service along with the resources operant within themselves and their social networks. Workers, on the other hand, tended top view clients as *reactive* organisms with continuing problems, weaknesses, and limited potentialities. (p. 399)

But even Maluccio assumes that, for the most part, competencies and skills have to be developed. Were they already extant, clients would not be stuck in their attempts to adapt to life transitions and environmental demands.

But, more currently, there are moves away from the problem or pathology perspective. The solution-focused approach is one example. In essence, it regards clients in the light of what they have done well, those times that the "problem" has not been apparent, or those times when exceptions to difficulty have occurred. Furthermore, client goals and visions are the centerpiece of the work to be done. It is not unusual for solution-focused practitioners to ask how things would be positively different if a miracle occurred overnight and the "problem" no longer held sway (De Jong & Miller, 1995; Miller & Berg, 1995). The literature on resilience, briefly discussed above, also provides conceptual and clinical ground for employing client strengths as a central part of the helping process. In the words of Benard (1994; see also chapter 11),

> . . . using resilience as the knowledge base for practice creates a *sense of optimism and hope.* It allows anyone working with troubled youth to, as poet Emily Dickinson urges, "dwell in possibility," to have confidence in their futures and, therefore, to convey this positive expectation to them. (p. 4)

Finally, the research on the effectiveness of a strengths approach, although preliminary, suggests that it is an effective and economical framework for practice (Rapp, 1996; Chamberlain & Rapp, 1991). Research done from the vantage point of a strengths approach includes the views and concerns of the stakeholders (subjects and clients) from the outset. The results of the research are to be used to achieve stated objectives of the stakeholders and/or to aid in the solving of identified problems.

In chapter 15, I will discuss in more detail some of the converging lines of research and practice that are reinforcing the strengths perspective. I will also address some of the persistent and significant criticisms of it.

CONCLUSION

This revised edition is intended to extend our knowledge of a subject that has been part of social work lore for decades, namely, the importance of building on client strengths. Such an endeavor affirms to the core values of the profession; it brings together clients, communities, and helpers in a relationship that exploits the best in all; and it restores a sense of hope and optimism in working with clients.

The strengths perspective is not yet a theory—although developments in that direction become bolder (Rapp, 1996). It is a way of thinking about what you do and with whom you do it. It provides a distinctive lens for examining the world of practice. Any approach to practice, in the end, is based on interpretation of the experiences of practitioners and clients and is composed of assumptions, rhetoric, ethics, and a set of methods. The importance and usefulness of any practice orientation lies not in some independent measure of its truth, but in how well it serves us in our work with people, how it fortifies our values, and how it generates opportunities for clients in a particular environment to change in the direction of their hopes and aspirations. The authors believe and hope that you will see the fecundity of the strengths perspective in initiating such opportunities for clients and the workers who serve them.

DISCUSSION QUESTIONS

1. What characteristics define the strengths approach?
2. What are the most significant contrasts between a strengths approach and a problem-focused one?
3. If you were to employ the strengths perspective in your practice, how would your approach to clients change?
4. Which of the principles of the strengths perspective do you already employ in practice? How do they affect the way you work with clients?
5. What do you consider to be your strengths? How do they energize your practice? How do they shape your personal life?

REFERENCES

American Psychiatric Association. (1994). *Diagnostic and statistical manual of mental disorders IV*. Washington, DC: American Psychiatric Association.

Becker, H. (1963). *Outsiders: Studies in the sociology of deviance*. New York: Free Press.

Benard, B. (1991). *Fostering resiliency in kids: Protective factors in the family, school, and community*. San Francisco: Western Regional Center.

Benard, B. (1994). *Applications of resilience*. Paper presented at a conference on the Role of Resilience in Drug Abuse, Alcohol Abuse, and Mental Illness. Dec. 5–6. Washington, D.C.

Bledstein, B. (1978). *The culture of professionalism*. New York: Norton.

Chamberlain, R., & Rapp, C. A. (1991). A decade of case management: A methodological review of outcome research. *Community Mental Health Journal, 27*, 171–188.

Conrad, J. (1900). *Lord Jim*. Edinburgh & London: William Blackwood & Sons.

Cousins, N. (1989). *Head first: The biology of hope*. New York: Dutton.

De Jong, P., & Miller, S. D. (1995). How to interview for client strengths. *Social Work, 40*, 729–736.

Freire, P. (1973). *Pedagogy of the oppressed*. New York: Seabury.

Gazzaniga, M. (1992). *Nature's mind*. New York: Basic Books.

Goffman, E. (1961). *Asylums: Essays on the situation of mental patients and other inmates*. Garden City, NY: Anchor/Doubleday.

Goldstein, H. (1992). Victors or victims: Contrasting views of clients in social work practice. In D. Saleebey, (Ed.), *The strengths perspective in social work practice* (1st ed.). White Plains, NY: Longman.

Hepworth, D. H., & Larsen, J. (1990). *Direct social work practice: Theory and skills* (3rd ed.). Chicago: Dorsey Press.

James, W. (1902). *The varieties of religious experience*. New York: Modern Library.

Kaplan, L., & Girard, J. (1994). *Strengthening high-risk families*. New York: Lexington Books.

Kretzmann, J. P., & McKnight, J. L. (1993). *Building communities from the inside out: Toward finding and mobilizing a community's assets.* Evanston, IL: Northwestern University, Center for Urban Affairs and Policy Research.

Lee, P. R. (1929). Social work: Cause and function. *Proceedings of the National Conference of Social Work*, 3–20.

Maluccio, A. (1979). *Learning from clients: Interpersonal helping as viewed by clients and social workers*. New York: Free Press.

Miller, S. D., & Berg, I. K. (1995). *The miracle method: A radically new approach to problem drinking*. New York: Norton.

Mills, R. (1995). *Realizing mental health: Toward a new psychology of resiliency*. New York: Sulzburger & Graham.

Ornstein, R., & Sobel, D. (1987). *The healing brain*. New York: Touchstone/Simon & Schuster.

Parsons, R. J., & Cox, E. O. (1994). *Empowerment-oriented social work practice with the elderly*. Newbury Park, CA: Sage.

Peele, S., & Brodsky, A. (1991). *The truth about addiction and recovery*. New York: Simon & Schuster.

Pinderhughes, E. (1994). Empowerment as intervention goals: Early ideas. In L. Gutierrez & P. Nurius, (Eds.), *Education and research for empowerment practice*. Seattle, WA: University of Washington School of Social Work, Center for Policy and Practice Research.

Rapp, C. A. (1996). *The strengths model: Case management with people suffering from severe and persistent mental illness* Unpublished manuscript, The University of Kansas at Lawrence.

Rappaport, J. (1981). Research methods and the empowerment agenda. In P. Tolan, C. Keys, F. Chertak, & L. Jason (Eds.), *Researching community psychology*. Washington, D.C.: American Psychological Association.

Rappaport, J. (1990). In praise of paradox: A social policy of empowerment over prevention. *American Journal of Community Psychology, 9*, 1–25.

Reynolds, B. C. (1951). *Social work and social living: Explorations in philosophy and* practice. Silver Spring, MD: National Association of Social Workers.

Saleebey, D. (1989). Professions in crisis: The estrangement of knowing and doing. *Social Casework,* 70, 556–563.

Scheff, T. J. (1984). *Being mentally ill: A sociological theory* (3rd ed.). New York: Aldine.

Schön, D. A. (1983). *The reflective practitioner*. New York: Basic Books.

Specht, H., & Courtney, M. (1993). *Unfaithful angels: How social work has abandoned its mission*. New York: Free Press.

Szasz, T. (1978). *The myth of psychotherapy*. Garden City, NY: Anchor/Doubleday.

Walzer, M. (1983). *Spheres of justice*. New York: Basic Books.

Weil, A. (1995). *Spontaneous healing*. New York: Knopf.

Werner, E., & Smith, R. S. (1992). *Overcoming the odds*. Ithaca, NY: Cornell University Press.

Wolin, S. J., & Wolin, S. (1993). *The resilient self: How survivors of troubled families rise above adversity*. New York: Villard.

chapter 2

Victors or Victims?

Howard Goldstein

BERTHA

> I would never have been a victim. I think I was born with a chip on my shoulder. To think my mother had to die and we were taken and put in that place. Now I understand it was a matter of necessity; my father couldn't help himself. So in a way it was a blessing that there was a place to go because our aunts who were poor had their own kids and you know goddam well that they cater to their kids before they give you anything. So in a way it was a godsend and it was what you made of it. You could either be a sniveling little nothing or you could be mischievous and upset people around you. You had to have a sense of humor or you'd be creamed. I'm not bitter. What saved me were the tricks I pulled on the superintendent. If I could outwit him, I could overlook a lot of other stuff.

These are Bertha's words, her response to my request that she tell me what it was like to have been a ward in a bygone orphanage, to have spent most of her first 16 years in an institution. Bertha was one of almost 40 elders, alumni of the Children's Home who eagerly shared the stories of their lifetimes with me (Goldstein, 1996).

A widow on the outer edge of her seventh decade, she was still mischievous, funny—but now in ways tempered by irony. Although the setting of our conversation was the kitchen of Bertha's small, modest Florida retirement condo, I had the sense of speaking with a larger and older version of a younger Bette Davis; she was in command, with well-practiced hauteur, and the smoke of her poised cigarette dramatized her answer to my question, "What was it really like growing up in the old orphanage?"

Nowadays, stories about survival have become so common as to wind up as fillers for the back pages of newspapers unless the latest cataclysm could be described in comparative and superlative terms—as a *more* devastating flood, *more* heinous killings, a *fiercer* fire. The world becomes a more threatening place and the numbers of remarkable people who have had to show the buoyancy, the immense vitality to overcome, outlast, and master their catastrophes increases. Still, traditional psychological thinking prevails: These signs of health and strength in the face of hardship are overlooked by a morbid interest in the defects, limitations, illnesses, and other presumed consequences of these "traumas." In other words, if one fails to adjust, it is obviously *because of* such insults to mind and body; but if one overcomes, it is explained that one does so *in spite of* these traumas. And so, human triumphs stand as oddities, exceptions to the received wisdom and are converted into the substance of Sunday supplements. I will give my attention to the reasons for this paradox.

I use Bertha's rejoinder as an introduction. Her life is not the journey of a heroine, the chronicle of a victor. I came to learn that her many years were scarcely exceptional: Married to Ed—it seemed to her like forever—she frequently had to take charge of his trucking business because of his chronic illness that finally left her a widow. They raised four children who had to make it through college on their own; money was never in excess. But what Bertha truly felt pride and success about was her many years of volunteer work with handicapped children. She poked me in the ribs to take a close look at her living room wall adorned with framed citations, honors, news clippings expressing gratitude for the difference she made in the lives of these children.

Consider this: It is the fact that Bertha (and the other graduates of the children's institution) succeeded, *did* live an ordinary life as a wife, mother, and citizen that distinguishes her. By most accepted psychosociological theories and expositions Bertha's life should have been otherwise. The inventory of her early years includes large servings of the classic maltreatment and trauma used to predict a less-than-ordered and secure adulthood. Not only did she openly deal with the obvious wounds of separation from and loss of a parent but resisted what could have been a more insidious affliction, an entire childhood as a ward of an archetypal orphanage.

Let me put this account in other terms to point to where this essay is heading. We know that a story like Bertha's is at risk because it can be interpreted, given meaning, to fit the presumptions of the reader. On telling this story, as I have done, to an ordinary audience of, say, friends or family, the listeners typically react in buoyant and affecting ways: "What spirit and perseverance," one says; another, "She reminds me of my dear old aunt who outlived two wars and four husbands"; and a third, "And she didn't have anything like the safety net we have."

Tell this story to professionals, however, and the reaction is quick and critical: "She reminds me of a really difficult patient who always avoided the facts"; "Look, this is just denial in action"; or, "Read Bowlby's book about early loss. There is lots more she isn't saying."

There is yet a third group—not easy to define or label—who, in plain talk, allude to something like the strength and resilience (terms I will use interchangeably) of spirit and self. They are neither Pollyannish about nor are they blind to the reality of vulnerability, frailty, adversity, and suffering. But what they are attuned to are the many paths that people seek out, alone or with help, that lead to, not away from, remarkable resources and talents, visions, and beliefs that allow for much more than mere survival. Responses from this group to Bertha's account take such forms as: "How remarkable that she could experience and live with both sorrow and joy"; "She could have used the same recollections to justify most any human failing"; "It's refreshing to hear about someone who is not a blamer, a victim"; "No question, life for her was a matter of choices—and tough ones, too."

Here we have three distinct perspectives on the same story. The first might be called "folk talk," in sympathy with what Jerome Bruner (1990) refers to as "folk psychology . . . or culture's account of what makes human beings tick [including] a theory of mind, one's own and others' [and] a theory of motivation." "Folk talk" is just another way of alluding to the manner in which people, like Bertha, define themselves and their worlds. In what we now call narrative terms, they speak the language and idioms of culture and suggest the personal frame of reference or beliefs that govern the understanding and meaning attributed to experience.

It is not the human sciences but literature—the novel (or poetry or drama)—that best tells us about the resilience and strength it takes to be a person. Consider the story of the coming of moral and psychological age as epitomized in, say, Dickens's *Great Expectations* or Woolf's *To the Lighthouse*. Should not the Humanities and Arts at least be included in professional education considering that, in practice, we typically relate to not artificial constructs but the earthy terms of the story, the personal drama?

Returning to the idea of multiple interpretations, the responses of those I called professionals tend to use the language of what can be called a medico-scientific model that classifies and treats defects, pathologies, and disabilities. The first and third groups share what I will call a humanistic perspective that gives greater importance to the resilience and strength in circumstances of adversity. Such a contrast is not a matter of word play or argument for the sake of argument: at stake is the well-being of our clients (however it is defined) since each perspective is itself a prescription of sorts for how we understand and therefore work with problems of living. Simply, the language of the theories, concepts, philosophies, and other perspectives we choose to use to describe, explain, or classify our clients has something to do with the nature, direction, and style of the helping experience.

In this regard, and in accord with the idea of "folk talk" and culture, ordinary people have considerable leeway in the terms and images they use to express how they see things. When it comes to explaining or accounting for human peculiarities, all sorts of metaphors, allusions, and idioms are available. Sure, they might use "psychotic." But reflecting relationship, attitude, and culture they are as likely to be more colorful when they speak of being daft, nuts, committable, loony, loco, tetched, unhinged and unglued, a couple of cards short of a full deck, mishuga, flaky, weird, to name a few. "Alcoholic" prompts an even larger spread of idioms.

The helping professions do not enjoy this freedom of expression or the use of idiom, nuance, and color. But they do have their own proprietary jargon. Professional communication and dominion require precision in terms used for description, explanation, and planning. To float such terms as "transference," "conditioning," "object relations," and the like also signifies a certain membership in an inner circle.

My observations here about the contrast between psychopathological and strength perspectives on the human predicament are hardly unprecedented. Given the polarities represented by the two perspectives, controversies about the plausibility, the strengths and weaknesses of either position have waxed and waned—at times, raged—over the past many years without much apparent change. In these pages, I will stay with plausibility as the major theme. Thus, since neither of the two perspectives represents a fact of nature nor were they created out of thin air, the place to start is their derivations. The epistemologies of the two modes, what they imply as rhetorical constructs, and their relevance for social work practice deserve at least brief examination.

Unlike the physical sciences wherein hypotheses about phenomena are tested and (optimally) where the proven will displace the others, our two disparate assumptions represent a brand of philosophical thinking that doesn't consider it strange that two or more diverse, even contradictory world views can coexist and persist. In this instance, the reason is that neither can show any real evidence or proof of its essential "goodness," "truth," or "effectiveness." In other words, the persistence of each form depends on a set of rhetorical assumptions about the nature of the human state that, typically, are unquestioned, ingrained, and unchallenged by its own adherents. There is the temptation to refer to these systems as "paradigms"; if one succumbs, it is an admitted metaphor since neither can be characterized by the rigor and internal logic and consistency that a true paradigm represents. I start with a definition of terms and their origins and rationale.

If veridicality is the watchword of the medico-scientific establishment, then the term "psychopathology" is a misnomer. Literally, the term means "illness of the mind" (or if we use Freud's definition, "of psyche," or "of spirit or soul"). Not long ago when brain–mind relations were considered in naive and speculative terms, theorists were free to imagine and fabricate their own versions of mind and behavior, both seemingly independent of the contents of the cranium and their operations. More than that, radically different versions of the mind and behavior—Freudian, Jungian, Rankian, Sullivanian, and other psychological systems—competed with one another, each positing its own unarguable etiology of and cure for the various neuroses and psychoses.

Recent explorations into disorders of thought, affect, and behavior show the concept of "illness of mind or brain," to be clumsy and inapt. Louis Sass (1992), for example, among the many investigators of schizophrenia, argues that it is likely a heterogeneous illness: All cases may have different etiologies; any of several theories may be true, but only as they apply to special subgroups; and it may suggest organic brain dysfunction and/or psychological reactions. For the sake of argument, let us say that schizophrenia or other pathologies are indeed caused by purely physiological conditions (for instance, genetic, chemical, structural). Such an illness, however, cannot be separated from what is the essential nature of the particular human being. To be sure, one may indeed "break": But even a purely physical ailment—arthritis or cancer, as examples—involve the whole person and depend, in some part, on the integrity and strength of that person as a source of healing and repair.

I suggest that political and proprietary reasons coupled with the noble status of a medical science have some say in sustaining the stature of the psychopathological or medical model; it is not uncommon for social work educators to insist on courses in psychopathology "because social workers need to understand how this orientation applies in psychiatry." And so, when students who are eager to gather in the contrivances of respectable professionalism are exposed to the doctrines of the pathological model as they are inscribed in the *Diagnostic and Statistical Manual,* can they argue against or have any reason to resist the finely wrought and morbid taxonomies of human defects and flaws? They undoubtedly would be impressed by the medical idiom although it is an apparent tautology: For example, the classification of "avoidant personality disorder" seems more rigorous and professional than the common and understandable folk language like "self-conscious," "fearful," or "shy." Compare this jargon with the folk language of the strength or resilience perspective. As I will show, its many synonyms—competency, wellness, effectiveness, for example—are friendly words that do not require resorting to manuals or taxonomies for definition. Which is as it should be when we talk about people, not objects.

As I am working out this rhetorical argument an opportunity presents itself—in the form of the arrival of the profession's monthly newsletter—to make my position slightly more graphic. Among the advertisements for doctoral programs and software for billing patients, announcements for seminars on the future of psychotherapy and the like, I am struck by a professionally designed advertisement announcing a new personality disorder so new that it has "not yet been codified in the DSM." The new disorder was, what? discovered? invented? experimentally tested? clinically based on an $n = 1$? The last is intimated by reference to two-years' therapy with a patient; the videotape of these sessions (that includes "diagnosis-specific interventions") can be ordered along with a viewer's guide for a 30-day free trial. Is this an example of medico-scientific protocols for the discovery and diagnosis of a new disease, illness, or virus? Can it be mailed in to the *Diagnostic Manual?*

In any case, despite these sharp differences, the two perspectives *do* share a common and demonstrated fact: Neither is securely anchored in fact—whether it be scientific proof, empirical evidence, or conformity with some established truth. As will be shown, "strength" or "pathology" are themselves metaphors, figures of speech that do not have specific referents, but make their point by comparison with or similarity to some arbitrary—often culturally defined—criterion. That they are metaphors does not diminish their usefulness; without such forms of communication, we could not speak meaningfully and intelligently about indefinable and everambiguous human conditions.

The best example is the story the client tells about herself, the problem, or some experience. In figurative more so than factual terms, we are presented with an account, a recollection, or an impression that often is seasoned with all sorts of images. They might include similes ("I feel like a lost dog"), metaphor ("my mind is just a blob of nothingness"), irony ("my husband is such a sweet bastard"), euphemisms ("I'd call it social drinking"), and symbols in all shapes and sizes. Depending on the client's intent, these terms, in turn, may confide or camouflage something as hard to pin down as a state of mind, a puzzled feeling, or a forbidden impulse, themselves figures of speech.

To rephrase this overview, I propose that our professional activities are not, as we would prefer to believe, rational consequences of a set of established and tested theories, constructs, and techniques. Rather, we are the inheritors of abstractions and concepts—a professional language comprising value-laden metaphors and idioms. It is a language that has far more to do with philosophic assumptions about the human state, about the ideologies of professionalism, and, not the least, the politics of practice than with some objective and rational hypothesis. The rhetoric of the two perspectives inevitably dictate (at least in broad terms) the professional's role vis-à-vis that of the client's. In so doing, unavoidable ethical questions come forward about the allocation of power and authority (and the matter of self-determination) in the helping experience. As happens with a medico-scientific approach to practice, the weight of influence is set by the expertise of the practitioner. In the case of the humanistic, strength-oriented approach, the issues of power and authority are the natural interpersonal conditions of the helping process that, optimally, can be shared by client and worker.

A useful way of pursuing the issues and questions raised thus far would be to redefine the two perspectives on practice as social constructions that reflect public and professional attitudes and beliefs: It is here that the question of plausibility comes forth. How well does each of these perspectives and their constructions serve us in our work with people? To what extent do they approximate and reflect the real-life human circumstances we encounter in practice? In what ways does the influence of these orientations intrude on the ethical and political climate of the helping relationship? For purposes of argument and contrast the commentary will need to be framed in polar terms.

STRENGTH/RESILIENCE AND PATHOLOGY AS SOCIAL CONSTRUCTIONS

As defined by Gergen (1985), social constructionist inquiry attempts to understand the processes by which people explain and define themselves and their world. Dismissing the notion that there is a firm and objective basis for conventional knowledge and language, social constructionism argues that the terms in which the world is understood are social artifacts, the products of cultural, symbolic and historical interchanges among people. Such artifacts have currency only as long as there is consensus about their value: Simply put, we continue to depend on the conventional knowledge and language. While they serve our varied social, adaptive, and professional purposes, we have no need question the verity of such "truths."

As social constructions, the language of each perspective attributes its own meaning to the human condition. By definition, "strength" and "psychopathology" denote what might be thought of as complementary states of being. That is, health makes sense in its relation to illness. According to *Webster's New World Dictionary, Third College Edition* (1994), strength refers to moral courage, fortitude, physical force, and vigor among other virtues; psychopathology covers abnormality, disorder, and disease.

Allow me a moment to examine the root sources of these terms, since their origins are informative. Strength is a word that derives from the Anglo-Saxon, an earthy and unadorned language that reflects the natural world of living. Etymologically, strength is a relative of other terms that express normalcy, assertiveness, proactiveness, and integrity. Resilience is Latin in origin—from *salire,* to leap—changing to *resilire,* to leap back or "recoil"; all concerned with active movement. Pathology, in contrast, derives from the early Greek that is elite, scholarly, abstract, and in some ways above the worldly experience. Its root is *pathos,* which connotes suffering, endurance, and sorrow.

As an inherited construct, how did it happen that the biomedical term "pathology" came to be applied to something as ambiguous as human mental states? Although the term has a long history in general medicine, it did not come into usage by medical psychiatry until the mid-nineteenth century. At that point, its adoption as a medical classification and its consequences were as political as medical.

By the mid-nineteenth century the study of brain anatomy took over and the positivistic sciences came into ascendance. Within this scientific revolution, medicine became institutionalized and standardized. Swept along with this change was the formal medicalization of mental disorders (Ellenberger, 1970).

> Ernest Becker (1964) sums up the rise of the medical prerogative: Nineteenth-century diagnosticians redoubled efforts to keep man under medical wraps and dress his behavior disorder in Greco-Latin cant. Thus the science that knew least about total symbolic man and most about the animal body fully established its sacrosanct domain. We are coming to know that it had no business there. . . . The result of this lopsided jurisdictional development was that human malfunction has continued to be treated largely in nineteenth-century disease categories up to the present day. (pp. 9–10)

There is one special consequence of the medicalizing or mechanizing of what, as a catchall of human distress and conflict, is called "mental disorders": The medical model as a rational, empirical, scientific method for diagnosis and treatment has little room for the intangible, immeasurable spectrum of personal beliefs and convictions. Such beliefs might include images as varied as personal faith and convictions, myths—both private and cultural, a spiritual sense of trust, whether secular or religious, the hope and promise of divine intercession, images and projections of self in a more sympathetic future, and other inner agencies. Falling outside the official taxonomy, such exclusively human propensities are at risk of being considered "irrational" or "metaphysical." Fairness demands that I not be overly wholesale in such judgments: Certainly the empirical practitioner, the precise behaviorist, even the organically oriented professional are sentient beings in their own right who respect and value such transcendent levels of existence. Whether these are used in practice as credible motivations is another question.

Strength and resilience are social constructions with some vintage built into, over time, the ordinary, plebian, or folk vocabulary. Terms—or really value judgments—such as virtue, willpower, integrity, fortitude, are common, culturally defined ways of referring to the character and worth displayed in the face of the travails of living. Curiously, although scientific or psychological terms have more prestige, the use of ordinary modes of characterization can make us more touchy, uneasy. I believe we would rather be considered "depressed," "anxious," or "compulsively driven" than for someone to suspect that we are, say, "spineless" or "domineering." It is more comforting and face-saving to be told that no matter how troubled I feel, it is "because" of something that "makes" me be that way. The alternative, of course, hits hard as a judgment of character.

As novel perspectives (at least within the helping profession), what we call "strength" and "resilience" are, by definition, value-laden, subjective constructs: They may express personal standards of excellence and/or prevailing social norms or standards. The obverse of these principles is, of course, a sense of failure, inadequacy, or low self-esteem. Even so, these are not judged as defects but as possible motivations for personal responsibility, growth, and realization. In either instance, the construct encourages and implies an expansive (rather than a reductionistic) and inclusive mode of understanding. As I will make clearer, "resilience" is not an inborn attribute as far as we can tell; even if it were, its significance can be appreciated best within a social context. Further understanding of this human quality is enriched by listening closely to the client's definition of what life has been and is all about: by regard for apparent potentials, expectations, visions, hopes and desires; by the *meanings* one gives to or finds in his or her circumstances, and not the least, the quality and extent of *relationships.* No matter how well we succeed in how we think we are deepening our understanding, humility must be ever-present.

Implications for Social Work Practice

Let us consider, first, the shape practice would take should it adopt either persuasion. I have already mentioned that the logical follow-through of a perspective that one learns, elects, or finds sympathetic to his or her world view should result in a peculiar social arrangement (whether it is called a psychotherapy, casework, counseling, or advocacy relationship). The nature of this arrangement or structure with its procedures and ground rules will quickly—but perhaps subtly—inform the client about how to be, what to expect, where he or she stands, and other undercurrents of the human relationship.

Specifically, if my metaphor for practice is the medical model, the logic of this model will lead me from the general to the specific—as might occur in a visit to a family physician. Of course, I will want to know from the outset as much as possible about yourself, the presenting problem, and perhaps what it is like for you to be in this situation. But as we proceed together, my intent to reach a diagnosis (or assessment or evaluation) of what is wrong (and, hopefully, the cause) will lead me to narrow the inquiry if I am to arrive at a plan of action or treatment. Along the way, I will do my best to involve you in all stages of the event.

Admittedly, the elaborate theoretical structure and technique-centered features of this model leaves it open to greater critical analysis than the more earthbound nature of the strengths perspective. But before I comment on certain risks and hazards, I must say that practitioners who draw from the medical model and its notions of pathology bear no resemblance to computer programmers. There is a natural and very human gap between theory and what it advises about practice, between the abstract and the real life. Although in this perspective, caring and amity are not excused, it is so much of a closed system the advantages and values of alternative approaches to helping may be overlooked.

As to what I see as pitfalls, first is the presence of a sense of detached objectivity, distance and control in the endeavor to assess you, your problem, and its cause. There is a suggestion in this process that I, as the human-relations expert, can in certain respects "know" you better than you can understand yourself. This being the case, you need little convincing about who in this relationship has earned the special knowledge and authority of professionalism, who is in charge. Let us not overlook the possibility that there are some rewards—certain comforts and relief—when one is in the hands of a maestro conducting the score. Such comfort does not come without risk: In an asymmetrical relationship where power is unevenly held, critical moral and ethical questions about responsibility, rights, and informed consent may not receive their proper due.

At any rate, my commentary is surely an oversimplification of a complex and convoluted process. But however this mode of practice unfolds, keep in mind that it is *linear* in its logic: Causes will bring about effects; diagnosis will lead to treatment that should effect cure; development is sequential, one stage following another, and so on.

In thinking about the alternative approach of the strengths/resilience perspective, it is impossible to make a one-to-one comparison with the medical model or to talk about which "works better." Since each is based on its own unique assumptions about the human condition, any judgment would be as pointless as trying to say that the English language is better than the Japanese or that, geographically, oceans are better than mountains. True, both perspectives have similar purposes; both are centered in a sentient, human relationship. Beyond these essential commonalties their world views diverge considerably.

Strength and Resiliency

Although I have used strength and resilience interchangeably, it is time now to mark, not their difference, but what they illuminate in the larger picture. As a perspective on human problems of living, I have referred to the strength perspective as an organizing construct that embraces a set of assumptions and attributes about health and potential. Although I am not sure there is consensus about this definition, I see resilience as the attribute that epitomizes and operationalizes what the strength perspective is all about.

Only recently has the theory of resiliency claimed a small corner of the literature of the behavioral sciences. George Vaillant (1993) defines resilience as the "self-righting tendencies" of the person, "both the capacity to be bent without breaking and the capacity, once bent, to spring back" (p. 248). Reflecting on a 50-year longitudinal study of men whose childhoods were marked by severe risk, Vaillant tells how he was struck with their ability to "spin straw into gold, laugh at themselves, display empathy . . . and worry and plan realistically," characteristics that apply equally to Bertha and her cohorts. Gail Sheehy (1986) carries this definition a step further in her tribute to what she calls the "victorious personality":

> One may be born with a naturally resilient temperament, but one develops a victorious personality. Those who do often come to believe they are special, perhaps meant to serve a purpose beyond themselves. Among the elements that contribute to a victorious personality are the ability to bend according to circumstance, self-trust, social ease . . . and the understanding that one's plight is not unique. (p. 26)

The concept of resiliency might not strike everyone as particularly novel, enlightening, or as a breakthrough in the field of psychology (or as a threat to professional authority). It is, after all, merely a high-flown version of what our culture and its folk psychology has always admired—and often expected—about the hardiness and pliability of the human spirit. While Social Darwinism has taken this standard to an extreme, in a more kindly sense, society as a whole has always assumed that, perhaps with some help and support, its members will literally stand up and be counted. Nevertheless, when Anthony and Cohler (1987) set out to edit a text on resilience, they were astonished at the sparseness of the literature on this topic:

> One would have thought that the picture of children triumphing over despairing, degrading, depressing, depriving, and deficient circumstances would have caught the immediate attention of both clinicians and researchers, but the survivors and thrivers appear to pass almost unnoticed amidst the holocaust of disadvantage and the tragedies of those who succumbed to it. (p. 28)

As was the intent of my study of the graduates of the Children's Home, previous behavioral scientists sought to sort out the characteristics of people who appear to be of the resilient mold; those who, as children, struggled with adversity without special help and eventually found their way into rewarding adulthood. There is agreement about one thing: As children, they were not exceptional "superkids."

These investigators focused largely on the personality characteristics of resilient children such as temperament, cognitive skills, self-esteem, and their social skills involving curiosity about people, cooperativeness, and friendliness. These features, however, tend to perpetuate the myth of causality: *If* one has any of these characteristics *then* certain resilient behaviors should follow. Even accepting this formula, it is, of course, hard to know what came first: whether these personal and social attributes begot resiliency or whether resiliency itself was the outgrowth of experience and trial. The researchers also allowed that the traits of resiliency do not add up like collecting grades or varsity points. Rather, they tend to swell exponentially. When a child or adult takes risks or survives a serious threat, new skills and greater self-confidence accrue. These gains fuel the individual to dare and test herself in other venues of her life; and so the adventures of living multiply (Garmezy, 1985; Rutter, 1987).

From an implied feminist standpoint, Judith Jordan (1992) also contests the causal idea, saying that the roots of resilient attitudes and behavior are not entirely located within the person or his social supports. More in line with the experience of the Home's children and the importance of the social context mentioned earlier, the sources of mastery and resilience are seen as the give-and-take, the dialectics and mutualities of interpersonal relationships. The former wards put this explanation in homier terms: "it was camaraderie . . . my group"; "there was always someone among us who cared what happened"; "by my rules, I never put myself first"; "other kids came to me for help and advice"; "I had to be the mother and fight for my sibs." In these terms, resilient behavior is not effected by something or someone: As a complex form of flexibility and mastery, it arises out of and is nourished by interpersonal and social processes.

In this view, Jordan argues that current studies of the psychology of resilience are too limited, since they focus largely either on the *individual's* acculturation or the gains of social support. Concentration either on personality (how one turns inward to find strength) or social support (turning outward for assistance and comfort) is a "separate self" model of development that works in one-directional ways. Jordan contends that this model is an *individualized*—even isolated—conception of what it means to be resilient and, for that matter, what it means to be a person. Resilience, in her terms, is a relational dynamic nurtured by a two-way process of mutuality and empathy—a process of "sharing with" more so than "getting from." As Bertha told me, "we all took an interest in each other . . . took up for each other." This unspoken bond did more than ease one's misfortune and sadness—the penalties of orphanage life. Such fellowship (often with irony or comedy) encouraged and applauded any show of talent for battling with trial and hardship, rewarded even a flicker of courage and self-confidence, and set the norms for how people were supposed to "be" with one another. Although this trust and caring perhaps were not complete substitutes for the affection and intimacy of a family, such sympathies could be depended on as proofs that someone was there, that trust among people was possible, that security was possible.

In case I am giving the impression that institutional life, as described by its graduates, was altogether a children's garden of delight, I must report on its larger and darker side: A harsh and crude pecking order meant that there were lots of bloody battles. Kids stole, cheated, lied, and played mean tricks. There were snotty-faced kids, whiners, bedwetters, complainers, blamers—the unkempt, pimply, un-washed kids. But given these dire conditions, the fostering of a resilient attitude is all the more impressive.

How does resilience translate into the more mundane, immediate, and pur-poseful processes of the helping situation? Whether or not resilience is a strength or attribute that one is endowed with in some measure or degree, Jordan gives greater weight to resilience as a state of mind. This means that basic principles of helping begin with a primary focus on—or better, a commitment to—how clients perceive their world. Don't let this imply that this principle will result in easy good-will, be-nevolence, or altruism. It might not take long before discouragement sets in, espe-cially when the less-than-inspired client conveys something less than a grateful view of the helper, the helping situation, and of what, if anything, lies ahead. In such (to put it lightly) challenging circumstances, the easy out on the part of the helper through the exit of that all-purpose loophole, the client's "resistance" (of the intractable type, of course), might be resisted. Trust, even a trace, in what may pos-sibly be ahead—expressed firmly, expectantly, reassuringly, insistently or in any genre that is proper to the circumstances—offers at least some probability that nar-row self-consciousness might gradually give way to greater openness.

It is a relationship of this kind and quality that makes the difference. Patients (subjects in a study) who believed they benefited from the services of a mental health center attributed the primary reason for their improvement to their therapists' genuine acceptance of their real-life worth and strength (Kunin, 1985). Mahoney (1991) in his authoritative book on change puts it in more sober terms:

> . . . the optimal therapeutic relationship creates a special human context—
> a context in and from which the client can safely experiment with and ex-plore familiar and novel ways of experiencing self, world (especially interpersonal), and possible relationships. Such experiments and explora-tions—which are individualized to match the client's current competencies and experiential horizons—are constrained only by the requirements that they be self-caring and socially responsible. (p. 267)

And he sums up: "Optimal helping respects the power and resilience of the human spirit" (p. 271).

Unquestionably, every model of practice is guided by an externally shaped code of ethics, its rules for avoiding any transgression that might prove harmful or insidious. It seems to me that a strengths perspective is by its very nature an ethical and moral enterprise. To repeat, the down-to-earth, interpersonal nature of strength and resilience is always contextual; it is centered on people's behavior in the real world, in palpable interpersonal affairs that, if they are to be civil and meaningful, must be guided at all times by clear moral obligations that are intrinsic to the proc-ess. Vacant of such principles, what may appear as one's strength and resiliency would be at best self-serving and at worst the misuse of power and exploitation.

WHAT KIND OF MODEL OF PRACTICE
FOR SOCIAL WORK?

I think I have shown that a health or strength perspective, although rooted in the philosophy of humanism, is also sympathetic to the emerging world views of scientists who are critical of Newtonian language, concepts, and assumptions that describe a linear world—a cause that effects a problem that suggests a "cure." The image of the resilient, vibrant, and ever-variable human being supplants the suppositions that one could or should be reduced to classifications, diagnoses, or prediction. Resilience represents the intertwining of strength in action and a state of mind that requires that clients' meanings, perceptions, self-definitions, and explanations and other substance of their narratives be given credibility in place of our own expert presumptions. It doesn't even need to be said that some grievous circumstances we know will be interpreted not only differently but what we might consider outrageously by different clients: Some will merely resign themselves; others may just hope to make it, to survive; a few are ready to fight for their lot in life.

It is not some defect or scar that determines or predicts the reach of hope and possibility in anyone's image of self. Rather, it is that well-worn term, values, that count. I am not speaking of some abstract notion of virtue or righteousness but more critically, the power of active *choice;* true values are rooted in belief but are made real by performance. And what differentiates a value choice from ordinary preferences and decisions is consciousness of our moral obligation that energize the intellectual and sensual images of how and what we ought to be.

Social work, then, is fundamentally an ethical and moral enterprise—one that is all too often camouflaged by all sorts of technical, faddish, or theoretical embroidery. Academic jargon and pseudo-technology become irrelevant once we are willing and able—lest we forget, invited or permitted—to enter the client's metaphoric and moral world. Often, this world is torn by the struggle with moral anguish, with value conflicts. They involve the conditions and qualities of living that one will risk or settle for—especially when life seems too chaotic and out of control, when the integrity of self is at risk and when former values and beliefs seem to be no longer reliable.

Rereading what I write, these words look like the many philosophical musings that take up space in professional literature—ideas that limply lead to the "oughts," "musts," and "shoulds" of what social workers do. They are not. The real-life world is (almost literally) shot through with effects of a human science that offers—even recommends—justifications for the right of any client to be a hapless victim. Reasons, causes, and responsibility for one's conflicts and troubles are (theoretically, of course) located somewhere outside the person in the environment, oppression, the perils of childhood loss and dependency, genetics, chemicals, dysfunctional families, repression, the ill-fortunes of race, poverty, social class, or most any other affliction you might think of. One consequence, as Daniel Patrick Moynihan (1993) proposes in his article, "Defining Deviancy Down" is the "normalizing" of outrageous deviant behavior *because of* a natural consequence of any of the above. Public tolerance of increasingly extreme atrocities increasingly stretches.

To be sure, these conditions are painfully, punitively real and toxic, certainly not helped by the hardening of political attitudes and the diminution of resources, by societal divisions and discriminations. How ever else we address these conditions—economically, legislatively, or with social programs, for example—morbid focus on the social or internal plagues people face will hardly help clients to de-victimize themselves, or enable them to discover their own island of strength, their innate resilience, and moral responsibility in their personal and social worlds.

As helpers, we first create the climate in which consumers can rediscover that one is worthwhile and has the right and incentive—and, in fact, the obligation—to hope and stretch for something of value and to carry these beliefs into action. Fortunately, this observation is not a revelation for so many humanistic practitioners and educators whose eyes are on the basic mission of their profession.

In summary, the vulnerable human beings who intentionally or by others' requirement find their way into the purview of social work bring with them the evidence of a reality that is painfully brutish, degrading, vitiating—even corrupt. Its source is often hard to determine: it might be psychologically and physically within the person, between people, between people and their community and society, between people and a depleted environment—or any combination of the above. Let us call this state of affairs the *ordeal*. But, despite the lure of simple explanations, do not confuse the *ordeal* with the *problem*. Many folks who don't find their way into a professional's office or agency endure similar or even more painful ordeals and even come out all the better for their efforts: community, culture, relationships and friends, a reflective nature among other resources may make the difference.

The readiness to think of such ordeals as the problem revives the whole specious notion of linear thinking: the idea that something—divorce, job loss, abandonment—somehow causes the client's sorrows, behaviors, denial, victimhood, and so on. Yes, I agree: These conditions are intrinsically dreadful. But the problem, simply put, may be the client's personal sense of failure, moral or otherwise, irresponsibility, flight, resignation, lack of needed resources, a caring someone or whatever stands for his or her inability to cope with, take control of, manage life's circumstances. The respondents of Kunin's (1985) study who believed things were better were not particularly indifferent to the "presenting problem" that first prompted their request for help; "getting better" to them meant that they now felt able, as they put it, to "take charge of my life," "get out of my failure mode," "no longer take it out on my kid," and so on. Their personal sense of strength and moral worth was undeniable as was the excuse of oppression and victimhood. Recall, also, the consequences of resilient behavior noted before, "These gains fuel the individual to dare and test herself in other venues of her life; and so the adventures of living multiply."

Last words: You can't say that the strengths/resilience perspective is "better than," "more effective than," "works better than" other practice models. Comparison is pointless. The perspective, however, by its very nature naturally embraces and operationalizes the essential and enduring precepts of social work: self-determination, starting where the client is, the importance of relationship, and so on. The perspective does not abstract, objectify, or theorize the client's circumstances; it uses the client's language, idiom, and narrative; it strives to understand and be sympathetic to the client's real-life ordeal as it is *experienced:* It not only gives credibility to subjective understanding but strives to refine this way of making sense and finding meaning through the development of reflective thinking.

Long ago, in my first casework class, our instructor began by giving his definition of social work: It is, he said, helping clients to help themselves. "That doesn't sound very professional," I thought at the time, "it is so simpleminded." I continue to learn just how complex and challenging that simple phrase is.

DISCUSSION QUESTIONS

1. What does it mean to say that both strength and pathology are social constructions?
2. How would your practice be different if you thought that most clients were probably victors rather than victims?
3. What do you think were the roots of the resilience of the survivors of the orphange experience?
4. What is the difference between thinking of clients as going through an ordeal as opposed to thinking of them as having problems?

REFERENCES

Anthony, E. J., & Cohler, B. J. (Eds.). (1987). *The invulnerable child.* New York: Guilford Press.

Becker, E. (1964). *The revolution in psychiatry.* New York: Free Press.

Bruner, J. (1990). *Acts of meaning.* Cambridge, MA: Harvard University Press.

Ellenberger, H. (1970). *The discovery of the unconscious.* New York: Basic Books.

Garmezy, N. (1985). Stress resistant children: The search for protective factors. In J. Stevenson (Ed.), *Recent research in developmental psychology.* Oxford: Pergamon Press.

Gergen, K. J. (1985). The Social Constructionist Movement in modern psychology. *American Psychologist, 40,* 266–275.

Goldstein, H. (1996). *The home on Gorham Street and the voices of its children.* Tuscaloosa, AL: University of Alabama Press.

Jordan, J. V. (1992, April). *Relational Resilience.* Paper presented as part of the Stone Center Colloquium Series, Wellesley College, Wellesley, MA.

Kunin, R. (1985). *A study of clients' self-reports of their experience of personal change in direct practice.* Unpublished doctoral dissertation, Case Western Reserve University, Cleveland, OH.

Mahoney, M. J. (1991). *Human change processes.* New York: Basic Books.

Moynihan, D. P. (1993, Winter). Defining deviancy down. *American Scholar,* 17–30.

Rutter, M. (1987). Psychosocial resilience & protective mechanisms. *American Journal of Orthopsychiatry 57*(3), 316–331.

Sass, L. A. (1992). *Madness & modernism.* New York: Basic Books.

Sheehy, G. (1986, April 20). The victorious personality. *New York Times Magazine,* p. 26.

Vaillant, G. E. (1993). *The wisdom of the ego.* Cambridge, MA: Harvard University Press.

part II

The Strengths Approach to Practice

chapter **3**

Putting Problems in Their Place: Further Explorations in the Strengths Perspective

Ann Weick
Ronna Chamberlain[1]

As a profession that grew out of an organized impulse to help those in need, social work has a long familiarity with human problems. While the focus of its attention has varied over time, its scope has remained wide and inclusive. Virtually every human trouble is encompassed within or touched by social work's interests. Given this investment in the well-being of society, it is worth examining what social work has brought to this history of response to problems and to ask whether its current preoccupations take advantage of the profession's wisdom and insight about the nature of human and social change.

This assessment is particularly appropriate in light of the development of a strengths perspective in social work. If social work is to more consciously focus on the strengths of people and their communities, where do problems fit? Critics claim that the strengths perspective ignores people's problems and glosses over their real pain. If we don't learn all there is to know about a person's problems, it seems that the very nature of helping is in jeopardy. Moreover, the profession's knowledge about human difficulties appears to be diminished if problems are no longer the central focus of work.

Fascination with the troubled, anomalous, and paradoxical aspects of human existence is rooted in cultural phenomena that extend well beyond social work (Weick, 1992). The profession is not alone in fastening its attention on what's wrong with people and society. Other professions, social institutions, and the popular culture seem mesmerized by the search for fallibility. Personal and social problems appear overwhelming and obvious, while personal and social resources seem insub-

---

[1] The authors gratefully acknowledge the contributions of their research assistant, Theresa Cote, to the development of this paper.

stantial and limited. The problems loom large; the solutions seem invisible. Our only defense seems to be an overactive vigilance in searching out, monitoring, and reporting all the ways in which people's capacity to do and endure harm is present among us.

In order to clarify the place of problems within the strengths perspective, it is important to develop a larger understanding about the place of problems within social work. The ways that the profession has defined its work have changed over time. Examining this history can provide a broader context for determining how social work can most appropriately view problems within its practice and how a strengths perspective can reveal the profession's essential insights about the power of our work.

THE SHAPE OF PROBLEMS

Social work has developed as a profession through a multiplicity of voices. Moralistic admonitions, scientific exhortations, and humanistic beliefs have all coexisted throughout the course of our history, with none being completely removed or silenced. The historical involvement of social work with those who were marginalized by virtue of poverty, race, age, nationality, or mental condition has never been an entirely clear commitment. Bertha Reynolds's (1951) observation about the tendency of social agencies to move away from the very poor and highly disadvantaged has been part of a long-term trend in social work. From the beginning, those who saw possibilities and those who saw liabilities both spoke for the profession.

Social work's interest in human problems began in very ordinary ways. At the end of the nineteenth century, the effects of industrialization and the large waves of immigrants arriving on American shores created, in numbers and intensity, a different level of visibility for age-old human issues. Unemployment, child maltreatment, homelessness, and poverty took on new dimensions and called for an organized response. Workers in charity organizations and settlement houses developed family-oriented and community-oriented strategies to help those who were caught in the tide of this major social upheaval.

The definitions of these problems took two general directions. For some social workers, the problems were squarely moral: Individuals who were poor or addicted, violent or insane were morally, and perhaps, constitutionally, defective. The character of the person was of central concern. But others saw the social dimensions and believed that resources such as housing, sanitation, education, neighborly assistance, and enriched social interactions would enable people to move beyond the limits of their situations. Both of these convictions rested on the positive value of the social work relationship as the medium for constructive change.

This orientation received renewed vigor through the writings of Bertha Reynolds (1951). She placed an emphasis on the problems of daily living, particularly within the context of the "conscious struggle of the person to deal with the facts of life confronting him" (p. 120). This orientation on problems reinforced both the everyday focus of work and the capacities of people to respond creatively within the constraints of their lives. The importance of the social work relationship was seen as the means by which personal and social resources could be activated. Charlotte Towle (1965) added another dimension to this sturdy base through her book, *Common Human Needs*. Although the focus was on the rights of those receiving public assistance, her philosophy embodied a strong belief in providing "opportunities for self-development" (p. xiii) and in human beings' "strong and inevitable impulse toward progression" (p. 43).

The tradition of problems as ordinary aspects of human life was continued in the writings of Helen Harris Perlman (1963), who conceived of social work as a problem-solving process, and Harriett Bartlett (1970), who emphasized the notion of life tasks common to all and the need to use rational, conscious processes for dealing with the problems presented by life situations. This view is sustained in the present day by the work of Carel Germain and Alex Gitterman (1980) who, in their life model, emphasize "problems in living" in three interrelated areas: "life transitions, environmental pressures, and interpersonal processes" (p. 11–12). The essence of the approach is that human troubles can be assessed by letting people talk about their problems and discover through this process courses of action that energize individual, family, and community resources necessary for resolution.

From its earliest days in the Settlement Movement, social group work has sounded another strong chord in the social work tradition. The process envisioned by Gisela Konopka (1963), Helen Northen (1969), and others of that era highlighted the idea of unleashing human potential through group support and strengthening the ideal of participatory democracy and social justice (Northen, 1969, p. 2). The voices of William Schwartz (1971), Ruth Middleman (1974), Larry Shulman (1992), and Judith Lee (1994) have kept alive and extended this view.

Beginning in the 1920s, the profession's understanding of human problems began to be influenced by the burgeoning fields of psychology and psychiatry. These professions no longer viewed human behavior as transparent or easily explained. Quite the reverse. Psychological and psychiatric theories made human actions mysterious, complex, and rarely what they seemed. The causes of behavior moved from simple categories like moral character, family origins, social habits, and economic situation to a new language of explanation that only a select few knew. This language was based on ideas about human motivation, the development of personality, and on intrapsychic aspects of everyday behaviors. In the world of human behavior, nothing was ever as it appeared.

The psychologizing of human behavior had a powerful impact on the nature of the helping process. If human problems were caused not by everyday troubles and challenges but by deeply seated, complex behavioral patterns, then the persons affected could not be expected to understand their own actions. People's inner lives became both inaccessible and differently accessible to them. The understandings they may have had were seen as mistaken and naive. The new understanding given to them was packaged by another: Someone else became the interpreter of what one was feeling and why. A new class of experts appeared, who, through professional training and perhaps through personal therapeutic analysis, were able to decipher the intrapsychic cause of one's difficulties. Moreover, the cause was thought to be connected to the cure so that no constructive action could be taken until the cause had been unearthed. The only work to be done was psychic excavation. Once the "ruins" were discovered, it was assumed that resolution and reconstitution would follow.

This redefinition of human problems has been the persistent legacy of psychologically oriented practice. What had been regarded as universal aspects of human experience throughout history evolved into new classes of behaviors, isolated from their context and viewed through the lens of pathology. Because these behaviors are removed from their larger social context, they appear to be unique failures and dangerous symptoms instead of pervasive, if frightening and puzzling, parts of human life. Psychological definitions hide from view the fact that human troubles, in all their guises, are predictable parts of social living. Saying this does not lessen our responsibility or concern. What it does suggest is that our interest in why problems exist has caused us to focus on the most intriguing but least useful aspect of work. In doing so, precious energy is used to understand problems and less attention devoted to determining creative ways to reduce their presence and ameliorate their effects.

The quest for psychological causes has not been successful. As the title of Hillman and Ventura's (1992) book suggests, *We've Had One Hundred Years of Psychotherapy and the World is Getting Worse.* Perhaps it is time once again to refocus our attention on results. The profession's historic commitment to working with people in the midst of their daily lives, with all their trials and cares, is a place to begin. The strengths perspective builds on this tradition by meeting people where they are and joining with them in discovering and reaffirming the talents, abilities, and aspirations that will form a path away from the problem.

PUTTING STRENGTHS INTO ACTION

Beginning with an identification of strengths leads the plan for work in a different direction than using the problem definition as the starting point.

KATHY

Kathy, age 43, had been hospitalized 17 times in 14 years for treatment of schizophrenia. Kathy's primary problems were identified as mental illness; noncompliance with treatment and medication regimen; and serious destructive behaviors such as fire-starting. Each discharge followed approximately the same course. Discharge plans included intensive treatment and supervised living in a congregate setting to monitor medication and behaviors. Each time, Kathy discontinued medication and began drinking alcohol and destroying property. All discharges ended with a hospital readmission in less than two months of the previous discharge.

Two years ago, Kathy was discharged with a plan built on a strengths approach and, to date, she has not been rehospitalized. The initial planning process began with conversations in which the social worker learned some important things from Kathy. She discovered that Kathy, although not a Native American herself, felt greater trust in Native Americans. She learned that Kathy enjoyed being with people but wanted to live alone; that she did not want to be involved in any mental health programs at a clinic, and that she loved animals and was very interested in having a pet. While Kathy understood that medication helped her symptoms of mental illness, she did not like taking it because of side effects.

The worker took seriously each of these wishes and began by arranging to have a Native American community social worker assigned to Kathy. Together, they found a small house that would accept pets and that Kathy could afford to rent on her own. Kathy adopted a kitten and began her life in the community. Since her discharge, she has been working at a volunteer job a few hours every week, keeping up her pet and her house, and socializing with her neighbors. She sees the psychiatrist every couple of months and meets with her social worker regularly, outside the clinic, to work on her goals. Kathy has her ups and downs. However, considering the stability of her psychiatric symptoms, the clinic professionals feel safe in assuming that she does not drink alcohol and is taking her antipsychotic medication.

Kathy's success illustrates some of the major differences between a strengths and a problem approach. While mental illness itself remains a mystifying phenomenon, Kathy's understanding of what she wanted or needed was not mysterious. Working with Kathy on goals related to her daily life, based on her interests and aspirations, helped her to find the path beyond her problems.

Kathy's problems did not disappear, but their impact on the quality of her life were significantly minimized. Kathy, like many people with mental illness, seemed more willing to endure the negative aspects of medication when she began shaping a life she valued. Building a daily life full of some personal satisfaction is based on enhancing a person's distinctive interests and talents. Satisfaction and contentment are less likely to occur by applying proscriptive solutions to the problem. While Kathy's schizophrenia is most certainly a problem, a critical portion of the solution rests in ignoring that problem.

Relegating problems to a secondary position may seem difficult when the problem appears to be too grave to be ignored. Such is the case with behaviors that might cause injury to the client or to others. When an individual is at risk of suicide or hurting others, the problem situation demands immediate attention to resolve the potential crisis by securing the safety of those involved. Unfortunately, because the behavior is often expected to recur, these critical problems tend to dominate assessment and case planning even after the crisis situation has abated.

LORETTA

Loretta, age 34, was diagnosed as having a borderline personality disorder. She had multiple hospitalizations on a yearly basis following suicidal threats, gestures such as cutting of wrists, other forms of self-injury, overdosing on medications, and two more serious suicide attempts. In recent years, she had also begun to threaten to hurt other people. Loretta had been in treatment for many years. Creative social workers and psychiatrists had worked diligently with her to help her get jobs and move from her family home into her own apartments. In spite of years of treatment focused on understanding and coping with her depression and suicidal impulses, and exploring different ways of managing her feelings, each job or new living arrangement ended abruptly with a dramatic crisis involving threats and/or self-destructive behaviors requiring hospitalization.

A newly assigned social worker decided that Loretta's destructive behaviors dominated not only her life but also the years of case planning. In an attempt to rid both the client and herself of the emphasis on "the problem," they worked together to arrive at a detailed action plan involving a crisis team to respond to Loretta's calls and threats and to arrange immediate hospitalization during crises. Once the crisis plan was put into place, the worker's sole focus was to assist Loretta in defining her considerable talents and in helping her find ways to express them in work, her home life, and social activities. In the four years that this plan has been in place, Loretta has had two brief hospitalizations. Fortunately, they were not accompanied by the usual spectacle of mental health professionals and emergency vehicles so she has been able to return to her job and apartment following discharge. With the social worker's refusal to be involved in the problem, Loretta has slowly learned to shift her attention to building more satisfying activities in her daily life. For Loretta, putting the problem in its place may, in fact, have saved her life.

The lesson to be learned from Loretta's situation is that, although some problems are too critical to be ignored, they need to be consigned to a position secondary to the person's strengths once a crisis has passed. The dilemma for both the client and the social worker is that the problem is sufficiently frightening that the details of daily life seem to be of little significance by comparison. The paradox appears to be that the problem will defy control until the client has a daily life providing enough gratification to make it worth the arduous task of overcoming a problem as powerful as impulses toward mutilating or violent behavior.

Sometimes more problems are actually created or exacerbated through the use of the problem model. In Kathy's case, when psychiatric discharge plans ceased "placing her" in environments she disliked, with days filled with structured activities in which she had no interest, she no longer damaged property or started fires. These behaviors appeared to have been a reaction against the professional solutions to her problems. Similarly, Loretta's destructive behaviors were minimized when attention to them was curtailed and she was assisted in focusing her attention on other matters.

By focusing work on client strengths in the assessment and planning process, problems are less likely to be invented or exacerbated. When a problem does appear, it is seen as an obstacle to the pursuit of a goal important to the client. In this kind of specific context, a problem becomes more relevant to the client, as was exemplified by Kathy's willingness to take medications in order to maintain the life-style she had designed for herself.

ERNEST

Twenty-six-year-old Ernest presented another kind of challenge. He wanted to work but unfortunately his ability to get a job was impeded by the wires that he insisted on wrapping around his head, limbs, and various articles of clothing to protect himself from evil spirits. From a problem-solving perspective, the medication he was taking was successful in stabilizing many of his symptoms of mental illness, but his problematic delusions continued unabated. A common conclusion would be that Ernest was "not ready to go to work." A typical solution would be to continue to treat Ernest by adjusting his medication in the hope that these delusions would finally be controlled so that he would then be ready to get a job.

A strengths perspective suggested a different strategy. Ernest seemed to have the basic skills necessary to work. However, his delusion related to wearing wires was an obstacle to his goal of getting and keeping a job. Ernest's vocational counselor helped Ernest to understand the social drawbacks of the wires. His wearing them made people uncomfortable and fearful. The strategy they worked on was locating a socially acceptable container in which his wires could be carried. Ernest felt frightened at the significant risk of carrying, rather than wearing, his wires but was able to make this accommodation for job interviews and, eventually, to the workplace. Ernest continued in treatment to control many of his symptoms, but he did not have to postpone enriching his life until his problem of having delusions was solved.

Key Strategies in Strengths-based Practice

As one examines the orientation to problems embraced by the strengths perspective, it becomes clear that problems are no longer in the center of the stage. Instead of being the star performer in a play, they become minor characters with small roles. The strengths perspective is anchored in the belief that a problem does not constitute all of a person's life. Whether the name of the problem is schizophrenia, addiction, child abuse, or troubled family relations, a person is always more than his or her problem.

In tandem with this belief is the acknowledgment that focusing on problems usually creates more problems. The longer one stays with a problem-focused assessment, the more likely it is that the problem will dominate the stage. Both Kathy and Loretta had long and unsuccessful treatment histories where this was the case. However, problems do have a role to play. Just as actors with a few lines are important in a larger drama, problems produce uncomfortable emotions such as pain, anger, shame, and confusion, which serve to get our attention and put us on notice. They are signs that something needs to change. But the problem is not a complete signpost: It signals "danger," "beware," "trouble ahead." It does not include directions about how to get beyond the problem. Complicated diagnoses about human problems can mask the more potent areas of strength, as well as small victories as the person experiences them. A problem orientation begins to look like an exercise serving the needs of professionals, rather than the needs of the people with whom professionals work.

Working from a strengths perspective is linked to three strategies for putting problems in their place. It requires that *we recognize problems only in their proper context,* find simpler ways to talk about problems, and pay less attention to them. By identifying problems when they become obstacles to the attainment of client-determined goals, the problem becomes situation-specific and, thus, more relevant to the client. This was exemplified by Loretta's situation. Her destructive behavior needed to be handled by a very specific action plan. When her behavior precipitated a crisis, both she and her worker knew what steps would be taken to insure her and others' safety. In this way, the attention to problems was contained. Helping her move beyond the crisis was accomplished by working in a single-minded, collaborative way on goals that she determined would make her life more satisfying. Deciding what she wanted for her life and having the experience of accomplishing her goals gave her reason to take medication, even with its negative side effects. Her hopes and dreams provided the larger context for her life; her mental illness became a bit player in this drama.

Adopting simpler ways of talking about problems is another useful strategy for making human problems less mysterious and more manageable. This approach harkens back to the early days of social work, where people were seen to have problems of daily living. Even though we may use more complicated ways of defining them, people's lives are still filled with such issues and opportunities. In some cases, problems arise because basic needs are not met. People are without adequate food, housing, employment, and medical attention. In other cases, problems develop because there are insufficient social supports in areas such as child care and activities for young people, or help for parents in rearing children and caring for family members whose physical or mental conditions require special assistance. Finally, there are the ongoing interpersonal challenges of life as a member of a family, neighborhood, or workplace. By seeing these aspects of social living as part of the predictable fabric of human life, they take on a more manageable form. They move from esoteric categories of psychological diagnosis to the very real, life-size challenges that come with being human beings and living in human communities. Using simple, everyday language or the person's own words to talk about and name the issues people bring is an important step in giving back to them a sense of control over their lives.

Paying less attention to the problem produces new energy for work. In order to get beyond the negativity of the problem, one must mobilize those individual, family, and community resources that make it possible for someone to create a different life. The bridge to doing so is an unrelenting focus on people's strengths. Focusing on people's aspirations, capacities, and skills is a powerful act. The attention itself is reaffirming. Through the eyes of another, people can see themselves in a new light and gain energy for the difficult work of human change. Implicit in this approach is a deep respect for the reservoir of potential inherent in each person and an understanding of the approach that supports and frees that potential for use.

The social worker's belief in this capacity for growth-oriented change is an essential ingredient in the dynamic of the relationship. Stimulating this positive energy begins first with the act of belief. The person, family, or community, deeply mired in the complexities of the trouble, typically does not believe that they possess any resources that would be useful in resolving the problem. They have already tried to fix the situation without success. Social workers' communicating their belief in the inner strength and resourcefulness of a person, family, or community becomes the beginning step in restoring people's faith in themselves and in their capacity to influence the shape of their lives. The power of belief has been eloquently documented by Jerome Frank (1963) in his exploration of the process of healing. But in contrast to his focus on belief in the power of the healer, the strengths perspective depends on the activation of people's belief in the power they themselves possess.

From a strengths perspective, having the problem is not the problem. The real test comes from figuring out constructive ways to meet, use, or transcend the problem. In strengths-based practice, the goal is to mobilize personal, family, and community resources in order to move beyond the problem. An important ingredient in achieving this goal is to learn what people want for themselves. Usually the problem they bring is keeping them from having the kind of life they imagine for themselves. If they did not have mental illness, an abusive partner, or a hyperactive child, they would be more satisfied and feel better about themselves. Helping people to begin talking about this vision of life without the problem taps into their aspirations, hopes, and dreams. Instead of worrying about how they came to have the problem, they can use the positive energy of their aspirations to pare the problem down to size and begin to envision a life beyond the problem.

This vision of a satisfying life, defined in people's own terms, and the steadfast support of social workers who believe in their capacity to achieve it, reveals the essence of the profession's long-time commitment to society's welfare. With that commitment comes a radical appreciation of people's personal potential and of the vast reservoir of supporting resources existing within families, groups, neighborhoods, and communities. Shifting our attention to these strengths will require us to turn away from the seduction of pathology-dominated thinking. But through this new determination, social work can reclaim its distinctive value orientation and bring its own considerable strengths to the task of improving human and social well-being.

DISCUSSION QUESTIONS

1. Definitions of human problems have changed throughout the history of social work. How have these changes affected clients?
2. How can the use of a problem focus create more problems for people?
3. What are three strategies for putting problems in their place?
4. What resources must be mobilized to get people beyond their problems?

5. From a strengths perspective, how can social workers respond in a responsible way to situations in which clients are causing serious harm to themselves or others?

REFERENCES

Bartlett, H. (1970). *The common base of social work practice.* Silver Spring, MD: National Association of Social Workers.

Frank, J. D. (1963). *Persuasion and healing.* New York: Schocken Books.

Germain, C., & Gitterman, A. (1980). *The life model of social work practice.* New York: Columbia University Press.

Hillman, J., & Ventura, M. (1992). *We've had one hundred years of psychotherapy and the world is getting worse.* San Francisco: HarperSanFrancisco.

Konopka, G. (1963). *Social group work: A helping process.* Englewood Cliffs, NJ: Prentice Hall.

Lee, J. A. B. (1994). *The empowerment approach to social work practice.* New York: Columbia University Press.

Middleman, R., & Goldberg, G. (1974). *Social service delivery: A structural approach to social work practice.* New York: Columbia University Press.

Northen, H. (1969). *Social work with groups.* New York: Columbia University Press.

Schwartz, W., & Zalba, S. R. (1971). *The practice of group work.* New York: Columbia University Press.

Shulman, L. (1992). *The skills of helping* (3rd ed.). Itasca, IL: F. E. Peacock.

Perlman, H. H. (1963). *Social casework: A problem solving process.* Chicago: University of Chicago Press.

Reynolds, B. (1951). *Social work and social living.* New York: Citadel Press.

Towle, C. (1965). *Common human needs.* Silver Spring, MD: National Association of Social Workers.

Weick, A. (1992). Building a strengths perspective for social work. In D. Saleebey (Ed.), *The strengths perspective in social work practice.* White Plains, NY: Longman.

chapter 4

The Strengths Approach to Practice

Dennis Saleebey

The chapters in parts II and III describe and discuss strengths-based practice with a number of different populations, including people with chronic mental illness, people with addictions, elders in long-term care, youth at risk, residents of public housing, people with physical and developmental disabilities. While you will perceive differences among these approaches, you will see throughout the chapters a vital and unmistakable belief in the capabilities of individuals, groups, families, and communities. It comes across in many ways, but the following ideas are resoundingly clear from beginning to end:

- Given the difficulties they have, and the *known* resources available to them, people are often doing amazingly well—the best they can at the time.
- People have survived to this point—certainly not without pain and struggle—through employing their will, their vision, their skills, and, as they have grappled with life, what they have learned about themselves and their world. We must understand these capacities and make alliance with this knowledge in order to help.
- Change can only come when you collaborate with clients' aspirations, perceptions, and strengths, and when you firmly believe in them.

As Rappaport (1990) puts it:

To work within an empowering ideology requires us to identify (for ourselves, for others, and for people with whom we work) the abilities they possess which may not be obvious, even to themselves. . . . It is always

49

easier to see what is wrong or what people lack. Empowering research [and practice] attempts to identify what is right with people, and what resources are already available, so as to encourage their use and expansion under the control of the people of concern. (p. 12)

To recognize the strengths in people and their situation implies that we give credence to the way clients experience and construct their social realities. We cannot impose from without our own versions (or those of the agency or other social institutions) of the world. This appreciation of context and construction is an acknowledgment of the special and distinctive social circumstances of each client or group (Saleebey, 1994). Seeking out the strengths of individuals and groups is one way to discover the stories, narratives, and systems of meaning that guide clients. This puts practitioners in the position of discovering the language, the symbols, the images, the perspectives that move clients—for good or ill. You will see in the chapters that follow the high level of commitment and resolve that is required to get you into the client's lifeworld authentically and respectfully. Other themes that abound in the following chapters include the importance of genuine dialogue; forming positive expectations of clients; helping clients participate more fully in their world of people, institutions, and communities; identifying natural resources in the clients' world; and learning from clients. One thing becomes clear in reading these chapters: Operating from a strengths perspective is *good, basic social work practice*. There is nothing here that is not coincidental with the core of values that energizes and drives the profession. All that we can do in these pages is to give these principles more conceptual and practical vigor.

SOME BEGINNING OBSERVATIONS ABOUT STRENGTHS-BASED PRACTICE

These observations are meant to answer some basic questions that have been asked over the years about generic practice from a strengths perspective. First of all, assume that it will take genuine diligence on your part to begin to appreciate and utilize client strengths in practice. The system is against you, the language and metaphors of the system are against you, consumers are sometimes against you because they have been inscribed with the hallmark of disease, and, not insignificantly, the culture is against you. Pursuing the ideas that formulate and celebrate strengths, resilience, rebound, challenge, and transformation is difficult because they are not now natural to much of the social service, health, and mental health systems and their membership.

What Are Strengths?

Almost anything can be considered a strength under certain conditions, so this list is not meant to be exhaustive. Nonetheless, some capacities, resources, and assets do commonly appear in any roster of strengths.

What people have learned about themselves, others, and their world as they have struggled, coped with, and battled abuse, trauma, illness, confusion, oppression, and even their own fallibility. People do learn from their trials, even those that they seem to inflict upon themselves. People do not just learn from successes but from their difficulties and disappointments as well. For example, most people quit or moderate their drinking on their own not only because they do not like what they see in the mirror, but also because they have come to cherish other values, and possibilities—some long forgotten (Peele & Brodsky, 1991).

Personal qualities, traits, and virtues that people possess. These are sometimes forged in the fires of trauma and catastrophe, and they might be anything—a sense of humor, creativity, loyalty, insight, independence, spirituality, moral imagination, and patience to name a few (Wolin & Wolin, 1993). These skills and attributes might well become sources of energy and motivation in working with clients.

What people know about the world around them from those things learned intellectually or educationally to those that people have discerned and distilled through their life experiences. Perhaps a person has developed skill at spotting incipient interpersonal conflict or soothing others who are suffering. Perhaps life has given an individual the ability to care and tend for young children or elders, or it could be that a person can use an artistic medium to teach others about themselves. Again, we have no way of knowing what it might be without observing and asking.

The talents that people have can surprise us sometimes (as well as surprising the individual as some talents have lain dormant over the years). Playing a musical instrument, telling stories, cooking, home repair, writing, carpentry (who knows what it might be?) may provide additional tools and resources to assist individuals or groups in reaching their goals. In addition, they may be assets that can be shared and given to others to foster solidarity, to strengthen mentorship, or to cement friendship.

Cultural and personal stories and lore are often profound sources of strength, guidance, stability, comfort, or transformation and are often overlooked, minimized, or distorted. It is now often told how the stories of women have been shrouded through domination but how they are, when recounted and celebrated, sources of profound strength and wisdom (Aptheker, 1989). Cultural approaches to helping, to cite another example—whether the sweat lodge, medicine wheel, or curanderismo—may be powerful sources of healing and regeneration. Cultural stories, narratives, and myths, accounts of origins and migrations or trauma and survival may provide sources of meaning and inspiration in times of difficulty or confusion. Personal and familial parables of falls from grace and redemption, of failure and resurrection, of struggle and resilience may also provide the diction, the metaphors from which one may construct a more vibrant vision of the self and world.

Pride. People do have pride; people who have leapt over obstacles, who have rebounded from misfortune and hardship often have what the Wolins call "survivor's pride." Often this self-regard is buried under the heap of blame, shame, and labeling, but it is often there waiting to be uncovered. "Pride drives the engine of change; shame jams the gears!" (Wolin & Wolin, 1994).

The community is frequently overlooked as a physical, interpersonal, and institutional terrain full of riches to be tapped into (see chapters 12, 13, 14). The informal or natural environment is an especially rich landscape, full of people and organizations, who, if asked, would provide their talents and knowledge in the service of helping and supporting others. The work of community development (see chapters 11–14) and organizing is, in part, dedicated to germinating the roots of strength and resourcefulness in the community.

How Do You Find out about Strengths?

Sounds difficult, but the discovery of strengths depends on some simple ideas. *Look around you.* Do you see evidence of client interests, talents, competencies?

MICHAEL

A student working with a middle-aged man with moderately severe retardation who lived in a group home was visiting "Michael" one day in his apartment and noticed some fabulous maps of the local area, the state, and the nation on the wall. They were extremely detailed, beautifully balanced, and, the student discovered, hand-drawn from memory by—Michael! He had been drawing these maps for years but no one who had worked with him had bothered to ask or show any curiosity about them. They had not looked around. Through the gradually deepening relationship between Michael and his student social worker, and through hard work and deep belief, Michael's maps eventually were exhibited at a museum, and his story was recounted in several newspapers. The last I heard, there was some interest from a major greeting card company in having Michael's maps, and the artwork of others with physical challenges, become the basis of a new line of cards.

Listen to clients' stories instead of zipping through an assessment protocol. Stories and narratives often contain within their plots and characterizations evidence of strengths, interests, hopes, and visions.

BILL

Bill was in his early forties, in and out of state hospitals since the age of 17 with a variety of diagnoses (chronic undifferentiated schizophrenia seemed to be the favorite). Single, living in a big city with no relatives nearby (or very interested in him), he worked as a dishwasher in a midtown bar and grill. He became hooked up with a community support program at the behest of a hospital social worker who was interested in keeping him out of the hospital. Bill was taking Halpenidol.

He was assigned a first year MSW student as a case manager. The student was learning the strengths approach to practice and was anxious to try it. She began by encouraging Bill to "tell his stories"—how he got to be where he was, what interesting things he had done, and how he had survived with a serious illness. She learned many interesting things about Bill, and some of his stories clearly revealed a resourceful, motivated person. He had a serious problem with alcohol but quit drinking on his own. Yet he continued to frequent a local bar "because that's where all my buddies are," and being with his buddies was one outpost of connection and stability for him.

Bill also, on one occasion, saved enough money from his modest salary to take a trip to Norway. He had seen some of Norway's marvelous statuary in an old *National Geographic* magazine and wanted to experience it for himself. He arranged and took the trip on his own. On his trek, he discovered a joy in flying. A dream began to form in his mind—he could see himself flying a plane.

He revealed his reverie to the social worker, who, given what she had come to learn about Bill, took it to heart. Together they began taking some modest steps toward his desire. In a few months, Bill got a job as a dishwasher at the airport, a busy international terminal, even though it involved an hour-long bus ride each way. He loved being around pilots and planes. At last account, Bill was working toward getting a job on the tarmac, perhaps as a baggage handler. Besides listening to his stories and searching within them for inklings of strength, character, and knowledge, the social worker did something else extraordinarily important to this kind of work: She let Bill know that she was *genuinely interested in the hopes and dreams* that he nurtured.

In trying to discover the strengths within and around, *what sort of questions might one ask?* There are several kinds of questions one might ask including:

Survival questions. How have you managed to survive (or thrive) thus far, given all the challenges you have had to contend with? How have you been able to rise to the challenges put before you? What was your mind-set as you faced these difficulties? What have you learned about yourself and your world during your struggles? Which of these difficulties have given you special strength, insight, or skill? What are the special qualities upon which you can rely?

Support questions. What people have given you special understanding, support, and guidance? Who are the special people on whom you can depend? What is it that these people give you that is exceptional? How did you find them or how did they come to you? What did they respond to in you? What associations, organizations, or groups have been especially helpful to you in the past?

Exception questions.[1] When things were going well in life, what was different? In the past, when you felt that your life was better, more interesting, or more stable, what about your world, your relationships, your thinking was special or different? What parts of your world and your being would you like to recapture, reinvent, or relive? What moments or incidents in your life have given you special understanding, resilience, and guidance?

---

[1] Thanks to the practitioners of solution-focused therapy for this terminology. We did not know what to call these kinds of questions (see P. De Jong and S. D. Miller, "How to interview for client strengths," *Social Work, 40*, 729–736, November, 1995).

Possibility questions. What now do you want out of life? What are your hopes, visions, and aspirations? How far along are you toward achieving these? What people or personal qualities are helping you move in these directions? What do you like to do? What are your special talents and abilities? What fantasies and dreams have given you special hope and guidance? How can I help you achieve your goals or recover those special abilities and times that you have had in the past?

Esteem questions. When people say good things about you, what are they likely to say? What is it about your life, yourself, and your accomplishments that give you real pride? How will you know when things are going well in your life—what will you be doing, who will you be with, how will you be feeling, thinking, and acting? What gives you genuine pleasure in life? When was it that you began to believe that you might achieve some of the things you wanted in life? What people, events, ideas were involved?

These obviously do not exhaust likely questions. And they are not meant to be a protocol, only possibilities.

What Are Some of the Elements of Strengths-based Practice?

What follows is a sampler of the steps in practice. The next six chapters will approach practice in more detail.

Acknowledge the Pain.   For many individuals and families, there is real use and purpose in addressing, acknowledging, reexperiencing, and putting into perspective, the pains and trauma of one's life, especially those that seem now insistent. Catharsis, grieving, expression of rage and anxiety, and reconstruction are important in developing an understanding of where individuals have been, what their current struggles are, and what emotional and cognitive baggage they carry with them. This is also an important step in letting go of the past, and revisioning a present and future that is different and organically better. For some, it may even be beneficial to explore the roots of trauma in family, community, and culture. But the purpose is always to look for the seeds of resilience and rebound, the lessons taken away from the adversity—the cultural, ethnic, and familial sources of adaptability.

Stimulate the Discourse and Narratives of Resilience and Strength.   There is often great resistance to acknowledging one's competence, reserve, and resourcefulness. In addition, many traits and capacities that are signs of strength are hidden by the rubble of years of self-doubt, the blame of others, and, in some cases, the wearing of a diagnostic label. Sometimes the problem of discovering strengths lies with the lack of words, sometimes it is disbelief, and sometimes, lack of trust. The social worker may have to begin to provide the language, to look for, address, and give name to those resiliencies that people have demonstrated in the past and in the present (the Wolins's [1993] language of the seven resiliencies is helpful here). The daily struggles and triumphs of one's life as revealed in stories and narratives is useful (for example, what they have done, how they survived, what they want, what they want to avoid). At some point in this process, people do have to ac-knowledge their strengths, play them out, see them in the past and the present, feel them, and have them affirmed by the worker and others. In a sense, what is hap-pening at this point is the writing of a better "text." *Reframing* is a part of this; not the reframing of so many family therapies, but adding to the picture already painted, brush strokes that depict capacity, ingenuity, and that provide a different coloration to the substance of one's life.

LASHAWN

LaShawn and her two sons had lived in public housing for years. She came from a background of serious abuse and battering—by a father early, and later, by a husband and two other men with whom she had relationships. A brief contact with a child welfare worker left her with the impression that she would always be subject to being sucked into abusive relationships, that she was a perpetual "victim." Her children had a variety of physical and learning prob-lems, and she was told that these were probably a result of their having been exposed to the battering that she suffered.

A fortuitous contact with another social worker (around community issues in the public housing complex) led to a developing relationship, and the worker began to see the enormous promise in LaShawn and her children. LaShawn's intelligence, wit, desire to make her life better, to help her children grow strong were all attributes that had been somewhat obscured by experience and a la-bel. Without ever working on "abuse issues," the relationship between the so-cial worker and LaShawn evolved around leadership in the community and community development. LaShawn became an effective leader in the commu-nity, a voice for the residents, and a force to be reckoned with. Although not without her troubles and the scars of her past, LaShawn began to formulate a different picture of her future and began to understand what skills, talents, and resources she might employ to get to that future.

In all of this, the close and collaborative relationship with the social worker revolved around the recognition, affirmation, and employment of LaShawn's strengths toward the underwriting of her hopes for the future. Today, LaShawn is out of public housing, works for the city government in a responsible posi-tion around housing issues, and is on her way to her dream of owning a Bed and Breakfast. Who knows how much of this was related to a "reframing" of a story of victimization?

In a sense, then, the stimulation of a strengths discourse involves at least two acts on the part of the worker: providing a vocabulary of strengths (in the language of the client), and mirroring—providing a positive reflection of the client's abilities and accomplishments, and helping the client to find other positive mirrors in the environment (Wolin & Wolin, 1994).

Act in Context: Education, Action, Advocacy, and Linkage. The education continues about the capacities and resilient aspects of the self. Now these are linked up to the person's hopes, goals, and visions. The individual is encouraged to take the risk of acting on one's expectancies using the newly found or articulated competencies as well as already active ones. It is through action with the worker—collaborative and continuous—that individuals really begin to employ their strengths as they move toward well-formed, achievable goals. This is precarious business for many people who have been through a figurative hell. But as they decide and act, they continue to discover and enrich their repertoire of aptitudes. They also discover the limits of their resilience and the effect of still-active sore spots and scars. But, in the end, it is their decision making and activity that lead to changes in thinking, feeling, and relationship that are more congruent with their goals and their strengths. Important as well, is that the individual (we could also be talking about a group or family) begins to use naturally occurring community resources to move toward their goals.

For the social worker, this means advocacy: discovering what natural or formal resources are available, accessible, and to what extent they are adequate and acceptable to the client (Kisthardt, 1993). The assumption here is that the environment is rich with resources: people, institutions, associations, families who are willing to and can provide instruction, succor, relief, resources, time, and mirroring. When people begin to plan fully to achieve their goals and to exercise their strengths, the effect is synergistic: They can do more personally, and they find themselves closer to connection to a community. For example, a receptionist at a physician's office begins to help an elderly woman with insurance forms, arranging transportation to and from the doctor's office so that she is more likely to keep appointments and to keep a level of health she believes is highly desirable. The synergistic effect is that the receptionist begins to do this for other elders as well and eventually finds other volunteers to assist them. For many of the older persons involved, this is an important support for the maintenance of relative independence—an important strength to be sure (see chapter 8).

Move toward Normalizing and Capitalizing upon One's Strengths.   Over a period of time, often a short period of time, the social worker and client begin to consolidate the strengths that have emerged, reinforce the new vocabulary of strengths and resilience, and bolster the capacity to discover resources within and around. The purpose is to cement the foundation of strengths, to insure the synergy of the continuing development and articulation of strengths, and to secure a place for the person to be. For many who have been helped through a strengths-based approach, one important avenue to normalization is teaching others what one has learned in the process. Finally, this is a process of disengagement for worker and client. Done with the assurance that the personal strengths and the communal resources are in place, disengagement is the ritual transition to normalization.

In summary, to assume a strengths perspective requires a degree of consciousness raising on the part of social workers and their clients—a different way of regarding what they do together. One thing is certain, however, from reports of many of those people who apply the strengths perspective in their professional work: Once a client is engaged in building up the strengths within and without, a desire to do more and to become more absorbed in daily life and drawn by future possibilities bursts forth.

DISCUSSION QUESTIONS

1. With a friend or client, use some of the methods for discovering strengths described in this chapter. What was the outcome? How would you personalize such methods so they would be more useful to you?

2. Do you think that the way one goes about finding out about strengths has a different feel to it than methods for determing symptoms or problems? What, if any, is the difference?

3. Do we assume that problems are real? How would you go about balancing the effort to discern problems and the need to discover strengths?

4. Do you know practitioners who approach clients from a strengths perspective? If so, what do you notice about their practice that is distinctive?

REFERENCES

Aptheker, B. (1989). *Tapestries of life*. Amherst, MA: University of Massachusetts Press.

Kisthardt, W. E. (1993). A strengths model of case management: The principles and functions of a helping partnership with persons with persistent mental illness. In M. Harris & H. Bergman (Eds.), *Case management for mentally ill patients: Theory and practice*. Langhorne, PA: Harwood Academic Publishers.

Peele, S., & Brodsky, A. (1991). *The truth about addiction and recovery*. New York: Simon & Schuster.

Rappaport, J. (1990). Research methods and the empowerment agenda. In P. Tolan, F. Chertak, & L. Jason (Eds.), *Researching community psychology*. Washington, D.C.: American Psychological Association.

Saleebey, D. (1994). Culture, theory, and narrative: The intersection of meanings in practice. *Social Work, 39*, 351–359.

Wolin , S. J., & Wolin, S. (1993). *The resilient self: How survivors of troubled families overcome adversity*. New York: Villard.

Wolin, S. J., & Wolin, S. (October, 1994). *Resilience in overcoming adversity*. Workshop for Employee Assistance Program members, Kansas City, MO.

chapter 5

Assessing Client Strengths:
Assessment for Client Empowerment[1]

Charles Cowger

The proposition that client strengths are central to the helping relationship is simple enough and seems uncontroversial as an important component of practice. Yet deficit, disease, and dysfunction metaphors are deeply rooted in social work, and the emphasis of assessment has continued to be the diagnosis of abnormal and pathological conditions.

Review of the social work literature on human behavior and the social environment reveals little theoretical or empirical content on strengths. Much of the social work literature on practice with families continues to use treatment, dysfunction, medical, and therapy metaphors and ignores work on family and community strengths developed in other disciplines. The assessment literature, including available assessment instruments, is overwhelmingly concerned with individual inadequacies. Taking a behavioral baseline of client deficits and examining the ability of social workers to correct those deficits have become the standard for evaluating the effectiveness of social work practice (Kagle & Cowger, 1984). The focus of assessment has "continued to be, one way or another, diagnosing pathological conditions" (Rodwell, 1987, p. 235). Hepworth and Larsen (1990) highlighted the incongruity between social work theoretical perspectives and practice when they stated "social workers persist in formulating assessments that focus almost exclusively on the pathology and dysfunction of clients—despite the time-honored social work platitude that social workers work with strengths, not weaknesses" (p. 157).

There is, on the other hand, very little empirical evidence indicating the extent to which practitioners consciously make use of client strengths in their practice.

---

[1] This chapter is based on C. D. Cowger, Assessing client strengths: Clinical assessment for client empowerment, *Social Work, 39*(3), 1994, 262–268. Copyright 1994, National Association of Social Workers, Inc.

Maluccio (1979) found that social workers underestimated client strengths and had more negative perceptions of clients than clients had of themselves. It seems unlikely that client strengths would have an impact on worker activity, considering the preponderance of deficit assessment instruments as opposed to the dearth of assessment tools that consider client strengths. A library search for assessment tools that include client strengths is a particularly unrewarding experience, as is reviewing collections of assessment, diagnosis, and measurement instruments in book and monograph form. And, of course, various versions of the American Psychiatric Association's *Diagnostic and Statistical Manual,* from volumes I to IV, have emphasized client pathology.

THE LINK BETWEEN ASSESSMENT AS POLITICAL ACTIVITY AND EMPOWERMENT

This chapter is based on a mainstream contextual understanding that the primary purpose of social work is to assist people in their relationships with one another and with social institutions in order to promote social and economic justice (Council on Social Work Education, 1994). Practice, thus, focuses on developing more positive and promising transactions between people and their environments. However, taking seriously the element of promoting social and economic justice in those transactions may not lead to a mainstream conception of practice. Indeed, practice that considers social and economic justice suggests a type of practice that explicitly deals with power and power relationships (see chapter 10). This perspective understands client empowerment as central to social work practice and client strengths as providing the fuel and energy for that empowerment. Client empowerment is characterized by two interdependent and interactive dynamics: personal empowerment and social empowerment. Although social work theories that split the attributes of people into the social and the psychological have considerable limitations (Falck, 1988), such a differentiation is made in this chapter to stress the importance of each element.

The personal empowerment dynamic is similar to a traditional clinical notion of self-determination whereby clients give direction to the helping process, take charge and control of their personal lives, get their "heads straight," learn new ways to think about their situations, and adopt new behaviors that give them more satisfying and rewarding outcomes. Personal empowerment recognizes the uniqueness of each client.

The social empowerment dynamic recognizes that client definitions and characteristics cannot be separated from their context and that personal empowerment is related to opportunity. Social empowerment acknowledges that individual behavior is socially derived and identity is "bound up with that of others through social involvement" (Falck, 1988, p. 30). A person empowered socially is a person who has the resources and opportunity to play an important role in his or her environment and in the shaping of that environment.

A person achieves personal and social empowerment simultaneously. For the client to achieve empowerment assumes that the resources and opportunity for that empowerment are available. Social justice, involving the reasonable and equitable distribution of society's resources, is directly related to the social empowerment of clients and, therefore, simultaneously, to personal empowerment.

Social work practice based on empowerment assumes that client power is achieved when clients make choices that give them more control over their presenting problem situations and, in turn, their own lives. However, empowerment-based practice also assumes social justice, recognizing that empowerment and self-determination are dependent not only on people's making choices but also on their having available choices to make. The distribution of available choices in a society is political. Societies organize systems of production and distribution of resources, and that organization affects those choices differentially. Across societies, production and distribution are based on varying degrees of commitment to equity and justice: "Some people get more of everything than others" (Goroff, 1983, p. 133). Social work practice based on the notion of choice requires attention to the dynamics of personal power, the social power endemic to the client's environment, and the relationship between the two.

Assessment as Political Activity

Assessment that focuses on deficits presents obstacles to the exercise of personal and social power for clients and reinforces those social structures that generate and regulate the unequal power relationships that victimize clients. Goroff (1983) persuasively argues that social work practice is a political activity and that the attribution of individual deficiencies as the cause of human problems is a politically conservative process that "supports the status quo" (p. 134).

Deficit-based assessment targets the individual as "the problem." For example, from a deficit perspective the person who is unemployed becomes the problem. Social work interventions that focus on what is wrong with the person—for example, why he or she is not working—reinforce the powerlessness the client is already experiencing because he or she does not have a job. At the same time such an intervention lets economic and social structures that do not provide opportunity "off the hook" and reinforces social structures that generate unequal power. To assume that the cause of personal pain and social problems is individual deficiency "has the political consequences of not focusing on the social structure (the body politic) but on the individual. Most, if not all, of the pain we experience is the result of the way we have organized ourselves and how we create and allocate life-surviving resources" (Goroff, 1983, p. 134).

Personal pain is political. Social work practice is political. Diagnostic and assessment metaphors and taxonomies that stress individual deficiencies and sickness reinforce the political status quo in a manner that is incongruent with a practice that attempts to promote social and economic justice. Practice centered on pathology is reminiscent of "blaming the victim" (Ryan, 1976). Practice based on metaphors of client strengths and empowerment is also political in that its thrust is the development of client power and the more equitable distribution of societal resources, those resources that underlie the development of personal resources.

Client Strengths and Empowerment

Promoting empowerment means believing that people are capable of making their own choices and decisions. It means not only that human beings possess the strengths and potential to resolve their own difficult life situations, but also that they increase their strength and contribute to society by doing so. The role of the social worker is to nourish, encourage, assist, enable, support, stimulate, and unleash the strengths within people; to illuminate the strengths available to people in their own environments; and to promote equity and justice at all levels of society. To do that, the social worker helps clients articulate the nature of their situations, identify what they want, explore alternatives for achieving those goals, and achieve them.

The role of the social worker is not to change people, treat people, help people cope, or counsel people. The role is not to empower people. As Simon (1990) argued, social workers cannot empower others: "More than a simple linguistic nuance, the notion that social workers do not empower others, but instead, help people empower themselves is an ontological distinction that frames the reality experienced by both workers and clients" (p. 32). To assume a social worker can empower someone else is naive and condescending and has little basis in reality. Power is not something that social workers possess for distribution at will. Clients, not social workers, own the power that brings significant change in social work practice. A social worker is merely a person, with professional training on the development, accumulation, and use of resources, who is committed to the empowerment of people and willing to share his or her knowledge in a manner that helps people realize their own power, take control of their own lives, and solve their own problems.

Importance of Assessing Strengths

Central to a strengths perspective is the role and place of assessment in the practice process (see chapters 4, 7, 8). How clients define difficult situations and how they evaluate and give meaning to the dynamic factors related to those situations set the context and content for the duration of the helping relationship. If assessment focuses on deficits, it is likely that deficits will remain the focus of both the worker and the client during remaining contacts. Concentrating on deficits or strengths can lead to self-fulfilling prophecies. Hepworth and Larsen (1990) articulated how this concentration might also impair a social worker's "ability to discern clients' potentials for growth," reinforce "client self-doubts and feelings of inadequacy," and predispose workers to "believe that clients should continue to receive service longer than is necessary" (p. 195).

Emphasizing deficits seriously limits the scope of professional work, but focusing on strengths provides considerable advantages. Strengths are all we have to work with. The recognition and embellishment of strengths is fundamental to the values and mission of the profession. A strengths perspective provides for a leveling of the power relationship between social workers and clients. Clients almost always enter the social work setting in a vulnerable position and with comparatively little power. Their lack of power is revealed by the very fact that they are seeking help and entering the social structure of service. A deficit focus emphasizes this vulnerability and highlights the unequal power relationship between the worker and the client.

A strengths perspective assumes client competence and thereby mitigates the significance of unequal power between the client and social worker. In so doing, a strengths orientation implies increased potential for liberating people from stigmatizing diagnostic classifications that promote "sickness" and "weakness" in individuals, families, and communities. A strengths perspective of assessment provides structure and content for an examination of realizable alternatives, for the mobilization of competencies that can make things different, and for the building of self-confidence that stimulates hope.

GUIDELINES FOR STRENGTHS ASSESSMENT

These guidelines for strengths assessment are presented with the understanding that assessment is a process as well as a product. Assessment as process is helping clients define their situations (that is, clarify the reasons they have sought assistance) and assisting clients in evaluating and giving meaning to those factors that affect their situations. It is particularly important to assist clients in telling their stories. The client owns that story, and if the social worker respects that ownership, the client will be able to more fully share it. The assessment as a product is an agreement, in many cases a written agreement, between the worker and the client as to the nature of the problem situation (descriptive) and the meaning ascribed to those factors influencing the problem situation (analytic and interpretative).

The following guidelines are based on the notion that the knowledge guiding the assessment process is based on a socially constructed reality (Berger & Luckmann, 1966). Also, the assessment should recognize that there are multiple constructions of reality for each client situation (Rodwell, 1987) and that problem situations are interactive, multicausal, and ever-changing.

1. *Give preeminence to the client's understanding of the facts.* The client's view of the situation, the meaning the client ascribes to the situation, and the client's feelings or emotions related to that situation are the central focus for assessment. Assessment content on the intrapersonal, developmental, cognitive, mental, and biophysical dynamics of the client are important only as it enlightens the situation presented by the client. It should be used only as a way to identify strengths that can be brought to bear on the presenting situation or to recognize obstacles to achieving client objectives. The use of social sciences behavior taxonomies representing the realities of the social scientists should not be used as something to apply to, thrust on, or label a client. An intrapersonal and interpersonal assessment, like

data gathered on the client's past, should not have a life of its own and is not important in its own right.

2. *Believe the client*. Central to a strengths perspective is a deeply held belief that clients ultimately are trustworthy. There is no evidence that people needing social work services tell untruths any more than anyone else. To prejudge a client as being untrustworthy is contrary to the social work-mandated values of having respect for individuals and recognizing client dignity, and prejudgment may lead to a self-fulfilling prophecy. Clients may need help to articulate their problem situations, and "caring confrontation" by the worker may facilitate that process. However, clients' understandings of reality are no less real than the social constructions of reality of the professionals assisting them.

3. *Discover what the client wants*. There are two aspects of client wants that provide the structure for the worker–client contract. The first is, what does the client want and expect from service? The second is, what does the client want to happen in relation to his or her current problem situation? This latter desire involves the client's goals and is concerned with what the client would perceive to be a successful resolution to the problem situation. Although recognizing that what the client wants and what agencies and workers are able and willing to offer is subject to negotiation, successful practitioners base assessments on client motivation. Clients' motivation is supported by expectations of the achieving of their own goals.

4. *Move the assessment toward personal and environmental strengths*. Obviously there are personal and environmental obstacles to the resolution of difficult situations. However, if one believes that solutions to difficult situations lie in strengths, dwelling on obstacles ultimately has little payoff.

5. *Make assessment of strengths multidimensional*. Multidimensional assessment is widely supported in social work. Practicing from a strengths perspective means believing that the strengths and resources to resolve a difficult situation lie within the client's interpersonal skills, motivation, emotional strengths, and ability to think clearly. The client's external strengths come from family networks, significant others, voluntary organizations, community groups, and public institutions that support and provide opportunities for clients to act on their own behalf and institutional services that have the potential to provide resources. Discovering these strengths is central to assessment. A multidimensional assessment also includes an examination of power and power relationships in transactions between the client and the environment. Explicit, critical examination of such relationships provides the client and the worker with the context for evaluating alternative solutions.

6. *Use the assessment to discover uniqueness*. The importance of uniqueness and individualization is well articulated by Meyer (1976): "When a family, group or a community is individualized, it is known through its uniqueness, despite all that it holds in common with other like groups" (p. 176). Although every person is in certain respects "like all other men [sic], like some other men, and like no other men" (Kluckholm, Murray, & Schneider, 1953, p. 53), foundation content in human behavior and social environment taught in schools of social work focuses on the first two of these, which are based on normative behavior assumptions. Assessment that focuses on client strengths must be individualized to understand the unique situ-

ation the client is experiencing. Normative perspectives of behavior are only useful insofar as they can enrich the understanding of this uniqueness. Pray's (1991) writings on assessment emphasize individual distinctiveness as an important element of Schön's (1983) reflective model of practice and are particularly insightful in establishing the importance of this in assessment.

7. *Use language the client can understand.* Professional and social sciences nomenclature is incongruent with an assessment approach based on mutual participation of the social worker and the client. Assessment as a product should be written in simple English and in such a way as to be self-explanatory. Goldstein (1990) convincingly stated, "We are the inheritors of a professional language composed of value-laden metaphors and idioms. The language has far more to do with philosophic assumptions about the human state, ideologies of professionalism, and, not least, the politics of practice than they do with objective rationality" (p. 268).

8. *Make assessment a joint activity between worker and client.* Social workers can minimize the inherent power imbalance between worker and client by stressing the importance of the client's understandings and wants. The worker's role is to inquire and listen and to assist the client in discovering, clarifying, and articulating. The client gives direction to the content of the assessment. The client must feel ownership of the process and the product and can do so only if assessment is open and shared. Rodwell (1987) articulated this well when she stated that the "major stakeholders must agree with the content" (p. 241).

9. *Reach a mutual agreement on the assessment.* Workers should not have secret assessments. All assessments in written form should be shared with clients. Because assessment is to provide structure and direction for confronting client problem situations, any privately held assessment a worker might have makes the client vulnerable to manipulation.

10. *Avoid blame and blaming.* Assessment and blame often get confused and convoluted. Blame is the first cousin of deficit models of practice. Concentrating on blame or allowing it to get a firm foothold in the process is done at the expense of getting on with a resolution to the problem. Client situations encountered by social workers are typically the result of the interaction of a myriad of events: personal interactions, intrapersonal attributes, physical health, social situations, social organizations, and chance happenings. Things happen; people are vulnerable to those happenings, and, therefore, they seek assistance. What can the worker and client do after blame is assigned? Generally, blaming leads nowhere, and, if relegated to the client, it may encourage low self-esteem. If assigned to others, it may encourage learned helplessness or deter motivation to address the problem situation.

11. *Avoid cause-and-effect thinking.* Professional judgments or assumptions of causation may well be the most detrimental exercises perpetrated on clients. Worker notions of cause should be minimized because they have the propensity to be based on simplistic cause-and-effect thinking. Causal thinking represents only one of many possible perspectives of the problem situation and can easily lead to blaming. Client problem situations are usually multidimensional, have energy, represent multidirectional actions, and reflect dynamics that are not well suited to simple causal explanations.

12. *Assess; do not diagnose.* Diagnosis is incongruent with a strengths perspective. Diagnosis is understood in the context of pathology, deviance, and deficits and is based on social constructions of reality that define human problem situations in a like manner. Diagnosis is associated with a medical model of labeling that assumes unpopular and unacceptable behavior as a symptom of an underlying pathological condition. It has been argued that labeling "accompanied by reinforcement of identified behavior is a sufficient condition for chronic mental illness" (Taber, Herbert, Mark, & Nealey, 1969, p. 354). The preference for use of the word "assessment" over "diagnosis" is widely held in the social work literature.

THE ASSESSMENT PROCESS

The assessment process suggested here has two components, which are similar to Mary Richmond's (1917) distinction between "study" and "diagnosis." She proposed that the social worker first study the facts of the situation and then diagnose the nature of the problem. Correspondingly, the first component here is a process whereby a worker and a client define the problem situation or clarify why the client has sought assistance. The second component involves evaluating and giving meaning to those factors that impinge on the problem situation.

Component 1: Defining the Problem Situation

Defining the problem situation is only the beginning of the helping process and should not be confused with evaluation and analysis of the problem situation. It is particularly important at this time to assist the client in telling his or her story. The following list outlines what the worker and client might do to define the problem situation. Items 2, 3, and 4 are based in part on guidelines developed by Brown and Levitt (1979), and later revised by Hepworth and Larsen (1990, p. 14).[2]

Defining the Problem Situation or
Discovering Why the Client Seeks Assistance
1. *Brief summary of the identified problem situation.* This should be in simple language, straightforward, and mutually agreed upon between worker and client. If written, it should be no more than a brief paragraph.
2. *Who* (persons, groups, or organizations) is involved, including the client(s) seeking assistance?
3. *How* or in what way are participants involved? What happens among the participants before, during, and immediately following activity related to the problem situation?

---

[2] Hepworth and Larsen use items 2, 3, and 4 as "questions" to identify other people and larger systems that are involved in the problem situation and/or interacting with the problem. These questions are given more assessment import in this chapter because they are seen as defining the problem rather than simply identifying involvement or interaction with the problem.

4. What meaning does the client ascribe to the problem situation?
5. What does the client want with regard to the problem situation?
6. What does the client want/expect by seeking assistance?
7. What would client's life be like if problem were resolved?

This outline assumes clients know why they seek assistance. With a little help from a worker, a client can clarify, or perhaps discover some new insight, and articulate the nature of the problem situation. These questions are based on a model of practice whereby social workers believe their clients, trust their clients' judgment, and reinforce their clients' competency. The orientation also assumes that when dealing with problem situations, what you see is what you get; that hidden, deep-seated, intrapsychic, and/or unconscious phenomena, if real, are irrelevant.

The word *situation* has a particularly important meaning because it affirms that problems always exist in an environmental context. To focus on the problem situation is to avoid a perception and subsequent definition of the person as pathological that may lead, for the client, to a self-fulfilling prophecy and, for the worker, to ascribing blame. However, using the word *problem* does not suggest that one therefore assumes environmental or situational pathology and continues with a pathological model by simply redirecting pathological assessment to the relevant environment. *Problem* here means only that there exists a mismatch or disequilibrium between the client's needs and environmental demands and resources that is causing difficulty, puzzlement, and often pain. Focusing on the individual alone is inappropriate and may hinder problem solution. Problem situations have a life of their own and are generated by combinations of unpredicted contingencies, incongruities, and systems disequilibrium. Understanding problem situations in this way allows the worker and client the freedom to capitalize on personal and environmental strengths to resolve the problem.

Component 2: Framework for Assessment

The second assessment component involves analyzing, evaluating, and giving meaning to those factors influencing the problem situation. The model proposed here revolves around two axes. The first axis is an environmental factors versus personal factors continuum, and the second is a strengths versus obstacles continuum (see Figure 5.1).

Concerns about emphasizing either end of the obstacles–strengths axis have been discussed previously. A new theoretical interest in how environmental factors affect practice has been increasingly evident in the literature since the early 1970s. However, like renewed interest in client strengths, this interest has not been fully realized in actual practice as practice guidelines, and specific practice knowledge has lagged behind theoretical development. The lack of knowledge of, or interest in, the relevant environmental factors, in actual practice, is evident when one reviews available assessment instruments.

When the axes in Figure 5.1 are enclosed, each of the four quadrants that result represents important content for assessment (see Figure 5.2). Because assess-

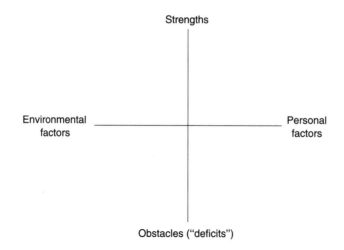

FIGURE 5.1 Assessment Axes

ment instruments themselves have tended to focus on the elements of quadrant 4, most practice today emphasizes personal deficits. A comprehensive assessment would have data recorded in each quadrant. The version of the assessment axes in Figure 5.2 has been used as a recording tool in teaching, workshops, and agency consultation and has demonstrated that workers and clients can readily identify content for each quadrant. However, quadrants 1 and 2 are *emphasized* when practicing from a strengths perspective. Indeed, *deficits* is probably a misnomer and the end of that continuum is better understood as *"obstacles"* to problem resolution.

Exemplars of Client Strengths (Quadrant 2)

Quadrant 2, personal strengths, includes both psychological and physiological strengths. For illustrative purposes, psychological factors are further developed here by listing a set or personal strength exemplars (see below). The taxonomy of strengths; cognition, emotion, motivation, coping, and interpersonal relationships, is used to organize and structure these exemplars. The categories are quite traditional and are not free of conceptual problems. For example, it is important to note that although these items are designated as "personal" factors, they do not represent intrapersonal attributes devoid of environmental and or physiological interaction (e.g., motivation is dependent on a unique set of environmental and personal dynamics). Physiological factors, not included in this list, are particularly important for some clients, such as the elderly or individuals with developmental or other disabilities.

The following list suggests exemplars of personal strengths workers and clients might consider during the assessment process. These items were arrived at through

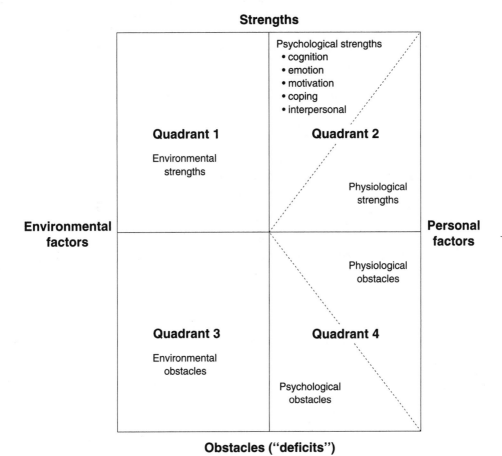

FIGURE 5.2 Framework for assessment

literature review (for example, Brown & Levitt, 1979; Hepworth & Larsen, 1990) and workshops with agency practitioners.

Assessment of Client Strengths (Quadrant 2 of Assessment Axes)
A. Cognition
  1. Sees the world as most other people see it in his culture.
  2. Has an understanding of right and wrong, from her cultural, ethical perspective.
  3. Understands how one's own behavior affects others and how others affect her. Is insightful.
  4. Is open to different ways of thinking about things.
  5. Reasoning is easy to follow.
  6. Considers and weighs alternatives in problem solving.

B. Emotion
   1. Is in touch with feelings and is able to express them if encouraged.
   2. Expresses love and concern for intimate others.
   3. Demonstrates a degree of self-control.
   4. Can handle stressful situations reasonably well.
   5. Is positive about life. Has hope.
   6. Has a range of emotions.
   7. Emotions are congruent with situations.
C. Motivation
   1. When having problems, doesn't hide from, avoid, or deny them.
   2. Willing to seek help and share problem situation with others he can trust.
   3. Willing to accept responsibility for her own part or role in problem situations.
   4. Wants to improve current and future situations.
   5. Does not want to be dependent on others.
   6. Seeks to improve self through further knowledge, education, and skills.
D. Coping
   1. Persistent in handling family crises.
   2. Is well organized.
   3. Follows through on decisions.
   4. Is resourceful and creative with limited resources.
   5. Stands up for self rather than submitting to injustice.
   6. Attempts to pay debts despite financial difficulty.
   7. Prepares for and handles new situations well.
   8. Has dealt successfully with related problems in the past.
E. Interpersonal
   1. Has friends.
   2. Seeks to understand friends, family members, and others.
   3. Makes sacrifices for friends, family members, and others.
   4. Performs social roles appropriately (e.g., parents, spouse, son or daughter, community).
   5. Is outgoing and friendly.
   6. Is truthful.
   7. Is cooperative and flexible in relating to family and friends.
   8. Is self-confident in relationships with others.
   9. Shows warm acceptance of others.
   10. Can accept loving and caring feelings from others.
   11. Has sense of propriety, good manners.
   12. Is a good listener.
   13. Expresses self spontaneously.
   14. Is patient.
   15. Has realistic expectations in relationships with others.
   16. Has a sense of humor.

17. Has sense of satisfaction in role performance with others.
18. Has ability to maintain own personal boundaries in relationships with others.
19. Demonstrates comfort in sexual role/identity.
20. Demonstrates ability to forgive.
21. Is generous with time and money.
22. Is verbally fluent.
23. Is ambitious and industrious.
24. Is resourceful.

These exemplars of client strengths are not intended to include all the assessment content and knowledge that a social worker must use in practice. Indeed, important topics such as assessing specific obstacles to empowerment, assessing power relationships, and assessing the relationship between personal empowerment and social empowerment of the individual client are not considered. The use of the exemplars depends on given practice situations, and professional judgment determines their specific applicability. They are proposed to provide an alternative approach to existing normative and deficit models of intrapersonal diagnosis and treatment. The exemplars may also be of interest to practitioners who wish to use them to supplement existing assessment paradigms they do not wish to give up.

The framework and outline is proposed as a resource to assist workers and clients in considering those client strengths to be exploited in coping with the problem situation. In the initial contact, the worker should be able to begin identifying client strengths. Workers may wish to have a copy of the exemplars list readily available during an interview. Other workers may find a review of the list helpful during case reflection, recording, and planning. One worker reported to the author that he has used the list by going through it item by item with the client. Workers may use the list to (1) stimulate thinking about strengths and their importance in the practice process, (2) assist in identifying strengths that otherwise would not be thought of, (3) assist in identifying and selecting positive and supportive content to be shared with clients, (4) provide a foundation for a case plan that is based on client competency and capability rather than inadequacy, and (5) bolster worker confidence and belief in the client. The list is intended to be suggestive and heuristic in nature by illustrating the wide range of strengths that any given client might have. The language in the list is somewhat contaminated with professional and middle-class notions of reality and the desirable, and therefore will require either interpretation or revision when the assessment process is shared with clients, especially those from different cultures.

When using these exemplars, an additional qualifier needs to be emphasized. Realistically, many clients at risk and those most vulnerable in our society simply are no match for the environmental intrusions and disruptive external impingements on their lives. The use of this list to the exclusion of a thorough assessment of environmental strengths and obstacles (quadrants 1 and 3, Figure 5.2), provides little advantage over deficit models of practice. Indeed, focusing on individual strengths in the face of overwhelming environmental odds may be no less cruel than a practice model that reinforces client deficits. A comprehensive assessment would include content from all four quadrants. However, a strengths perspective would emphasize quadrants 1 and 2, elements often missing from assessment.

CONCLUSION

Inherent in the assessment guidelines is the recognition that to focus on client strengths and to practice with the intent of client empowerment is to practice with an explicit power consciousness. Whatever else social work practice is, it is always political, because it always encompasses power and power relationships.

In summary, social work literature has emphasized philosophy and theory that presents a strengths perspective, but is devoid of practice directives, guidelines, and know-how for incorporating this perspective into practice. Assessment based on a strengths perspective places environmental and individual strengths in a prominent position. Environmental and individual obstacles that hinder a resolution to a problem situation are viewed only as obstacles, and as such, they are not considered the primary content of assessment. Guidelines for assessing client strengths and exemplars of individual client strengths have been presented in an attempt to bridge the gap between philosophy and theory, which supports client strengths, and practice knowledge, which ignores it. Believing in client strengths can generate self-fulfilling prophecies.

DISCUSSION QUESTIONS

1. Take a client that you have worked with and, using the model in Figure 5.2, fill in the quadrants as best you can. Does this arrangment give you a different picture of your client?
2. What is meant by the politics of assessment? Have you seen it in operation in your practice or agency?
3. How can you use assessment to empower clients?
4. What do you think of the guidelines for assessment that direct you to give preeminence to the client's perspective and to believe the client? Does this level of belief in clients exist in your agency? How do you know?

REFERENCES

Berger, P. L., & Luckmann, T. A. (1966). *The social construction of reality*. Garden City, NY: Doubleday.

Brown, L., & Levitt, J. (1979). A methodology for problem-system identification. *Social Casework, 60*, 408–415.

Council on Social Work Education. (1994). Curriculum policy statement for master's degree program. In *Handbook of accreditation standards and procedures*. Washington, D.C.: Author.

Falck, H. S. (1988). *Social work: The membership perspective.* New York: Springer.

Goldstein, H. (1990) Strength or pathology: Ethical and rhetorical contrasts in approaches to practice. *Families in Society, 71*(5), 267–275.

Goroff, N. N. (1983). Social work within a political and social context: The triumph of the therapeutic. In S. Ables & P. Ables (Eds.), *Social work with groups: Proceedings 1978 symposium* (pp. 133–145). Louisville, KY: Committee for the Advancement of Social Work with Groups.

Hepworth, D. H., & Larsen, J. A. (1990). *Direct social work practice* (3rd Ed.). Belmont, CA: Wadsworth.

Kagle, J. D., & Cowger, C. D. (1984). Blaming the client: Implicit agenda in practice research? *Social Work, 29,* 347–351.

Kluckholm, C., Murray, H. A., & Schneider, D. M. (Eds.). (1953). *Personality in nature, society, and culture.* New York: Knopf.

Maluccio, A. (1979). The influence of the agency environment on clinical practice. *Journal of Sociology and Social Welfare, 6,* 734–755.

Meyer, C. H. (1976). *Social work practice* (2nd ed.). New York: Free Press.

Pray, J. E. (1991). Respecting the uniqueness of the individual: Social work practice within a reflective model. *Social Work, 36,* 80–85.

Richmond, M. (1917). *Social diagnosis.* New York: Russell Sage Foundation.

Rodwell, M. K. (1987). Naturalistic inquiry: An alternative model for social work assessment. *Social Service Review, 61*(2), 231–246.

Ryan, W. (1976). *Blaming the victim.* New York: Vintage Books.

Schön, D. A. (1983). *The reflective practitioner: How professionals think in action.* New York: Basic Books.

Simon, B. L. (1990). Rethinking empowerment. *Journal of Progressive Human Services, 1*(1), 27–40.

Taber, M., Herbert, C. Q., Mark, M., & Nealey, V. (1969). Disease ideology and mental health research. *Social Problems, 16,* 349–357.

part III

Using the Strengths
Approach with Individuals

chapter **6**

The Strengths Perspective and Persons with Substance Abuse Problems[1]

Richard Rapp

INTRODUCTION

The strengths perspective on case management has been implemented with persons experiencing various psychosocial and health-related difficulties, including: persistent mental illness, aging, emotional disabilities, need for public assistance, and substance abuse (Rapp & Chamberlain, 1985; Rapp, Siegal, & Fisher, 1992; Saleebey, 1992; Sullivan & Fisher, 1994; Sullivan, Jordan, & Dillon, 1994). The implementation of strengths-based case management with each of these populations has faced significant challenges—challenges that are frequently present in social service settings that focus on narrowly defined eligibility criteria, highlight client pathology, and maximize the importance of expert opinion and the gatekeeper role. Perhaps nowhere are these challenges more evident than in settings designed to provide services to persons who have substance abuse problems.

This chapter focuses on issues surrounding the implementation and practice of the strengths perspective of case management with persons who have substance abuse problems. As a backdrop to the discussion we examine a characteristic of substance abuse problems that *seems* to argue against the use of a strengths-based approach. This characteristic—the notion of denial and resistance to treatment—frequently leads to the belief that a strengths-based approach is inappropriate for these individuals. We conclude the chapter by examining some of the early findings that support the use of strengths-based case management with persons who have

---

[1] Acknowledgment: This research was supported by The National Institute on Drug Abuse (Grant No. DAO6944).

77

substance abuse problems. Issues to be considered in future implementations are also discussed.

THE STRENGTHS PERSPECTIVE AND
RESISTANCE TO TREATMENT

Whether in the popular media or scientific literature, virtually every reference to substance abusers is framed in the context of problems, chaos, and pathology. Lacking a more balanced presentation of the larger context for substance abuse problems—for instance, poverty, and hopelessness—most elements of society, treatment professionals included, have negative attitudes about substance abusers. For instance, while society may view persons with schizophrenia through an uncertain lens, they are generally perceived as not responsible for their situation and thereby need to be cared for, albeit in some manner that doesn't cause problems for the rest of society. On the other hand "drug addicts," "junkies," and somewhat more benignly, "substance abusers" are viewed much more skeptically, even by those charged with treating them (Bander, Goldman, Schwartz, Rabinowitz, & English, 1987; Ross & Darke, 1992).

The negative or at best guarded expectations held by substance abuse treatment professionals is usually expressed in the belief that clients will be resistant to treatment. It is axiomatic to any discussion of the treatment of substance abuse problems that substance abusers will deny the existence of a problem or even if they accept the presence of a problem be resistant to the steps necessary to correct it. As traditionally viewed in the field of substance abuse treatment, specific manifestations of treatment resistance abound, encapsulated in the concept of "denial." When clients do not recognize, or admit, the connection between problems in their life and their substance abuse, they are identified as being in "complete denial." Clients who do not participate willingly in treatment need to have their "denial confronted." Frequently, the primary goal of treatment is "breaking through denial." Denial has been added to the American Medical Association's definition of alcoholism, which in part, describes the abuse of this one particular substance as ". . . a primary, chronic disease with genetic, psychosocial and environmental factors . . . characterized by . . . use of alcohol despite adverse consequences and distortions in thinking, most notably denial. . . ." (Morse & Flavin, 1992, p. 1013). While the term *denial* has long been invoked to describe a client's resistance to and lack of success in treatment, there is growing sentiment that denial has been overemphasized in substance abuse treatment. An alternative view regards denial not as a reality of the client but as an artifact of the helper/therapist's expectations (Duncan, Solovey, & Rusk, 1992; O'Hanlon & Weiner-Davis, 1989). Practitioners of solution-focused approaches to psychosocial problems argue for dismissing the entire concept of psychological defenses and resistance (DeShazer, 1984).

The opportunity to systematically examine the effects of introducing strengths-based concepts to substance abuse treatment presented itself in a 1990 National Institute on Drug Abuse initiative whose goal was to test interventions that would reduce attrition from treatment and lead to better treatment outcomes. The Enhanced Treatment Project (ETP) was created to test the effects of a strengths-based approach to case management with persons experiencing substance abuse problems primarily resulting from the use of crack cocaine. Details surrounding the development of the Enhanced Treatment Project can be found elsewhere (Siegal, Fisher, Rapp, Wagner, Forney, & Callejo, 1995; Siegal, Rapp, Fisher, Cole, & Wagner, 1993).

STRENGTHS-BASED CASE MANAGEMENT—
ADDRESSING TWO ASPECTS
OF SUBSTANCE ABUSE TREATMENT

Initially, the intervention proposed for improving treatment participation and outcome was to be a traditional model of case management. Case management, widely described and defined, was seen as an intervention that would assist clients in identifying and accessing the resources they needed in order to function independently. The need for such assistance was unmistakable. Persons experiencing abuse and its effects are generally lacking in many of the basics of successful living: appropriate housing, occupational and educational opportunities, etc. (Oppenheimer, Sheehan, & Taylor, 1988; Westermeyer, 1989). It was planned that case management, as part of an overall treatment program, would assist clients with very real needs, such as for housing and employment. It was hypothesized that whatever a client' s acceptance of a substance abuse problem or whatever the degree of motivation for treatment, clients would stay involved because of assistance provided in appropriating needed services.

Four requirements were imposed on the selection of a model of case management. (1) The model must have demonstrated value with similar populations. Out of necessity the ETP had to settle for similar populations, because at that time little actual work had been conducted with case management and substance abuse. (2) Because of the prevailing attitudes regarding substance abusers, there would need to be a strong advocacy component to any model we selected. (3) Case management would focus on resource identification and acquisition as opposed to providing counseling or therapy. (4) Case management was to be an enhancement, or something additional when viewed alongside existing substance abuse treatment. Original plans called for this "extra" to be the exclusive focus on the search for needed resources. All four of these conditions were met in a strengths-based approach to case management developed at the University of Kansas School of Social Welfare. The strengths perspective of case management/advocacy was originally implemented with persons being discharged from long-term hospitalization for mental illness (Rapp & Chamberlain, 1985). The spirit of the perspective is found in five principles.

    1. *The use of client strengths, abilities, and assets is facilitated.* Central to the Strengths Perspective is the belief that clients are most successful when they identify and use their strengths, abilities, and assets. The process of enumerating and using personal strengths allows clients to appreciate their own past efficacy, encourages motivation, and sets the stage for identifying and achieving goals.

2. *Client control over goal setting and the search for needed resources is encouraged.* All goal setting is guided by the clients' perceptions of their own needs. The role of the case manager is to assist the client in making goals specific, to discuss alternatives, and to identify available resources. Underlying this principle is the belief that clients will participate most fully in treatment if they are in charge of goals which are really theirs, as opposed to goals which are dictated by others.

3. *The client–case manager relationship is promoted as primary.* The case manager serves as the consistent figure in the client's treatment experience and is thereby able to coordinate fragmented and poorly coordinated resources. A strong relationship allows the case manager to advocate for the client as necessary. Far from being exclusive, the client and case manager relationship will involve many other persons in the search for resources.

4. *The community is viewed as a resource and not a barrier.* The strengths perspective assumes that a creative approach to use of the community will lead to discovery of needed resources. In working with formal resources—housing agencies, job training programs—case managers assist clients by modeling and practicing behaviors that increase the likelihood of a successful contact. Whenever possible, case managers will encourage clients to explore informal resources—friends, neighbors, other clients—as sources of assistance.

5. *Case management is conducted as an active, community-based activity.* Office-based contacts are minimized; case managers meet with clients in the community—in their homes, at their work sites, etc. For the case manager, this activity will inevitably lead to an increased appreciation of the challenges clients face in making changes. For the clients, these meetings provide opportunities to develop and master skills where they actually live. In turn, this focus helps clients to break an all-too-prevalent reliance on institutional settings for assistance.

While conducting focus groups and developing training and clinical protocols prior to initiation of the project it became apparent that an additional "extra" would result from the implementation of a strengths-based model. It appeared that an approach so diametrically opposed to a pathology-based, medical model-driven substance abuse treatment would serve to reduce the level of resistance to treatment. At the time, it was unnecessary to prove whether this resistance was an artifact of treatment or rested in the individual. If resistance and denial were minimized, it was likely that more effective treatment would take place. Indeed, strengths-based case management borrows readily from theories (e.g., empowerment and self-efficacy) that seek to minimize the resistance often accompanying the helping process (Weick, 1983; Weick & Pope, 1988).

Anecdotal support for the decision to use a strengths-based approach occurred frequently during the pilot phase of the project. One client's comment summarized the belief of many when he said, "I really like lookin' at what's right about me. I've had so many problems and done so many first steps I forgot I was anything but a junkie." As project protocols were finalized, all practice interventions were designed in such a way as to address both resource acquisition needs as well as the client's relationship with treatment.

The Practice of Strengths-based Case Management

As a first step toward accomplishing the dual goals of resource acquisition and building a positive relationship with treatment, case managers were discouraged from reading the client's substance abuse assessment or medical record prior to their first meeting with the client. By not doing so, case managers were encouraged to not predefine the client in terms of their diagnoses and problems. While ignoring the problems and needs of clients would be negligent, it was an assumption of strengths-based practice that the most appropriate way to hear about those needs was directly from the client and not through the filter of records passed down from previous treatment episodes.

The case manager's initial contact with a client was usually a brief meeting in which the overall project was explained and the worker introduced the concepts of "case management," "advocacy," and "strengths approach." The case manager described examples of activities appropriate for case management/advocacy—employment searches, assistance with housing, etc. The case manager attempted to end this first contact by offering to assist the client in some immediate, tangible manner, such as helping the client's family avoid having electric service disconnected or retrieving clothing from a temporary housing situation.

Also during the first meeting with a case manager, clients rated themselves in each of nine domains: life skills, finance, leisure, relationships, living arrangements, occupation/education, health, internal resources, and recovery. Specific behavioral anchors define functioning on a nine-point scale in each of these. These scales, the "ETP Progress Evaluation Scales" (PES), were adapted from earlier work with mental health clients and incarcerated substance abusers (Ihilevich & Gleser, 1982; Martin, Isenberg, & Inciardi, 1993).

During the next several contacts, clients participated in an extensive strengths-based assessment. The ETP Strengths Assessment is the antithesis of most assessments. The aim of this assessment was to reacquaint, or in many cases acquaint for the first time, clients with their strengths and assets. Discussions were focused on a client's ability to accomplish a task, use a skill, and have a goal or fulfill a desire in one or more of the nine life domains described above. Discussions of topics such as arrest record, drug use, and failures were avoided. A strengths-based assessment provided clients with the opportunity to examine their personal abilities and the role those abilities could play in solving problems. Furthermore, case managers themselves were able to avoid being drawn into the skepticism and hopelessness that almost inevitably attached to a recounting of real or imagined failures.

Upon completion of the strengths assessment, clients once again rated their functioning in each life domain. At that time, the case manager also rated the client's functioning. Clients were encouraged to compare their self-ratings before and after completion of the strengths-based assessment. This comparison was intended to involve the client in a discussion regarding their strengths and abilities. Next, client and case manager determined a "consensus rating" for each life domain, a rating that came from a comparison of the case manager and client ratings. Clients then decided on a "goal rating" for each life domain. This rating reflected their desired level of functioning in 90 days and was reviewed at that time.

These numerical goal ratings were translated into specific action plans through use of the *Enhanced Treatment Project* Case Management Plan (CMP). From an open-ended question, "What do you need/want to accomplish?", clients began to identify goals in various life domains. Goal statements were written as broad, general, and perhaps never fully attainable, such as "Improve my opportunities to get the job I'm interested in." Objectives were always measurable, specific steps that lead the client toward the goal. Two specific objectives for the previous goal might include, "Objective 1: Take and pass the Graduation Equivalency Degree (GED) exam" and "Objective 2: Complete course on identifying job interests at Smith Vocational School." Strategies were specific activities that led to accomplishment of an objective. Examples of strategies used to accomplish Objective 1 included obtaining a GED application, studying a GED work guide 10 hours each week, and scheduling an appointment for taking the GED. The establishment of target and review dates for each objective and strategy prompted periodic review of client progress. While work on goals was always guided by the client's wishes, the case manager lent support to the process of goal setting by reminding the client of identified strengths, assisting in making objectives specific, discussing alternatives, contributing a knowledge of existing resources, and advocating for the client as he or she attempted to tap into those resources.

The detailed attention to the creation of objectives and strategies and systematic review of their outcome was powerful at two levels. First, clients learned an approach to solving problems that was easily transferable from the treatment setting to their own use outside the treatment milieu. Second, clients had the opportunity to evaluate their own progress in very personal, specific terms. Even in not completing some of their identified tasks clients had the support and feedback to learn from the experience. One former client discussed his work with his case manager: "I had a case manager who had me write every little step down, plan out every day what I was gonna do. I was so used to planning on big things and never seein' 'em get done. It was great to see some progress every day." The overall effect of this goal-setting process specifically and the strengths-based approach generally was that clients were in the position to take responsibility for their own treatment. This personal responsibility, while a stated intention of traditional medical model substance abuse treatment, is unwittingly negated by the way in which that model is frequently implemented (Rapp, Kelliher, Fisher, & Hall, 1994).

IMPLEMENTING A STRENGTHS-BASED MODEL

The impact of implementing case management, a strengths-based approach especially, in substance abuse treatment settings has been discussed recently (Siegal, Rapp, Fisher, Cole, & Wagner, 1994; Sullivan, Jordan, & Dillon, 1994). The barriers to implementation that have arisen are predictable, most frequently growing out of conflicts with the prevailing medical model. Difficulties in implementation surfaced at each level of the treatment system—philosophical orientation as implemented by treatment staff, strengths-oriented case managers, and clients.

Impact on Treatment Philosophy and Treatment Staff

The medical model, or disease concept-based, treatment for substance abuse problems follows a parallel course to that described for other health problems treated under the medical model (Peele, 1989; Sontag, 1978). Specifically, a diagnosis of some illnesses, in this case drug dependence, is required as a prerequisite to admission; there must be at least a tacit acceptance by the patient that he or she is sick, that is, an addict; and a detailed exploration of symptoms is conducted, here through a substance abuse assessment. Because the condition, addiction, is viewed as life threatening all other problems are frequently seen as secondary. The system often goes to great lengths to discourage "difficult patienthood" (Bachrach, 1994). This term, while coined in reference to psychiatric patients who challenged their treatment, could be applied to persons with substance abuse problems who do likewise.

The strengths- and client-based nature of our approach, as well as case management's emphasis on advocacy and resource acquisition, challenged many of these premises. Most directly, the case managers' focus on strengths and deemphasis of diagnoses created a situation where they and treatment staff were speaking a different language when it came to describing clients. The same client who was "Cocaine Dependent, 304.20, a multiple treatment failure and very treatmentwise" from the perspective of the medical model was "selective (in whom he trusted), able to maintain periods of abstinence of over two years and interested in becoming a gourmet cook" from a strengths-based approach. While both descriptions could be applied to the same client, strengths-based case managers believed the latter description would create fewer negative expectations about the client and allow more opportunity for positive movement. Given that strengths and abilities could be identified in these clients, it followed that they should have an active stake and voice in deciding the course of their treatment. Case managers were also designated as the veterans' primary point of contact in the search for needed resources. As such, case managers were frequently in the position of having to challenge the treatment resource itself.

The response of individual staff to the strengths approach varied greatly. Many members of the staff were excited to find out that they were already incorporating elements of a strengths-based approach in their work with clients. In addition, staff who were reluctant to implement certain disease concept tenets welcomed an alternative approach to working with clients. Other staff reacted negatively to the strengths-based approach. These reactions were based on staff assumptions about substance abusers' recalcitrance, concern over threats to expert status and professional turf, and deeply held beliefs about the value of the medical model approach. This view was summed up in a comment that one treatment staff person made to a case manager, "You always get to be the good guy."

These reactions were addressed in several ways. Overall, the remedy involved creating an approach to treatment that consisted of two parallel tracks, strengths-based case management and medical model-based core treatment. In this remedy, treatment staff were free to accept elements of a strengths-based approach to client care as they wished. Issues around patient care and staff cooperation were negotiated as necessary through ongoing administrative and treatment team meetings. At times, this parallel approach resulted in decisions being made more slowly, although the final result generally reflected a more considered result that supported the client's goals. Case managers also used these formal meetings, as well as informal communications with treatment staff, to convey information on the value of the strengths perspective. An example of several of these points can be found in the case of Michael.

MICHAEL

Michael was a 35-year-old, single, African-American male who requested inpatient treatment for problems relating to his polysubstance abuse. He indicated to the counselor who conducted the initial screening that he was "tired of feeling bad" and afraid members of his family were finally about to cut all ties with him. The results of the screening were presented in a screening team meeting (where treatment recommendations are made) and could be summarized as follows: almost daily crack, alcohol, and/or marijuana use intermittently for the last 10 years; lack of steady employment during that time; absence of specific vocational skills; one arrest on a drug abuse charge; and the breakup of a marriage due to his drug use. Against this problem-based history, Michael was accepted into inpatient treatment.

A strengths-based case manager, T. R., contacted Michael on his second day of treatment. Over several appointments, T. R. engaged Michael in completing a strengths assessment and progress evaluation scales. The most telling strength that Michael rediscovered about himself centered on his interest in helping young persons achieve their potential. This interest and ability was last expressed during four years as a lifeguard at a public pool. During that time, he acted as an informal big brother to several neighborhood boys, achieving what he believed was a significant positive impact in their lives. In response to the focus on abilities, Michael frequently related, "It's great to be able to remember things that I've done right with my life."

Michael's participation in case management activities was in sharp contrast to his involvement in the treatment component of the program. In treatment, he was sometimes late to scheduled meetings, asked frequent questions about the purpose of various activities, and was very verbal in expressing his belief that program rules were not responsive to the needs of clients. However, all treatment assignments were completed on time, and Michael participated actively in therapeutic activities.

As discharge plans were being discussed, Michael requested, and T. R. advocated for, placement in a residential vocational training program. Michael's primary counselor was opposed to the idea based on the belief that he was "resistant, unmotivated, and noncompliant," apparently in reference to his outspoken view of the treatment program. Other members of the treatment team supported the counselor's opposition and did not support a referral to the training program. Two days later, Michael completed the treatment program and was discharged to his brother's home where drug use was prevalent.

After two days of his living in this situation, Michael and T. R. agreed that Michael would go to hospital admissions the following day to request a screening for the vocational training program. At the screening, Michael described his participation in the treatment program in terms of the benefits he received from treatment as opposed to focusing on "denial." In addition, Michael expressed the strengths and assets that he had come to appreciate in himself and relate those to his suitability for the vocational program. Despite negative descriptions of his treatment participation that were contained in the medical record, he was accepted to the program, due perhaps to Michael's enthusiasm for his rediscovered assets and to T. R.'s advocacy. Michael completed the program, continued to maintain his sobriety, and remained employed in a food service position. He planned to seek employment in some aspect of working with troubled youth after he became more secure in his sobriety.

Many issues surfaced in this history that are pertinent to the previous discussion of the strengths perspective of case management/advocacy. The usual approach of focusing on substance abuse treatment—dwelling on problems, pathology, and negative history—during the initial screening punctuated the virtual hopelessness of seeking help. Perhaps more importantly, this view evidenced itself in staff's interpretation of Michael's behavior in treatment. In criticizing Michael's outspoken behavior in treatment, staff of the program discounted an obvious and very important strength—his willingness to speak up for himself. He would certainly have to be an assertive self-advocate to find and achieve access to the many resources (training, employment, housing) he needed. Michael's desire to seek a specific resource (vocational training program) was in line with the strengths perspective principle that supports a client's right to self-determination. While T. R.'s suggestion that Michael seek an alternative route to the resource he needed might be seen as an "end-run," it underscored the need for creative forms of advocacy to serve the client's best interests.

Impact on Case Managers

Members of various social service professions (social workers, psychologists) are frequently reminded of how their profession might enable a substance abuser—for instance, by not confronting defenses vigorously enough, allowing clients to dictate treatment, or protecting clients from the consequences of their behavior. In the substance abuse treatment field, enabling is defined as countertherapeutic; it is regarded as a set of actions that directly or indirectly encourage drug-using behavior.

Professionals from these disciplines who were hired as strengths-based case managers had usually been trained in this belief. While individuals selected to be case managers generally embraced the concept of working with client strengths, in the early stages of their training they frequently had difficulty reconciling the concepts of client-driven practice and enabling. Many situations prompted this uncertainty. Should a case manager actively support a client who is frequently critical of treatment or should the behavior be labeled as resistance and confronted? Should the case manager support or discourage an individual who seeks to apply for a substance abuse disability benefit? How active should a case manager be in discouraging or challenging a substance abuser who seeks to return to a spouse who is still using, in the hope of helping the spouse? Are some client goals too frivolous for a case manager to involve themselves with even if it is the client's wishes? A traditional approach would argue for confronting the criticism of treatment, discouraging an individual from seeking the disability benefit, challenging a substance abuser about returning to the spouse, and viewing some goals as frivolous.

In implementing the strengths perspective, case managers were encouraged to consider the client's perspective in each of these situations and look for healthy, adaptive reasons behind their decisions. Although case managers assertively encouraged clients to evaluate the advantages and disadvantages of certain decisions, they generally supported clients in their actions. In doing so, they placed responsibility squarely with the clients. Attempts to coerce clients toward some other end were almost always avoided. The clients' goals were operationalized in the case management plan; in the event that a goal was not achieved, alternative plans were formulated.

BRUCE

An example of a seemingly trivial client goal lies in the case of Bruce, a client who wanted assistance in learning how to market a system he had created for beating the state's lottery. Treatment staff had labeled this goal as grandiose, irrelevant, and "defocusing," an attempt to not look at his substance use and its consequences on his life. Their approach had been to confront Bruce and attempt to dissuade him from this goal. Conversely, Bruce's case manager assisted him in deciding on the specific steps necessary in order to market such a product. Objectives included learning about similar products, analyzing costs involved, learning about patents, etc. Although not achieving the overall goal of becoming self-employed, Bruce did accomplish several of the objectives he created. Completion of these objectives allowed him to become experienced in contacting several professional organizations and learning accounting skills—skills readily transferable to other situations. Other benefits accrued as well. First, debate over the value of this goal and the inevitable judgment of the client as misguided did not occur; a debate that had wasted time and created a great sense of mistrust. Second, during the course of the work on this goal, Bruce frequently acknowledged the need to stay sober in order to accomplish these objectives and from that realization he created a goal of maintaining sobriety. In addition, his interest in this goal appeared to encourage him to continue in treatment.

Supporting client decisions sometimes led to negative consequences for project case managers as in the case of Bruce and his controversial goal. Despite the benefits that resulted from his pursuit of this goal, his case manager was confronted about support of a controversial goal that was not completed. Confrontation of this type generally took place from colleagues who did not recognize the diverse benefits that accrued from setting a goal or who were envious of case managers being "the good guys."

Impact on Clients

Perhaps the greatest risk of this approach to clients resided in the stark differences presented by strengths-based case management and disease-concept substance abuse treatment. From the discussion of the strengths perspective's impact on treatment philosophy, treatment staff, and (strengths-based) case managers, it is obvious that there is a risk of clients' being caught in the middle. Michael's case posed a prime example. His outspoken concern over treatment was supported by his case manager. This affirmation, and the potential resulting escalation of his comments, could have threatened his continued presence in the treatment program. Even when he was coached on how to express his concerns in a constructive manner, there was no guarantee the system would react favorably. His creative use of resources (his application to the vocational program) could have created a negative backlash. Indeed, case managers had to continually anticipate the potential consequences to a client that a particular intervention might create. While this is certainly a routine part of planning any therapeutic intervention, it is usually not anticipated that the treatment system itself is a potential source of negative response. In case management generally and a strengths-based approach specifically, the service system's reaction must always be an anticipated part of any planning.

Beyond this issue, the one aspect of the strengths perspective that was difficult for clients was in assessing strengths. As described earlier, project protocols dictated that case managers would be persistent in helping clients recognize past situations where they made good decisions, demonstrated competence, or displayed skills. This task was frequently difficult for clients and at times created confusion over what treatment, or more accurately, case management was all about. The reasons were several. First, most clients had ample experience in the approach to reviewing their life, that is focusing on deficits. Clients who had previous treatment(s) under the medical model were especially prone to lapse into a recitation of problems. Second, many clients did not feel worthy of verbalizing strengths and were fearful of being accused of boasting or being grandiose. Third, and perhaps most prevalently, clients were not consciously aware of their strengths and abilities.

Whatever the cause of a client's difficulty in acclimating to the discussion of strengths, case managers had to become adept at prompting discussion of strengths. Techniques gleaned from solution-oriented approaches assisted in this process. These techniques included those that assisted the client in looking for alternative realities, searching for exceptions, expanding solutions, and exploring coping skills (Berg & Miller, 1992). Implicit in the use of these techniques was the need to guard against simply reframing pathology or labeling as a strength some quality or behavior that a client adamantly disliked about themselves.

Potential Difficulties in Implementing the Strengths Perspective

Perhaps the most common flaw attributed to the strengths approach is that it is not confrontive enough in dealing with some clients—that it is a naive approach. This complaint is usually leveled by professionals unfamiliar with the subtleties of how strengths-based, client-driven approaches can be used to heighten the responsibility placed on clients. In addition, they forget the obvious, that a client is ultimately the person who will or will not implement a suggested intervention or planned behavior. Strengths-based case managers recognize this and help clients remember how they have been successful in the past. In affirming the client's successes and abilities, the bridge to responsibility is built. In identifying the problems they wish to work on, clients will be more likely to walk across that bridge.

Similarly, some professionals view the philosophy of focusing on strengths as misguided when a client suffers from a serious problem and needs relief from that problem. It is neglectful, so the concern goes, to be discussing strengths and abilities while a client is suffering. While it is true that strengths-based case managers encourage clients to examine strengths, this does not mean that clients' problems are ignored. In fact, it can be assumed that in most cases where an individual presents for treatment of some type, he or she does have a problem. While the problem may or may not actually be intrinsic to the client, as opposed to some aspect of their environment, case managers do not ignore clients' concern over their problems. In fact, as has been stressed here, it is the client's perceptions and needs that are primary in this approach.

Underlying much of the criticism of the strengths-based approach seems to be the belief that it is incompatible with the predominant treatment culture. Indeed, a strengths-based approach can challenge the very foundation of treatment services that are predicated on systematically uncovering pathology and stressing the role and status of experts in a particular field. At the very least, the implementation of the two approaches in the same setting can lead to an inefficiency in the client's business being conducted. At the worst, power conflicts will arise and become permanent, a condition that benefits neither the treatment setting nor, more importantly, the client. The following section will present findings that provide a preliminary view on one aspect of client participation in a mixed strengths–disease setting.

FINDINGS

A total of 632 clients were admitted to the Enhanced Treatment Project between September 1991 and December 1994. All clients were veterans seeking treatment at a Midwestern Department of Veterans Affairs Medical Center. Eligibility was determined based on the veteran's use of any cocaine or heroin in the preceding 6 months or being a regular user of other drugs during that time and not being in treatment in the preceding 3 months. Random assignment resulted in 313 veterans being assigned to a case management (CM) group and 319 to a non-case management (NCM) group. The NCM group received core treatment activities only and no case management; veterans in the CM group received strengths-based case management services in addition to core treatment activities. Core treatment activities were based on a medical model of substance abuse and included didactic presentations about various aspects of substance abuse, group therapy focused on raising the veterans' awareness of their substance abuse problems, and collateral services such as vocational and family counseling. A total of 514 clients (81 percent of the original sample) completed a 6-month follow-up interview; follow-up rates for the two groups, CM and NCM, were similar (84 percent and 79 percent respectively).

An examination of process variables at six months following entry into the project yielded two markers of client participation in strengths-based case management that supported its value in improving both resource acquisition and resistance to treatment. First were the results from clients' work on case management plans. The case management plan proved to be an especially powerful tool that provided clients an opportunity to identify those areas they saw as most immediate to their well-being and a structure in which to operationalize their abilities as vehicles for accomplishing that work. Second, clients' continued participation in case management activities into the aftercare period (after completion of primary treatment) suggest a preference for a strength-based approach and/or the services available under case management.

Case Management Plans—Objective and Strategy Completion and Perceived Value

As discussed earlier, development of the case management plan was guided by clients' perceptions of their own needs. Goals were operationalized through the establishment of specific target dates for the objectives and strategies that comprised each goal. In addition, client and case manager affixed an outcome of "completed" or "not completed" to each objective and "used" or "not used" to each strategy. "Revised" was used when either an objective or strategy was altered before its termination date. Table 6.1 summarizes the frequency of goals, objectives, and strategies created within each of the nine life domains and the percentage completed or used.

Most evident in an examination of Table 6.1 is the high rate of objective and strategy completion that took place overall and within each life domain. Almost two-thirds of objectives (64 percent) and strategies (65 percent) were accomplished

TABLE 6.1 Strengths-based goals, objectives, and strategies by life domains (Clients represented = 236)

Life Domains	Goals	Objectives			Strategies		
Life Skills	33 (5%)	Completed	(67%)	34	Used	(73%)	96
		Revised		2	Revised		11
		Not Completed		15	Not Used		24
		Total		51	Total		131
Finance	41 (6%)	Completed	(70%)	50	Used	(75%)	126
		Revised		8	Revised		18
		Not Completed		13	Not Used		25
		Total		71	Total		169
Leisure	15 (2%)	Completed	(58%)	21	Used	(57%)	48
		Revised		1	Revised		5
		Not Completed		14	Not Used		31
		Total		36	Total		84
Relationships	27 (4%)	Completed	(53%)	32	Used	(60%)	85
		Revised		1	Revised		11
		Not Completed		27	Not Used		45
		Total		60	Total		141
Living Arrangements	117 (18%)	Completed	(77%)	204	Used	(76%)	625
		Revised		14	Revised		25
		Not Completed		47	Not Used		175
		Total		265	Total		825
Occupation/ Education	192 (30%)	Completed	(61%)	293	Used	(60%)	776
		Revised		33	Revised		91
		Not Completed		158	Not Used		426
		Total		484	Total		1293
Health	46 (7%)	Completed	(57%)	56	Used	(66%)	164
		Revised		4	Revised		9
		Not Completed		39	Not Used		75
		Total		99	Total		248
Internal Resources	21 (3%)	Completed	(71%)	40	Used	(63%)	82
		Revised		3	Revised		6
		Not Completed		13	Not Used		42
		Total		56	Total		130
Recovery	148 (23%)	Completed	(60%)	257	Used	(61%)	729
		Revised		11	Revised		21
		Not Completed		160	Not Used		452
		Total		428	Total		1202
Total	640 (100%)	Completed	(64%)	987	Used	(65%)	2731
		Revised		77	Revised		197
		Not Completed		486	Not Used		1295
		Total		1550	Total		4223

by clients. Ranges for completion rates for both objectives and strategies were quite similar ranging from 53 percent (relationships) to 77 percent (living arrangements) and 57 percent (leisure) to 76 percent (living arrangements), respectively. On average, 2.4 objectives were completed for each goal and 2.7 strategies developed for each objective. No comparable measure of goal attainment was available for the work undertaken by clients with other treatment staff, including substance abuse counselors. While treatment plans were developed, goals were not created or reviewed in such a way that allowed for systematic measurement of outcome.

Almost three-quarters (71 percent) of the goals developed by clients were in three life domains. The predominance of these domains—occupation/education (30 percent), recovery (23 percent), and living arrangements (18 percent)—was not unexpected as clients expressed attention to basic needs for a job and an adequate place to live. The fact that almost one-fourth of the goals focused on recovery was somewhat surprising because it was originally intended that case managers would leave recovery and relapse prevention issues primarily to clients' work with their substance abuse counselors. A more detailed examination of the recovery domain revealed that much of the work here was oriented to resource acquisition, the intended focus of case management. Resource acquisition in the recovery life domain usually focused on establishing a relationship with self-help groups or additional treatment resources.

Another source of information that spoke to the value of creating case management plans came from clients' views of what was beneficial in their work with case managers and with other treatment staff. As part of a series of questions administered at the six-month follow-up interview, clients were asked to respond to the question, "What is the single most helpful topic you worked on?" The question was asked of all clients about their work with their substance abuse counselors and, for those clients who were assigned case managers, for work with them as well. Client responses were recorded verbatim by project interviewers and then independently classified by two members of the project's scientific team. The raters then arrived at a consensus classification for each response. Although clients were asked to identify a single topic, they sometimes identified more than one; in these cases multiple classifications were assigned.

Originally the responses were to be placed into one of the nine life domains or one of two other categories of interest to the team. These two additional categories focused on (1) "neutral" presentation of cognitive, emotional, or psychological functioning or (2) presentation of "negative" or deficit-oriented cognitions, emotions, or psychological functioning—in other words, what terms clients used in presenting their own perceptions of what was helpful to them. It should be noted that "positive," healthy, or constructive terms were coded under life domain 8, internal resources. In addition, three other categories developed from client responses. These categories included (1) relationship with their case manager or substance abuse counselor, (2) no topic seen as most helpful, and (3) assistance in learning how to set goals. Of significance to our discussion here is the frequent mention of assistance in developing goals relative to work with case managers. Thirty-six percent of clients identified "working on goals," "setting life goals," etc. as the most helpful topic they worked on with their case managers. In contrast only 1 percent of clients recognized this type of assistance in their work with their substance abuse counselors.

These two findings, rate of objective and strategy completion and client perception of the value of goal setting, illustrate the practical importance of clients' controlling their own course of treatment. Simply put, clients were likely to complete those plans that they had been instrumental in creating and seemed to value the skills they had learned (goal setting) as well as other forms of assistance, for instance, accessing resources. Obviously, the ability to set goals systematically and successfully accomplish them are skills that can be used independently by the client. Of course, some limitations in these findings exist given the inability to compare the outcomes between plans created under the strengths perspective and core medical model treatment.

Continued Participation in Case Management

One of the motivations for implementing strengths-based case management was the belief that this approach would encourage clients to continue their participation in treatment activities, activities related to both primary treatment and aftercare. While a complete discussion of case management's role in retaining clients in treatment is beyond the scope of this chapter, several points warrant mention. Most clients (N = 349/394; 89 percent) completed a 4-week course of *primary inpatient* treatment with little difference accruing between case managed (N = 180/201; 90 percent) and non-case managed clients (N = 169/193; 88 percent). Conversely, attrition was quite high from *primary outpatient* treatment with only 50 percent of case managed clients completing a 6-week course of treatment as compared to 36 percent of non-case managed clients (31/62 vs. 21/58). Case managed clients were somewhat more likely to start *aftercare* treatment than non-case managed clients (52 percent vs. 49 percent) and on average stayed slightly longer (5.45 weeks vs. 4.54 weeks).

A closer examination of the case management group during the aftercare period revealed an interesting phenomenon. Case managed clients demonstrated a strong tendency to select participation in case management services during the aftercare period over participation in the relapse prevention activities. As noted above, only 52 percent of clients in this group attended at least one session of aftercare following their discharge from primary treatment. In contrast, 66 percent of the clients in this group attended at least one session with their case manager after completion of primary treatment. As Figure 6.1 demonstrates, the gap between attendance at relapse prevention activities and case management activities grows significantly as time progresses. Thirty-five percent of clients reported up to 20 weeks of contact with their case managers while only 11 percent of clients attended that amount of relapse prevention activities. A similar gap, up to 21 percent, between case management and relapse prevention attendance persisted until the end of the 6-month follow-up period.

At this juncture, we can only speculate about what factor(s) led clients who had the choice to select case management attendance over attendance in relapse

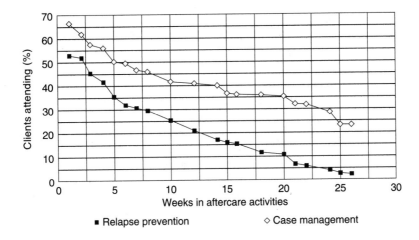

FIGURE 6.1 Participation in aftercare activities, case management and relapse prevention

prevention activities. Early analysis of other data suggests that it might be related to case managers' willingness to meet clients in their environments, as opposed to only in an office setting. In addition, clients had the opportunity to address recovery and multiple other life domains with their case managers. This "one-stop shopping" reflects the strengths perspective principle that encourages the case manager to be a central point in the client's search for resources. This would seem to be a welcome relief to clients who typically have been involved with numerous, disparate resources at any one time. Quite possibly, clients may have found that a focus on strengths and the opportunity to direct their own treatment in a highly individualized fashion was more attractive than relapse prevention activities that focus on pathology.

CONCLUSION

This discussion of strengths-based case management with persons who have substance abuse problems emphasizes the conceptual and practical differences that exist between this approach and the traditional pathology-oriented medical model. The differences are many, among them divergent notions of focusing on abilities versus focusing on disabilities and client-driven treatment versus treatment that emphasizes the role of experts. These differences coalesce around the issue of what leads to treatment resistance and denial and the interventions that should be used to address them. Whether resistance and denial stem from client factors or are artifacts of the helping process, or a combination of both, one thing is certain: Minimally the intervention should in no way engender treatment resistance. Ideally the implementation should both serve client needs for the task at hand (here, resource acquisition) and reduce resistance, whatever its cause.

There is early support for the idea that a strengths-based approach to case management meets both conditions. The evidence comes from (1) the high rate of success that clients experience in completing resource acquisition objectives and strategies and (2) the importance that clients assign to the goal-setting process. When given the opportunity to choose, case managed clients choose to participate in strengths-based case management activities during their aftercare as opposed to medical model-oriented relapse prevention. These process findings will need to be examined further through qualitative approaches that may clarify what aspect(s) of the strengths perspective are particularly valuable in diminishing resistance to treatment. In addition, the impact of this perspective, and case management generally, will need to be examined as it applies to longer tangible outcomes. Preliminary findings from the Enhanced Treatment Project suggest a relationship between strengths-based case management and improved outcome in two areas: reduced levels of cocaine use and improved occupational functioning. Additional studies are needed to support or refute these findings.

Since its inception and ascendancy during the last 30 years, the medical model approach to the treatment of substance abuse problems has served persons suffering from these problems well in one respect. It has given the treatment of these problems legitimacy in many quarters, albeit an ambivalent legitimacy. Ironically the very model that has served substance abuse treatment well has also served to impose a rigidity to that treatment. Strengths-based approaches, including strengths-based case management, may well provide a viable alternative.

DISCUSSION QUESTIONS

1. What are the potential limitation(s) of strengths-based case management as it is practiced with persons who have substance abuse problems?
2. In what ways might a strengths-based approach to case management be compatible with a medical model of substance abuse treatment? Is there room for an integration of these two approaches in the same treatment setting?
3. What are some specific avenues for future research into strengths-based case management's value with this population?

REFERENCES

Bachrach, L. L. (1994). What do patients say about program planning? Perspectives from the patient-authored literature. In J. R. Bedell (Ed.), *Psychological assessment and treatment of persons with severe mental disorders. The series in clinical and community psychology* (pp. 75–91). Philadelphia, PA: Taylor and Francis.

Bander, K. W., Goldman, D. S., Schwartz, M. A., Rabinowitz, E., & English, J. T. (1987). Survey of attitudes among three specialties in a teaching hospital toward alcoholics. *Journal of Medical Education, 62*(1), 17–24.

Berg, I. K., & Miller, S. (1992). *Working with the problem drinker: A solution-focused approach.* New York: Norton.

DeShazer, S. (1984). The death of resistance. *Family Process, 23,* 11–17.

Duncan, B. L., Solovey, A. D., & Rusk, G. S. (1992). *Changing the rules: A client-directed approach to therapy.* New York: Guilford.

Ihilevich, D., & Gleser, G. (1982). *Evaluating mental health programs: The Progress Evaluation Scale.* Lexington, MA: Lexington Books.

Martin, S. S., Isenberg, H., & Inciardi, J. A. (1993). Assertive community treatment: Integrating intensive drug treatment with aggressive case management for hard to reach populations. In J. A. Inciardi, F. M. Tims, & B. W. Fletcher (Eds.), *Innovative approaches in the treatment of drug abuse: Program models and strategies* (pp. 97–108). Westport, CT: Greenwood Press.

Morse, R., & Flavin, D. (1992). The definition of alcoholism. *Journal of the American Medical Association, 268*(8), 1012–1014.

O'Hanlon, W. H., & Weiner-Davis, M. (1989). *In search of solutions: A new direction in psychotherapy.* New York: Norton.

Oppenheimer, E., Sheehan, M., & Taylor, C. (1988). Letting the client speak: Drug misusers and the process of help seeking. *British Journal of Addiction, 83,* 635–647.

Peele, S. (1989). *Diseasing of America—Addiction treatment out of control.* Lexington, MA: Lexington Books.

Rapp, C. A., & Chamberlain, R. (1985). Case management services for the chronically mentally ill. *Social Work, 30,* 417–422.

Rapp, R. C., Kelliher, C. W., Fisher, J. H., & Hall, F. J. (1994). Strengths-based case management: A role in addressing denial in substance abuse treatment. *Journal of Case Management, 3*(4), 139–144.

Rapp, R. C., Siegal, H. A., & Fisher, J. H. (1992). A strengths-based model of case management/advocacy: Adapting a mental health model to practice work with persons who have substance abuse problems. In R. S. Ashery (Ed.), *NIDA Research Monograph* (pp. 79–91). Rockville, MD: U.S. Department of Health and Human Services.

Ross, M. W., & Darke, S. (1992). Mad, bad and dangerous to know: Dimensions and measurement of attitudes toward injecting drug users. *Drug and Alcohol Dependence, 30*(1), 71–74.

Saleebey, D. (Ed.). (1992). *The strengths perspective in social work practice.* White Plains, NY: Longman.

Siegal, H. A., Fisher, J. H., Rapp, R. C., Wagner, J. H., Forney, M., & Callejo, V. (1995). Presenting problems of substance abusers in treatment: implications for service delivery and attrition. *American Journal of Drug and Alcohol Abuse, 21*(1), 17–26.

Siegal, H. A., Rapp, R. C., Fisher, J., Cole, P., & Wagner, J. H. (1993). Treatment dropouts and noncompliers: Two persistent problems and a programmatic remedy. In J. A. Inciardi, F. M. Tims, & B. W. Fletcher (Eds.), *Innovative approaches in the treatment of drug abuse: Program models and strategies* (pp. 109–122). Westport, CT: Greenwood Press.

Siegal, H. A., Rapp, R. C., Fisher, J., Cole, P., & Wagner, J. H. (1994). Implementing innovations in drug treatment: Case management and treatment induction in the enhanced treatment project. In B. W. Fletcher, J. A. Inciardi, & A. M. Horton (Eds.), *Drug abuse treatment: The implementation of innovative approaches* (pp. 131–143). Westport, CT: Greenwood Press.

Sontag, S. (1978). *Illness as metaphor.* New York: Farrar, Straus & Giroux.

Sullivan, W. P., & Fisher, B. J. (1994). Intervening for success: Strengths-based case management and successful aging. *Journal of Gerontological Social Work, 22*(1/2), 61–74.

Sullivan, W. P., Jordan, L., & Dillon, D. (1994). Comprehensive drug and alcohol treatment programming: A bold new approach. *Journal of Health and Social Policy, 6*(2), 91–106.

Weick, A. (1983). A growth-task model of human development. *Social Casework, 64,* 131–137.

Weick, A., & Pope, L. (1988). Knowing what's best: A new look at self-determination. *Social Casework, 69,* 10–16.

Westermeyer, J. (1989). Nontreatment factors affecting treatment outcome in substance abuse. *American Journal of Substance Abuse, 15*(1), 13–29.

chapter **7**

The Strengths Model of Case Management: Principles and Helping Functions

Walter Kisthardt

We do clients a disservice when we insist that they have a problem for us to pay attention to them. Our first question to someone who comes to us for help should not be . . . "what problems bring you here today?" but rather, . . . "you have lived life thus far, tell me how you have done it."

— *Bertha Reynolds*

INTRODUCTION

This chapter explores the specific helping skills involved in the process of engaging, collaborating with, and empowering people who struggle with the difficulties engendered by persistent mental illness and poverty. The ideas that are presented for your consideration flow from research on the "strengths model" of case management (Kisthardt, 1992; Kisthardt, 1993; Rapp & Chamberlain, 1985; Rapp & Wintersteen, 1989). Training in this approach has been provided in 42 U.S. cities and five in Great Britain. This chapter focuses on specific strategies that have been highlighted by consumers as being meaningful and helpful to them in their journey to increased well-being and perceived sense of connectedness in the community.

The seven primary helping functions of the strengths model are (1) engagement, (2) strengths assessment, (3) planning, (4) implementation through advocacy and linkage, (5) monitoring (continuous evaluation), (6) counseling, and (7) graduated disengagement. These functions have been described generally in the sources noted above. In this chapter, we provide greater detail regarding the specifics of engagement, strengths assessment, and implementation through advocacy and linkage, and how these functions may serve as a foundation for effective support and transition to fuller membership and inclusion for consumers in the community. The six principles of the strengths model serve as the foundation for the delivery of these functions.

THE SIX PRINCIPLES OF THE STRENGTHS MODEL

There are six beliefs or values at the heart of the helping process in the strengths model. Many of these values have been expressed in many disciplines for a number of years. When taken together, they serve as a guiding beacon toward using individualized personal care to effect healthy connections in community. The six principles are as follows.

1. The focus of the helping process is on the strengths, interests, abilities, knowledge, and capacities of each person, not on their diagnoses, weaknesses, or deficits.

The human beings who enter your lives are so much more than a collection of symptoms and amalgam of problems. They are survivors. They are exceptionally adaptive. They fight a battle every day with the internal enemy of mental illness and the external enemies of poverty, public apathy, and even hostility. They are resourceful, knowledgeable, resilient, and courageous. They have not given up but have decided to press on despite the barriers society has placed in their paths.

A strengths perspective challenges us to assume a stance of respect and admiration for people. We are challenged to assume the role of student rather than expert. We are asked to validate peoples' dreams and aspirations. We are required to get to know each person as unique and valuable individuals; to learn what it is they want in their lives, what holds meaning for them, what they believe to be important. One consumer put it this way:

Mary (CM) was the first person I ever worked with who asked me what I wanted to do. She told me that she admired me because of how I have been able to get what I need, and that she had a lot to learn from me. She said I have a lot of strengths, and I guess she's right . . . but I didn't even see them as strengths . . . but I do now.

---

2. The relationship between consumers and case managers becomes an essential component of the helping process; and it is characterized by mutuality, collaboration, and partnership.

In this approach, the concepts of independence and dependence lose their utility. They are replaced by interdependence. Both case managers and consumers bring strengths, knowledge, experience, and human emotions to the helping encounter. We depend on having people to work with for our identity as helping professionals. We need the consumers as much, if not more, than they need us. By taking the time to develop helping relationships that model mutual interdependence, we are able to promote and nurture interdependent relationships with others in the community. One consumer spoke about the power of the relationship that evolved with her case manager:

> My case manager was more like a friend than doctors and therapists I have worked with in the past. She really seemed to care about me, and she did not force me to do things. We talked about our mothers, we smoked and laughed together. She helped me get my own place and she came to AA meetings with me. Now I go without her. She has been a gift from heaven, a real miracle in my life.

3. The people we are privileged to work with are viewed as the directors of the helping process.

People with persistent mental illness make decisions. To be sure, there are times when the illness has affected their thinking processes and consequent decision making. In general, however, people consistently make decisions regarding whether they come to your program, whether they take their medications, whether they use alcohol, and the like. A strengths perspective suggests that we acknowledge this individual decision making. Once acknowledged, we may better attempt to understand the motivation for people's actions as opposed to intervening to change them. This is particularly important when the person does not *want* to change, even though others may believe strongly that he or she *needs* to change.

In recent seminars, I have been suggesting that we eliminate the term case manager. This designation does not, in my view, capture the essence of mutuality, collaboration, and partnership. As more than one consumer has shared with me, "I am not a case . . . and they are not my manager!" In its place, I have suggested referring to the worker as a "community living consultant." This term includes integration into the community as the primary *raison d'être* of our helping efforts. Moreover, it emphasizes the roles of listener, advisor, mentor, and colleague in promoting maximum self-determination, autonomy, and sense of empowerment for each consumer. As one consumer stated:

> . . . she told me I was the boss! That although she got paid by the mental health center, she really worked for me. That made me feel real good, like I was in charge. I got pissed one day and fired her . . . when I calmed down the next day I called to hire her back. I never fired or hired anybody in my life. It was a weird feeling.

4. All human beings possess the inherent capacity to learn, grow, and change.

Despite the hardships, and years of living with frequent hospitalizations or without a place that could be called home, each person may, at the time you begin working with him or her, be on the verge of making conscious changes in his or her life. This principle calls us to harness the motivating power of positive expectations; the healing power that often comes with the faith and hope of one other human being, whose love and concern ignites the spark that resides in everyone.

A corollary of this belief is that people have the right to take supported risks, and that they have the right to fail. At times, professionals have been less than sanguine about supporting someone who is, in their minds, "setting themselves up to fail." To be human is, at times, to fail, to make mistakes, to be the author of bad decisions. But it is also to learn from them and, perhaps, grow a little wiser, a little more resilient.

5. The helping activities in this approach are designed to occur in the community, not in the confines of a building.

Case managers are encouraged to deliver each aspect of the strengths model outside of the office or "program" whenever possible. Integration will be promoted more effectively when skills are practiced "in vivo."

There are three possible outcomes when case managers spend most of their time outside of the program building: (1) They learn much more about the resources, both formal and informal, that are available in their community; (2) They are able to nurture collaborative relationships with potential resource people such as landlords, people at the housing authority, potential employers, relatives, and others, and; (3) They may observe skills and behaviors on the part of consumers that often do not occur when they are playing the role of client or patient. Many case managers I have spoken with around the country share that consumers often disclose things about themselves or their history when they are riding together in the car or just walking down the street . . . things they have not told others, including their therapists or doctors. Many community support programs expect their case managers to be out in the community 60 to 70 percent of the time. Research on models of case management has consistently demonstrated that meeting the person in various locations in the community is an important aspect of care (Bond, McDonel, Miller, & Pensec, 1991; Bond, McGrew, and Fekete, 1995; Bush, Langford, Rosen, & Gott, 1990; Kisthardt, 1993).

6. The entire community is viewed as an oasis of potential resources to enlist on behalf of consumers. naturally occurring resources are considered as a possibility before segregated or formally constituted "mental health" resources.

The recent trend toward "supported housing" in community support programming is a prime example of this principle in action (Carling & Ridgeway, 1987). Often a person wants to secure his or her own apartment, and others, including the treatment team at the mental health center, see this plan as "unrealistic" or view agreement with this goal as "setting the client up for failure." This principle challenges community workers to validate the desires of the person. It also challenges workers to creatively address barriers and advocate to help the person live where he or she wants to live, with the supports necessary to make it happen. In many situations this requires much more time, energy, and perseverance than placing someone in a residential treatment home where he or she usually does not want to be in the first place. As one consumer said to me:

> I was in a group home and I couldn't take it. I can't be around people. I don't like people. I went back to the hospital (state psychiatric hospital), I had more freedom there. My case manager helped me to get my own place. It's not much, just one room, but it's mine.

Each of these principles serves to guide and direct each element of the strengths approach. By focusing on individual strengths and personal desires, we get to know the person underneath the illness. By realizing that there is more in our humanity that binds us to consumers than separates us, we gain the courage to be warm, caring, empathic, and genuine. Case managers who exhibit a strengths-based approach are often viewed by consumers as friends. These case managers are expanding the traditional "boundaries" of mental health "treatment." As one consumer shared:

> He's like a brother to me. I know he care (sic) about me, he checks on me, comes to my place, makes sure I get my medicine . . . he send me a card at Christmas . . . I never got a card at Christmas . . . it meant so much . . . I showed it to my mom, I'm gonna keep the card forever . . . Tom's (CM) gone now, but I'll never forget him.

Mutual empowerment may be fostered by accepting and validating the right of people, despite illness and hardship, to make decisions about their own lives, and to learn and grow through experience. By becoming an agent for access to each and every resource in the community, not just those set aside for "the mentally ill," we begin to put our actions where our rhetoric is. The first opportunity to provide principle-based, strengths-oriented practice is during the engagement stage of helping.

STRATEGIES THAT PROMOTE EFFECTIVE ENGAGEMENT FROM THE CONSUMERS' PERSPECTIVE

Our research of the case management helping process has focused on the perceptions of consumers. We have learned much through enthnographic, qualitative inquiry based on conversations with the people who have been on the receiving end of case management. We have also had the good fortune to be able to talk with case managers from Baltimore to New Orleans to Los Angeles who have been successful in engaging people who struggle with the consequences of mental illness and poverty every day. Successful engagement appears to be promoted by the following specific activities:

- *Talk to people . . . do not interview them.* People appear to respond more comfortably to another human being who is being "real" and not playing the role of helper. The assumption going in to the initial conversation with a consumer is that they may have legitimate reasons to distrust. We must earn their respect, their confidence, and their willingness to allow us into their lives. The person who hesitates to engage is viewed in the strengths perspective as being "reluctant" rather than "resistive," "guarded," or "paranoid."

    The task here is not to place a number of conditions on your involvement. Programs often have many rules and regulations by which consumers must abide as a condition for assistance. In case management, we must allow consumers to have a say in the conditions that will characterize the helping relationship. We must become open to being influenced by consumers, without feeling that we are being used. It is interesting to note that when consumers attempt to express their own power in relationships, it is often viewed by professionals as "manipulation." When professionals attempt to influence consumers, however, it is called "treatment."

- *Try to make people see that you are not there to judge them, or even change them, but rather, to accept and validate them.* Here it is important to try to have people identify what they want in their lives, before identifying what they need from your perspective. You may believe that someone "needs" to stop using alcohol before that person is able to benefit from case management. This behavior may indeed be presenting a barrier to long-term change. During engagement, however, the primary task is to lay the groundwork for a collaborative relationship. Therefore, if the person does not wish to stop drinking, but they do want your help in securing a place to live, begin the process of helping them find a place to live. Anecdotal evidence suggests that consumers are more willing to accept recommendations regarding more adaptive behavior from case managers who have earned their trust and demonstrated their unconditional positive regard (Rogers, 1961).

- *Talk about things you both have in common.* Recognize that just as you are trying to gather initial data and to generate an assessment on consumers, they are, at the same time, doing their own assessment of you. Talk about yourself. Your ability to share parts of your own life with consumers appears to be a very important factor in the engagement stage. Talking about things you have in common seems to be less threatening and it can also be fun.

- *Engage in activities you both enjoy.* While you are attempting to gather information and get to know each consumer, try to do this in the context of a mutually satisfying activity. This may take many forms, including going for a walk together, riding in your car, listening to music, having coffee together, smoking together, shooting pool together—almost anything that people do to become more comfortable with each other.

- *Look for opportunities to help people with immediate wants and needs.* Helping people with transportation, food, clothing, shelter, companionship, entitlements, or other tangible resources helps to demonstrate your caring and competence. It is important to keep in mind that some people will be reluctant to accept these initial overtures due to a negative experience in the past. When another person accepts help from you, it is usually a signal of trust, and often patience and understanding are the two most important skills in our repertoire.

- *Be sensitive to consumers' culture, gender, age, and other factors of their distinctive being.* Interactions with people, especially in the early stages of the helping process, should reflect our understanding and acceptance of human diversity and developmental processes. Demonstrate to people that you value who they are and what they believe. Assume the role of student when interacting with someone from a different cultural or ethnic heritage. Remember during this stage that our primary task is to proceed at consumers' unique pace, to accept and validate them, not to get them to do something you think they should do. Every person we come in contact with is viewed as being motivated. The challenge is to discover what specifically motivates each person, and creatively provide opportunities for inclusion and involvement.

One way to discover the uniqueness and motivation in work during the engagement stage is to use a "strengths assessment" to guide the interaction. The strengths assessment tool is illustrated in Figure 7.1 (pages 104–107).

THE STRENGTHS ASSESSMENT AS HOLISTIC PERSONAL INVENTORY

The strengths assessment is a tool that was developed for case managers. It is designed to gather information regarding consumers' circumstances in six domains of community living. The goal is to gather information regarding current social circumstances, what people want in each domain, and what resources or successes they have realized in the past in each life domain.

The following sample of questions provides an illustration of the nature of the data gathering during the engagement and assessment process.

1. Where are you living now? Where are you going to sleep tonight? What does home mean to you? Where would you like to live? What part of town?
2. Do you have friends you can count on to be there for you?
3. What type of help does your family provide?
4. Do you have enough money to get the things you want and need? Are you on SSI? Medicaid? What jobs have you held in the past? What was your favorite job?

PARTICIPANT _____ DATE _____

PRIMARY TEAM MEMBER _____

A. HOUSING

1. Describe current housing arrangement:

2. How satisfied are you with current housing circumstances? Do you want to remain there for the next 6 months or do you want to move?

3. Describe the housing arrangements you have had in the past that have been most satisfying for you.

B. TRANSPORTATION

1. Currently, how do you get around?

2. Do you have any desires regarding expanding your transportation options?

3. What are different ways you used to get around?

C. FINANCIAL/INSURANCE

1. What are your current sources of income? List amount. What in-kind benefits do you receive (food stamps, Medicaid, etc.)?

FIGURE 7.1 Person-centered strengths assessment

2. What do you desire regarding your financial situation?

3. What was the most satisfying time in your life regarding your
   financial situation?

D. VOCATIONAL

1. Identify as many reasons as you can regarding why you have chosen
   to pursue getting a job at this time:

2. If you could design the job you get, what would it be? Let's try to be
   as specific as we can. Where are you? Indoors or outdoors? Do you work
   with a group of people or are you alone? Do you go to work in the day-
   time or at night?

3. Talk about your past job experience. What was the best job you ever
   held? How long were you there? Identify the particulars of this job
   that made it so good for you.

4. Why have you left jobs in the past? Let's try to identify if there
   is a certain pattern that has been evident in your employment history.

5. What supports do you think you need to be successful in getting and
   keeping a job?

FIGURE 7.1 (continued)

6. Talk about your use of alcohol and drugs. This includes drugs that are prescribed and those that are not.

7. Most people who are looking for a new job have mixed feelings about this process. How are you feeling about it? What kinds of things concern you or make you feel nervous or anxious about seeking employment?

8. What are the things you are good at? What things do you enjoy doing and believe you do well? Where is your favorite place to hang out? Why do you like it there?

E. SOCIAL SUPPORTS, RELATIONSHIPS, INTIMACY, SPIRITUALITY

1. Talk about the people who are most important in your life. How will getting and keeping a job affect these relationships?

2. What do you want in the nature of a close relationship? Can I help you achieve that?

3. How important is religion, church, or spirituality in your life? Would you like to strengthen your spiritual life? How can I help?

4. When you need support, understanding, or just someone to talk to, where do you go? Can we do more in this area?

FIGURE 7.1 (continued)

5. What do you want and need in the area of social relationships?

F. HEALTH

1. How is your health? What do you do to take care of your health? Do you smoke? What limitations do you experience because of health-related factors? What medications are you currently taking? How is your diet?

2. What do you want and need in the area of health?

G. LEISURE TIME

1. Talk about what you really enjoy doing to kick back and relax. When are you most joyful? When are you most peaceful?

2. Are there things you used to enjoy that you haven't done in awhile?

3. What do you want and need in the area of leisure time?

H. PRIORITIZING

1. With all we have talked about, let's decide on the area of your life with the most immediate and meaningful wants and needs.

FIGURE 7.1 (continued)

5. If you had three wishes, what would they be?
6. What kinds of things are important to you? When are you happiest? What things interest you?
7. What knowledge and skills do you have that help you "make it" each day?
8. What kinds of things do you do to help other people out?
9. Do you use smoking and/or drinking alcohol to help you maintain?
10. What do you do on a Sunday afternoon?
11. Is spirituality important in your life?
12. Where are the places you go in the community when you are feeling alone, nervous, or upset?
13. If you agree to work with me, what do I need to know about you to be an effective helper?
14. What do you do in your life to stay healthy?
15. What do you like to do for fun?
16. When do you feel really good about yourself?
17. What was your favorite subject in school?
18. Who are your heroes?
19. What do you do when you are bored?
20. What is your favorite food?
21. Who is your favorite author?
22. If you awarded yourself a medal, what would it say?
23. What kinds of music do you enjoy? Who is your favorite performer?

You are encouraged to develop these and other conversational questions that help to paint a holistic portrait of each human being you strive to help. Armed with the richness of personal, strengths-oriented data, the helping plan evolves around what people say they want. The planning and implementation functions then address the complex issues regarding what decisions people need to make, and what behaviors they need to engage in in order for their desires to become a reality.

The implementation process frequently involves advocating with other people on behalf of consumers. Your knowledge of community resources, legislation such as the Americans with Disabilities Act, and your skills in influencing resource people become essential in building the bridges between program and community.

CASE MANAGER AS COMMUNITY LIVING ADVOCATE

From interviews with case managers and supervisors across the nation, there appears to be a set of five questions that serve to guide effective advocacy in the case management process. Often these questions are discussed in the context of group supervision, an essential component of the strengths model (Modrcin, Rapp, & Chamberlain, 1985).

1. What naturally occurring as well as mental health and social services are available in my neighborhood and larger community that may satisfy a specific need related to a consumer goal?

Consider the consumers who state that they want their own apartments. Do they qualify for Section XIII homeless certificates? Do they know any landlords in their community? Are there friends or family who would be willing to help with material or social support? Are there church groups that provide emergency assistance? Are there specialized homelessness programs funded through United Way or McKinney Act funds? Does the mental health center have a transitional housing program? How many landlords do you know in your community?

2. What barriers exist (attitudes, policies, location, etc.) that minimize accessibility to this resource?

Do you sense active discrimination on the part of potential resource providers? Do local zoning laws work against community integration? Do public transportation routes promote access to available housing resources? Training in current regulations regarding Section XIII and SSI is extremely important. These policies are continually changing as policymakers become aware of the realities of homelessness and persistent mental illness.

Of course, one of the biggest barriers to accessibility is the lack of affordable housing in our cities. As the Chicago Coalition for the Homeless (1991) stated: "No combination of mental health, social services, case management, health care, or advocacy will be effective in meeting the needs of homeless mentally ill persons in the absence of the availability of affordable housing" (p. 1).

3. What accommodations need to be made for the consumer to be successful in using this resource?

The Americans with Disabilities Act requires employers with 25 or more employees to not discriminate against a qualified individual with a disability in any aspect of employment. The act requires employers to base their decisions on the ability of the individual to perform the job, not to rely on assumptions about what a person can or cannot do. The act further requires that employers "reasonably accommodate" to disabilities, if necessary, unless it would impose undue hardship on the employer.

This legislation provides further sanction for case managers to assume a more active advocacy role on behalf of people. Many case managers have become active educators, and their efforts have often paid dividends not only for consumers, but for landlords and employers as well.

4. How adequate is the resource?

The concern here is twofold. First, will connection to the resource be effective in meeting the stated need? Second, does the resource meet at least minimum standards of health and human decency? For example, does the apartment meet safety codes? Is there running water available? Is the living space clear of rats, roaches, or other carriers of disease? Is there a problem with asbestos, lead, and other toxins, especially if there are children involved?

5. How acceptable is the resource from the consumer's perspective?

Case managers sometimes expend many hours trying to effect a "placement" in a structured residential setting such as a group home, only to find that the consumer begins to act out or just leaves the setting. In some cases, this may be due in part to the fact that the consumer did not want to be placed in a group home. This was the plan, however, that professionals felt was "best."

It is important to recognize the ambivalence that consumers may experience with any transition into more responsible living circumstances. Consumers may have mixed feelings—wanting the freedom and autonomy but concerned about the new responsibility their new circumstances bring. Workers should explore with consumers how acceptable connecting to the given resource is.

Sometimes, consumers will want to live in an area that we do not think is safe. We may believe they could do better, and we try to influence them to accept a place in a more "structured" setting. When consumers do not agree with our assessment of what would be the best placement, we need to become aware of our own values, and how these may be interfering with creating an empowering helping atmosphere.

In influencing potential resource people, specific strategies have been found to be effective (Netting, Kettner, & McMurtry, 1993). First, the worker should maintain a positive attitude and approach. Conflict strategies are considered as a last resort. Second, it is critical to convey to people with a resource how making it available will benefit them. Third, make a decision about who on the community living team is best suited to approach a particular resource person. For example, someone on the team may have had prior experience with this individual, or someone on the team has more confidence and experience with employers in a particular field. Fourth, the resource person should be given the assurance that you or someone from the program will remain involved as long as necessary during the transition process. Fifth, there ought to be a trial period and, at a defined point, a reassessment of whether the placement is working out. Finally, when you enter into the advocacy effort, expect others to become involved, anticipate their concerns, and consciously attempt to address them.

SUMMARY

In this chapter, we have discussed specific components of the strengths model of case management. Moreover, we have given examples of how these principles serve to guide the functions of engagement, assessment, planning, and implementation through advocating on behalf of people who struggle with persistent mental illness, substance abuse, homelessness, or other conditions that act as barriers to community integration. These principles and functions are shared by many community programs throughout the nation. Programs that work with many different populations, such as Head Start, Welfare Reform, Aging, Developmental Disabilities, and Corrections, have received training in the strengths model and are reporting positive outcomes. In addition, a case management/outpatient project has been in place in Johnson County, Kansas for the past three years. Results indicate that the addition of case management in work with adults who carry diagnoses of border-line, dissociative, multiple personality, or mood disorder demonstrate improved so-cial functioning as measured by reduced emergency contacts and diminished use of inpatient care. The study is currently being submitted for publication.

In light of recent trends on the political and economic scene, it appears likely that states will be given greater discretion regarding the organization, funding, and delivery of services to vulnerable populations. It will be imperative for systems to develop integrated, cost-effective, efficient community caring responses. In Kansas, and in several other locations around the nation including Maricopa County, Ari-zona, and Marin County, California, providers from Vocational Rehabilitation, Men-tal Health, Substance Abuse, and Developmental Disabilities have attempted to come together around the employment of the philosophy, purpose, and principles of the strengths approach.

We must constantly strive to focus on strengths of people and of communities: to convey the belief that people want to be the directors of their lives; to view the entire community as our office; to value the partnership and mutuality that tran-scends traditional professional/client roles; to refuse to tolerate discrimination, seg-regation, and apathy regarding the preservation of human dignity and the promo-tion of social justice. We must be able to validate the pain, heartache, disappointment, frustration, and personal struggle of each person, while at the same time recognizing, celebrating, and learning from the strategies, resources, and competencies they have employed in their journey. In this way, an atmosphere that sustains personal growth and fulfillment will be created for consumers, as well as for ourselves. As the following poem suggests, we are bound to each other through our human experience.

WHO IS NOT RECOVERING?[1]

Who is not recovering, from something in their past?
From a painful loss, a relationship that didn't last?
Who is not recovering, from harsh words that cut, and scarred?
Or decisions that were made, that made the journey hard?

Who is not recovering, from setbacks and despair?
From a life crying out for healing, for mending, and repair?
Who is not recovering, from disappointment after a failed goal?
From illness of the spirit, or desperation of the soul?

We are all like pilgrims, on a journey, where we fall.
The road sometimes gets bumpy, sometimes we hit a wall.
We have much to teach each other, of lessons we have learned.
As we opted for the straight path, or the times we chose to turn.

---

[1] From *You Validate My Visions: Collected Poems of Helping, Healing, Crying, and Loving*, ©1995, Wally Kisthardt.

Recovering is discovering, that we have much to give.
That all of our experiences, have served to help us live.
Recovering is uncovering, the gifts we still possess,
And bringing them to the light of day, and basking in success.

Yes, we are all recovering, as we live from day to day.
And we all seek a caring hand, when we seem to lose our way.
Case managers and consumers, seeking comfort, and release.
Both pilgrims on the journey, together we'll find peace.

DISCUSSION QUESTIONS

1. What are the six principles of the strengths model of case management? Give an example from your own practice or program that illustrates these principles.
2. Compare the type of information gathered for a consumer at your program on the diagnostic or bio-psycho-social intake with the type of information gathered by a strengths assessment.
3. Discuss how information from both sources is used to generate an individualized care plan.
4. Describe three of the guidelines for effective advocacy and use helping examples to illustrate these points.

REFERENCES

Bond, G. R., McDonel, E. C., Miller, L. D., & Pensec, M. (1991). Assertive community treatment and reference groups: An evaluation of their effectiveness for young adults with serious mental illness and substance abuse problems. *Psychosocial Rehabilitation Journal, 15*(2), 31–43.

Bond, G. R., McGrew, J. H., & Fekete, D. (1995). Assertive outreach for frequent users of psychiatric hospitals: A meta study. *Journal of Mental Health Administration, 22,* 4–16.

Bush, C. T., Langford, M. W., Rosen, P., & Gott, W. (1990). Operation outreach: Intensive case management for severely psychiatrically disabled adults. *Hospital and Community Psychiatry, 41,* 647–649.

Carling, P. J., & Ridgeway, P. (1987). Overview of a psychiatric rehabilitation approach to housing. In W. Anthony and M. Farkas (Eds.), *Psychiatric rehabilitation: Programs and principles.* Baltimore: Johns Hopkins University Press.

Chronic mental illness and homelessness: Summary of recommendations for action. National Advisory Mental Health Council and National Mental Health Leadership Forum Hearing on Severe Mental Illness and Homelessness (1991) (testimony presented by the Chicago Coalition for the Homeless Mental Health Committee).

Kisthardt, W. E. (1992). A strengths model of case management: The principles and functions of a helping partnership with persons with persistent mental illness. In D. Saleebey (Ed.), *The strengths perspective in social work practice.* White Plains, NY: Longman.

Kisthardt, W. E. (1993). An empowerment agenda for case management research: Evaluating the strengths model from the consumers' perspective. In M. Harris and H. Bergman (Eds.),

Case management for mentally ill patients: Theory and practice. Langhorne, PA: Harwood Academic Publishers.

Modrcin, M., Rapp, C. A., & Chamberlain, R. (1985). *Case management with psychiatrically disabled individuals: Curriculum and training program.* Lawrence, KS: University of Kansas School of Social Welfare.

Netting, E. F., Kettner, P. M., & McMurtry, S. L. (1993). *Social work macro practice.* White Plains, NY: Longman.

Rapp, C. A., & Chamberlain, R. (1985). Case management services for the chronically mentally ill. *Social Work, 26,* 417–422.

Rapp, C. A., & Wintersteen, R. (1989). The strengths model of case management: Results for twelve demonstrations. *Journal of Psychosocial Rehabilitation, 13*(1), 23–32.

Rogers, C. R. (1961). *On becoming a person.* Boston: Houghton Mifflin.

chapter **8**

The Strengths Model with Older Adults: Critical Practice Components

Becky Fast
Rosemary Chapin

ANN

Ann Karlin got her wish. She went home after discharge from the cardiac care unit at a large inner-city hospital 75 miles from her small rural community. Ann is a 75-year-old African-American woman whose husband died last year. All of Ann's children moved out of the state shortly after their high school graduations. She lives on a small Social Security check and retirement pension that resulted from her husband's factory work in the city. Ann arrived home weak, depressed, and anxious about how she was going to manage, given her failing health resulting from congestive heart disease. Francis, Ann's neighbor, who is herself frail, also was deeply concerned about Ann and decided to contact the Area Agency on Aging (AAA) on her behalf.

Ann received a call from the social worker and refused the offered help. Despite Ann's unwillingness to accept or request formal services, the social worker from the aging social services agency decided to contact Ann again. The social worker was persistent in reaching out to Ann to see how she was doing and to find out if she needed any additional help. The precariousness of Ann's condition worried the social worker. She knew that a fall, insufficient nutrition, or lack of medication adherence could necessitate a nursing home admission. Slowly, a relationship developed between the two. Ann began to trust the social worker and believe that she was not secretly trying to put her in a nursing home. After being homebound for a week, Ann asked the social worker to find her a cleaning lady and someone to pick up some groceries for her at the local store. From Ann's perspective, she wanted to be sure that the social worker would respect what she wanted and needed before she agreed to any type of service arrangement.

115

Ann has entered into the complex and confusing web of long-term care services. Luckily, she has a seasoned social worker who uses a strengths-based practice model and understands the importance of developing rapport. When such an approach is absent, many older adults like Ann will not even consider looking at service options. The strengths model of case management is designed for people like Ann who will require different types of help and levels of intensity in caring and service provision as their health improves or deteriorates. Respect for the dignity and uniqueness of individuals like Ann is operationalized through the model's practice principles and methods. Furthermore, social workers using the strengths model are alert to the additional barriers to service access that African-American women may face. Workers operating from a strengths approach are interested in building on the strengths that have helped older adults overcome previous difficult times in their lives.

This chapter describes how the strengths model of case management is implemented in the long-term care of older adults, specifically in the provision of home- and community-based services. The application of the strengths model of case management with seniors living at home in the community has not yet been empirically tested; however, initial data gathered from consumers and long-term care social workers trained in the strengths model supports its applicability to older adults. The responses and observations the authors have received from social workers while providing training on and technical assistance for the strengths approach have been instrumental in identifying and developing those components of the strengths model that seem essential to effective practice.

The first section of this chapter presents the conceptual framework that guides and directs the helping efforts with elders. The next section delineates the critical practice components of a strengths-based case management approach in long-term care, especially practice methods designed to support older adults' autonomy, and meet resource-oriented needs while promoting cost-effectiveness and efficiency. The personal stories of individuals who have received case management are included to illustrate the usefulness of the strengths approach within a system accountable for reducing unnecessary institutional costs. Finally, the potential of the strengths model in changing long-term care environments is explored.

CONCEPTUAL FRAMEWORK FOR PRACTICE

For nearly a decade, the professional literature has occasionally considered the effectiveness and plausibility of using a strengths-based approach with older adults, children with severe emotional disturbance, and persons with mental illness and/or substance abuse problems (Perkins & Tice, 1995; Poertner & Ronnau, 1990; Pray, 1992; Rapp, Siegal, Fisher, & Wagner, 1992; Sullivan & Fisher, 1994). Strengths-based case management for older adults is derived from the basic principles and functions of the strengths model developed in the 1980s for persons with severe and persistent mental illness living in the community (Rapp, 1992).

Case management has been a part of social work practice since its inception (Johnson & Rubin, 1983). Like all social work practice, strengths-based case management for older adults rests on a foundation of values, knowledge, and skills. But there are several distinguishing features emanating from the values and philosophy of the model that set it apart from other long-term care case management practice approaches. These distinctive features include a shift from traditional models of helping based on medical necessity to a strengths-based model that addresses the whole person in his or her environment. In the strengths framework, discovering, developing and building on the person's internal and external resources is a focal point. In contrast to many other long-term care case management models, the strengths-based helping process emphasizes consumer participation and decision making.

Medical and rehabilitation models typically emphasize professional diagnosis and treatment of the symptomatology to eradicate or ameliorate the "problem." Authority for and control over decisions lies in the hands of the professional. The unspoken premise is that persons in need of assistance lack knowledge or insight about the identified physical or mental problem and certainly about how it might be resolved. Professional expertise is needed to assess and treat the troublesome condition (Freidson, 1988).

In contrast, the primary purpose of strengths case management is to help older persons maintain as much control over their lives as possible by compensating for what they cannot do and capitalizing on what they can do. The goal of strengths case management is to "normalize" the older person's routine within the bounds determined by the individual, often despite advancing disability. Assessment and planning strategies are woven from the social, psychological, and physical needs and strengths of an older person. For example, in a medical model case management system, a patient with a broken hip might be hospitalized, have the hip treated, and then be released. The medical needs may have been well met, but matters such as transportation, housing modifications, financial assistance, social isolation, and some physical limitations might never be considered. For most older adults, well-being is more than a medical matter. What is equally significant is the ability to contribute and feel useful, to prevent or cope with social isolation, and to normalize the routine of daily life despite the disease or illness (Smith & Eggleston, 1989). As a matter of fact, a person might be suffering from a serious chronic condition, but if these other needs are attended to, they might experience a sense of heightened well-being.

The assumption underlying the medicalization of aging services is that older people, and especially those with chronic disabilities, require the involvement of medical professionals to protect them from further injury and debilitation. In advanced age, chronic rather than acute illnesses are, for the most part, the major medical problems. The leading chronic conditions among older people include arthritis, heart diseases, high blood pressure, asthma, bronchitis, hearing or visual impairments, and ulcers (U.S. Bureau of the Census, 1991). However, these conditions merely irritate some older people as they lead relatively normal lives despite aches and pains. Others are not so lucky and are significantly limited in their ability to carry out daily activities, such as cooking, housework, yard work, and getting out of the house to socialize. Of course, many older people also are periodically afflicted with acute illnesses (that is, conditions lasting less than three months).

But over the long haul, the stress inherent in providing and receiving emotional support and getting help with household tasks and personal care are the most pressing challenges during later life transitions for older adults and their families. Medical problems of older persons may remain stable during long periods. The person may even experience years of relative remission, occasionally interspersed with episodes of crisis and declining mental or physical health. The day-to-day stress of aging results from dealing with functional disabilities—the degree of independence in functioning a person possesses in the face of illness. The performance of activities of daily living (ADLs) such as bathing, dressing, and eating, and independent activities of daily living (IADLs) such as shopping, walking, and getting out of the house must be addressed on a daily basis. Despite functional deficits, older people may demonstrate remarkable resiliency. They often possess an underutilized or untapped capacity for growth and change even in the context of their handicapping circumstances. Like younger persons with disabilities, some older adults need only minimal assistance to arrange and manage supports and resources so that they can remain in the community and lead the life to which they are accustomed.

The conceptual framework for the strengths model of case management with older adults places self-determination as the central value, and that directs the focus to personal goal achievement. In achieving goals, consumer authority is key to the case management relationship, and the elder as well as the community must be viewed as possessing valuable resources and strengths. Thus, the case managers' task is to help elders identify and achieve access to both formal and informal resources in order to reach the outcomes they desire. Table 8.1 presents key elements of the strengths model and delineates differences between it and traditional medical/rehabilitative models of helping.

Operationalizing the Conceptual Framework

Case managers cannot be truly effective with older clients unless they believe in the worth, dignity, and uniqueness of older people in the face of a society that too often relegates seniors to an inferior position. Allowing older persons to determine for themselves where they want to go, and when and how, demands faith in their ability and capacity to choose and to handle the consequences of their choices. Such attitudes affirm the dignity and worth of older adults in spite of prevalent myths and stereotypes that clearly represent bias and prejudice against elders.

Despite the strong preference of older adults to remain in their homes as long as possible, family and professional relationships can strongly affect the elder's sense of self and the type of long-term care they decide on. Assisting older persons with identifying and defining the problems at hand, while facilitating their participation in finding solutions, helps them to believe that continued community-based living is possible. An overarching goal of strengths-based case management, anchored in the value base of client self-determination, is facilitating consumer involvement

TABLE 8.1   The strengths conceptual model contrasted with traditional medical/rehabilitative models of helping

Factor	Strengths Model	Medical/Rehabilitative Models
Value base	Human potential to grow, heal, learn Human ability to identify wants Self-determination Strengths of person and environment Individuality and uniqueness	Problem resolution dependent upon professional expertise Compliance with prescribed treatments Patient lacks insight and knowledge about health
Focus	Combining personal and environmental resources to create situations for personal goal achievement	Professional diagnosis to determine the specific nature of the person's problem and to prescribe treatment
Solution to problems	Determined by consumer/ environment Natural community resources used first Consumer authority and investment	Professional-oriented assessment and service delivery
Social and cultural role	Consumer "Elders taking care of themselves"	Patient "Taking care of the elderly"
Case management relationship	Consumer choice and decision making Develops rapport and trust Case manager coaches, supports, and encourages Case manager replaces self when possible with natural helpers	Clients are passive recipients Professional contact limited to assessment, planning, evaluating functions Provider-directed decision making and interventions
Case management tasks	Identifying strengths and resources Rejuvenating and creating natural helping networks Developing relationships Provided within daily routines	Teaching skills to overcome deficits Monitoring compliance Medical management of identified problems
Desired client outcomes	Interdependence Quality of life Self-efficacy Consumer satisfaction	Problem resolution Maximum bodily functioning Meeting identified biomedical standards of treatment

and choice. Providing older people with plausible options and including them in decision making about possible institutional placement increases the likelihood of satisfaction with, and relevance of, the choices made. When the older consumer becomes more active in making medical and social decisions, both the consumer and the providers achieve greater satisfaction.

Asking for additional help can be extremely difficult for an older person. Motenko and Greenberg assert that "the ability to acknowledge the need for help and ask for help is evidence of mature dependence, a crucial transition in late life" (1995, p. 387). These authors suggest that older persons are better able to accept increased dependence if they are given authority to make decisions about the nature of the help needed and how it should be provided. Simply stated, being in charge or calling the shots is essential to personal pride, particularly for older adults who have been operating independently throughout their lives. The more older persons feel in control of their lives by solving their own problems, the less the likelihood of unnecessary dependency and learned helplessness—two outcomes that are too often the fate of older citizens.

In the strengths model, social workers identify consumer abilities and create or find situations to use those abilities in the achievement of personal goals. Change, we believe, can happen only when you collaborate with an individual's aspirations, perceptions, and strengths. Most consumers are competent and able to participate in the planning and delivery processes. Doing so brings renewed self-confidence and independence precipitated by moving with the elder in the direction he or she chooses and in situations and contexts where the person feels capable and willing. If consumers are experts in defining their needs, the role of the social worker must change to reflect a greater appreciation of that consumer expertise.

Helping individuals like Ann manage their own inevitable aging process and the physical and emotional losses involved assists them in being better equipped to make sound decisions regarding what type of help they want. When considering the needs of older person and their families, risk and security must be carefully balanced. The conflict between the two becomes even clearer for elders who are more severely disabled. The following case example, supplied by a strengths-oriented case manager, illustrates this dilemma.

SARAH

Sarah Nelson is 82 years old and lives alone on the family's farm several miles out of town with her six cats and two dogs. Since her stroke, she has fallen several times. At one point she fractured her hip. Even though Sarah is confined to her lazy boy chair during the day, she continues to create dried flower arrangements. She relies on the home health aide to get her in and out of the bath, into bed, and to help with meal preparation. Sarah calls in her grocery list each week and the grocery store delivers her groceries. Her case manager and daughters assist her with finding transportation, managing her finances, and overseeing the upkeep of her home and farm. Her daughter Mary insists that she should move into the assisted-living unit in town. Sarah replies that she would rather lie helpless on the floor for hours than have to share a room and bathroom with a complete stranger. Sarah's daughters are very concerned about her living all alone on the farm. They fear that she will hurt herself and no one will be available to help her.

Over and over again, older people like Sarah state that they value freedom, privacy, and the independence to make risk-laden decisions about their daily life far more than they value living in a safe and protective environment. Sarah, a strong-willed woman, has adamantly resisted her daughters' and her medical providers' pleas that she move into supervised housing, which would prevent her from hurting herself. In this situation, Sarah's decision to remain living in her own home has continued to be respected. Her case manager has helped make it possible by providing her with meaningful choices about long-term care. Sarah's life-long habits of self-care, preferences about daily tasks, and her considerable strength of character are respected through negotiation about the type and level of service she prefers.

Table 8.2 presents a continuum of possible behaviors available to case managers for facilitating higher or lower levels of participation and involvement by the consumer. This table is intended to provide guidance to social workers attempting to foster the participation of frail or disabled older adults who are competent in decisions about their care needs. The continuum ranges from absolute authority (having the locus of control with the case manager) to a self-directed care approach (shifting the control to an informed consumer). The midpoint indicates shared responsibility by both parties for managing the multiple effects of the consumer's disabilities and illnesses, and for individualizing the consumer's resources.

The goal of strengths-based case management is to encourage more active consumer participation in long-term care decisions. The case manager begins where the consumer is and moves with him or her on the continuum to the highest possi-

TABLE 8.2   Continuum of decision making

Absolute Authority	Imposing	Joint Action	Limited Constraints	Self-Directed Care
The case manager pressures the consumer to accept the problems or solutions without input or participation in the decision. The person's understanding of the issues are solicited, but the case manager retains absolute authority over decisions.	The case manager defines the problem and selects the solutions that are the most promising. Consumer preferences are taken into consideration.	Together, both parties brainstorm a possible range of solutions. The case manager and consumer are both responsible for identifying consumer strengths and resources for implementing the plan of care. Decisions are not made unless both individuals agree on them.	The consumer offers preferences about the type, role, and the level of service provision. Information and counseling is given by the case manager to assist the consumer in making informed decisions. The consumer retains the final decision within limits defined by the case manager.	Consumer choices are supported through being allowed to choose the mix, frequency, duration, and timing of formal/informal service provision within organizational boundaries. In this system, the case manager becomes a consultant to and resource for consumers to help make viable arrangements.
CASE MANAGER-DIRECTED DECISION MAKING		COLLABORATIVE DECISION MAKING		CONSUMER-DIRECTED DECISION MAKING

ble level of participation. Professional-directed decision making is seen as the least desirable state. The aim is to expand consumer confidence in making crucial decisions such as when to seek care and what options to select, and to move toward consumer-directed decision making. Ann had never taken care of the finances, the car, or fixing the house. She was at a loss about how to handle what she saw as traditionally male duties that her husband always had performed. In those arenas, she initially wanted the case manager to make more of the decisions. However, she wanted to retain the responsibilities that she had during her marriage. In time, she felt more confident about managing her late husband's duties and subsequently wanted less direction from the case manager.

At the self-directed end of the continuum (see Table 8.2) consumers determine what services they need and at what level they need to support themselves in the community. The example of Sarah illustrates how a consumer participated in and negotiated her care service schedule including what service would be performed. She did not want someone coming into her house to clean on a weekly basis. Sarah thought it was unnecessary for her to have a higher standard of living now than she had known previously in her life.

Self-directed care does not preclude the case manager from developing a supportive structure that enables individuals with disabilities, with the assistance of family, friends, and community members, to take responsibility for planning their own lives. Sarah, with the support of her case manager and several women who owned small businesses, was assisted in finding a market for her dried flower arrangements.

One difficulty lies with the minority of elders whose judgment is so impaired that increased responsibility for care decisions poses a danger to self and others. Questions inevitably arise about whether the person should participate in decision making and at what level. Frail or disabled older adults have the right to be involved in decisions about their long-term care. Even consumers with cognitive or psychiatric disabilities should be afforded as many choices as possible. The challenge is to be scrupulously aware of their rights and the *real* limitations of their physical and mental conditions. Given patience and time, a relationship can be established even with a very frail older person who fades in and out mentally. Their fears can be identified, concerns expressed, trust established, and actions taken in which the elder is a willing partner to the maximum of his or her potential and capacity. Strengths-based case managers strive to understand how their relationship supports or limits the autonomy of older persons.

CRITICAL PRACTICE COMPONENTS
OF EFFECTIVE CASE MANAGEMENT

The purpose of strengths-based case management is to assist seniors in identifying, securing, and sustaining external and internal resources that are needed for customary interdependent (as opposed to independent or dependent) community living (Kisthardt & Rapp, 1991). The strengths model's potential to increase case management effectiveness with older adults occurs through the following practice methods:

(1) personalized assessment and planning; (2) assertive outreach to natural community resources and services; (3) emergency crisis planning; and (4) ongoing collaboration and caregiving adjustments.

Personalized Assessment and Planning

Assessment from a strengths perspective is holistic rather than diagnostic. Consumer knowledge and motivation rather than professional expertise is the basis of the assessment and planning process (Pray, 1992). A standard functional assessment does not generate a complete picture of the older person's strengths, coping strategies, motivations, and potential for change (Kivnick, 1993). Eligibility for long-term care services based on functional limitations prompts social workers to view their consumers in terms of activities of daily living (ADLs) and independent living activities (IADLs) typologies. In fact, so much emphasis is placed on functional limitations that an older person's quality of life is often reduced to *nothing more* than a list of ADLs and IADLs. Vulnerable older adults soon realize that in order to receive help, they too must describe themselves in those terms. In Ann Karlin's case, an initial focus on the deficits in her activities of daily living could have reinforced suspicions about the social worker's intentions to find her incapable of remaining in her home. Careful attention to her desires during the initial relationship building created an environment where functional limitations as well as capacities could be acknowledged and used in the care planning process.

Strengths-based assessment and planning focuses on the optimization of the older person's strengths and resources. Applied helping strategies are implemented to support the individual's sense of control and capacity to function at home. This is accomplished through finding and trying out supports and resources that take the person's limitations into consideration but counterbalance them through discovering new and old strengths and activities that might fit with the individual's desires and interests (Sullivan & Fisher, 1994). For example, in assessing Sarah's strengths, the case manager learned of her past hobby even though it had been years since Sarah had created flower arrangements. She recultivated Sarah's interest in the hobby and helped her buy the necessary supplies. After several months, Sarah's depression lifted, very probably from pursuing her hobby, and her dried flower arrangements even brought in some additional income to fund her home care. The desired resources needed to optimize the person's capabilities may or may not be available on the menu of services offered by the social worker's agency. Strengths-based care plan development strives to be unrestricted by payment sources. Care planning driven by consumer interests and assets rather than steered by reimbursement is the desired outcome.

Most social workers are indeed committed to acknowledging their consumers' strengths. However, the majority of assessment and care planning tools provide little space or incentive for recording what the older person wants, is doing, has done, and can do to maintain his or her independence. This omission hinders even the best of intentions. Rarely, if ever, are consumer strengths seen as integral to the planning process so that services are provided and activities structured to maximize and promote existing or potential strengths. Subsequently, social workers can easily fall back into old habits. They fail to get to know the older person in a holistic way, whereas an appreciation of the whole person almost always creates a positive inter-action. When the necessary time is taken to develop this kind of relationship, the case manager is better able to assist the consumer in developing an individualized plan of action.

Given system barriers such as large caseloads and organizational policies, the strengths assessment and planning process with senior adults should, at minimum, cover these items:

- Exploring commonalties: shared values, experiences, interests
- Learning how the person has coped with difficulties in the past
- Visioning together what kind of life the consumer wants
- Focusing on the strengths within the person and his or her environment

Basic questions to ask include

- Who is important to you in your life?
- What do you do during a normal day?
- What makes life worth living for you?
- What is going well for you right now?
- If things could be different, what would you wish for?
- What has worked well for you in the past?

The strengths assessment process is not meant to replace existing standardized assessments for conferring and allocating benefits. However, it is unjust and arro-gant to suppose that the whole picture of a person is captured in diagnostic, func-tional, or psychotherapeutic assessments. Only through creating *life* plans rather than *care* plans will an older person be able to live meaningfully in the community. The above focal points and questions can serve as guides for gathering the informa-tion needed to develop such plans. An actual strengths assessment and personal plan can be seen in Kisthardt (1992, pp. 70–73).

Assertive Outreach to Natural Community Resources and Services

The strengths perspective on case management practice offers an alternative con-ception to resource acquisition. Before using formal paid services, the case manager is expected to determine first that naturally occurring, environmental and commu-nity resources are not available. Natural helpers include a collective of supporters to be developed and sustained such as neighbors, apartment managers, grocery store clerks, church or youth groups, adult children, and others with whom the older cli-ent comes into contact on a daily or weekly basis. The presence of naturally occur-ring resources is a strength of all communities and an available resource in *all* com-munities when actively pursued (Sullivan, 1992).

The strengths model advocates employing natural helpers and resources whenever possible. From the perspective of older adults, such help may be more acceptable because it is often based on friendship or a perception of mutual need, is easily accessible, lacks stigma, and is usually much cheaper. However, many seniors would rather not encumber their existing social network. In fact, when older persons are asked to help identify their helping networks, they will often tell you that no one is around who can help them. The avoidance of acknowledging dependency, combined with pride, may prevent older people from recognizing their extensive reliance on others for their daily survival. Therefore, it is imperative for strengths-oriented case managers to identify and support these helpers without undermining the older person's self-esteem and dignity. Special assistance when it comes from family, friends, employers, and colleagues often is not recognized by the older people as help per se because it is extended in such a subtle manner. This help is given by the informal social helpers as they interact with the individual during the normal rhythms of the day. These individuals may notice that their older friend is having some difficulty with walking, eating, or shopping and, without being asked, help the person with these tasks.

Social supports take on increased significance as elders become more frail. One of the losses experienced by elders is the shrinkage of the informal support system. Many of our consumers no longer have a full social support system that can help them. One of the critical functions of the social worker is to help secure and sustain their connection to informal resources. The social worker's goal is to facilitate a more adequate fit between the individual's desires and the resources in his or her environment. This includes the social worker's helping the individual and primary caregivers to recognize and map out what assets are already being used to some degree and to include other community capacities that have not yet been mobilized.

Acquisition of natural community resources is predicated on the belief that including consumers in the decision about who or what entity provides the service will further promote adherence to the form and direction of the help received. The challenge for most social workers is locating and expanding a natural support system for their consumers. In Ann's and Sarah's situation, most of their friends and acquaintances, except for their children, were equally frail. They too, are limited in their physical capability to conduct heavy cleaning or lift objects, and they are not able to come and go as they please. The social worker needs to be informed about the naturally occurring resources in the wider community, as well as in the consumer's personal network. It is important to generate as many potential resources as possible with consumers and their primary caregivers. Older persons may withdraw and withhold existing support network information out of pride and a desire to protect their privacy and maintain the appearance of independence.

A useful strategy for case managers to use in order to identify natural helpers is to accompany the older person through a typical day in order to learn what help is given, by whom, and how often (Lustbader & Hooyman, 1994). By going with the person to the doctor, hairdressers, etc., and by listening to the conversations, more often than not, a social worker will discover that the older person has more social contact than the social worker realized. Or, the case manager might discover a totally different personality outside the home than that seen at home in the "client" role.

In developing the service mix, caregiver burden is acknowledged. Support networks of family and friends should not feel overtaxed. Assertively working to relieve primary caregiver burden is basic to developing a workable care plan. Ongoing dialogue, assessment of perceived burden, and role adjustment must occur with informal caregivers when they are providing some of the major components of care. One of the chief problems with natural helpers is finding ways to limit their involvement because they are within easy reach on a potentially unlimited basis. Many who could help would rather not get involved because they fear being overwhelmed by the needs that may eventually occur. Occasionally, some older people alienate those who could help by complaining about the help or by expecting too much help.

Despite the emotional bonds linking older adults with their families, friends, and other established caregivers, these persons often lack the expertise to provide comprehensive long-term care. Further, a previous history of caregiver abuse and neglect in a given situation may necessitate agency assistance to care for and protect the vulnerable adult from any informal assistance. However, formal providers, while often equipped with the necessary technical skills, cannot fully satisfy affective needs or deliver the kind of idiosyncratic care that reflects a lifetime of shared values and experiences.

Balancing expensive formal care with less-expensive informal resources can help control costs while ensuring necessary assistance is provided in ways acceptable to the older adult. In Ann's case, the social worker discovered that the man who rented Ann's garage to store an antique car had a daughter in high school. With Ann's agreement, the social worker hired the girl to shop for groceries. Ann prepared a list that the girl's father picked up when he drove by on his way to work (he also usually dropped in to see how Ann was doing on these occasions). When the social worker explored with Ann what her experiences as an African-American woman had been in seeking formal service, Ann indicated that she was hesitant to try to negotiate a formal care system primarily staffed by white people. Her preference was to rely on friends or relatives to help her get services. The high school girl and her father were recognized both as a source of help and as trusted friends who could aid Ann in her efforts to gain access to other resources.

In addition, Ann's son, a school teacher, would spend a month with his mother in the summer. His work to keep her home repaired relieved many of his mother's concerns about basic household upkeep. The social worker had a chance to become acquainted with him during these visits. At the social worker's suggestion, he accompanied his mother to the senior center each week. This allowed time for Ann to become comfortable in the service environment. She continued to attend the center from time to time even after her son returned home. Ann's son now felt more confident his mother could continue to live in the community with the support of the social worker, the service center, and other informal resources. If he became concerned about her well-being, he knew he could turn to the social worker for help. Undoubtedly, there will never be enough paid formal services to meet the needs of a growing disabled elderly population. However, focusing primarily on the deficits and lacks in the social environment only further restricts the number of helping resources.

Emergency Crisis Planning

Most older persons come to the attention of a social worker at a time of crisis. Unfortunately, crisis frequently occurs as the result of an acute care hospitalization. This experience leaves frail older adults in a weakened state suffering from depression, anxiety, or a sense of failure if the admission was caused by a fall, medication mismanagement, or lapses in personal care. During these instances, when the person's resiliency is low, they are most ready to yield to accepting professional and caregiver choices and goals. Advocating for the person's wishes and increasing elder involvement in the decision-making process increases the likelihood that alternatives to institutional care will be chosen if available. High care costs often result because the case manager has not had time to deal with the problem before it becomes a crisis or because services are simply allocated to the consumer without trying to fully assess and resolve the situation. Kulys (1983) found that older adults typically do not plan for a health-related crisis. This potential for unwanted institutionalization precipitated by unexpected crises can be mitigated by planning ahead for crisis services.

In the strengths model, an emergency plan is discussed and negotiated with the consumer and the primary caregivers before a health crisis develops. This plan is rehearsed and reviewed. Specific behaviors are practiced to ensure that they are followed in an emergency. However, as the following examples illustrate, developing an emergency plan entails the careful building of a relationship. Emergency planning was initiated with a man who had fallen repeatedly. He was not interested in installing a medical alert system that could potentially cause a big scene in his neighborhood. Even though his pride prevented him from using a medical alert system, he did willingly agree to have his mail carrier alert his son if his mail did not get picked up. In Ann's case, she was willing to wear a medical alert pin that linked her to the small local rural hospital. She and Francis, her neighbor, discussed alternative emergency plans for nonmedical crises. In the event of such a crisis, one of them would alert the on-call worker at the aging social service agency who would then alert the staff nurse or social worker depending on presenting need.

An established emergency plan takes into consideration that most frail older adults will probably need time-limited, acute-care crisis services at various times. However, at a large number of crisis junctures, either low- or high-cost rapid response mechanisms can be selected, depending on how informed the consumer and caregivers are about the existing resources and their accessibility. When a structured plan for dealing with crises involving natural and formal resources is not in place, then high-cost services become the simplest and most readily available option. The strengths approach focuses on anticipating key crisis points as a strategy for providing effective case management and helping to contain unnecessary costs.

Ongoing Collaboration and Caregiving Adjustments

In the strengths perspective, monitoring is a continuous process that begins when care goals are established. The social worker frequently contacts and collaborates not only with the older person, but also with their family members, friendly visitors, senior citizen groups, nurses, and other support networks. The social worker's role goes far beyond that of "appointments secretary" to that of leader, trainer, and supervisor of a cadre of paid and unpaid helpers.

Skilled and effective case management presupposes that securing resources provides minimal benefits unless they are sustained and individualized to meet consumer preferences. Even after the older person has gained access to desired services and resources, a lot of work may need to be done to sustain that person. The challenge of strengths-based case management is to resolve or at least reduce the interpersonal conflicts within the personal support networks that inevitably arise. Relationship-driven collaboration recognizes the value of each person's input and the benefits of making the helping experience mutually advantageous for everyone. The goal of continuous contact is to strengthen the consumer's self-care capacities and the caregivers' ability to help through the transfer of knowledge and skills by social and medical service providers, all coordinated by the case manager.

For example, an older consumer with hearing difficulties may become extremely frustrated when the taxi driver, whom he calls for rides to the grocery store, leaves after momentarily honking the horn. Addressing the accommodation of the resource frequently involves educating the helper. Being careful to build partnerships with providers of resources, whether volunteer or paid, is very important. Tailoring the help to meet the needs of the consumer should be done in a nonthreatening way, not only for the sake of the present consumer but for all future consumers who may use that resource.

Ongoing contacts with the consumer and their helpers enable the case manager to influence cost-effectiveness through increasing, decreasing, or terminating any or all services expeditiously. Applebaum and Austin (1990) assert that rapid responsiveness to consumer changes can have a dramatic impact on service costs. The overutilization of services typically results from not adjusting prescribed amounts of delivered services to the current situation as it unfolds. Reduction in case management costs as well as paid services can be expected in the strengths model because efforts are reduced and shifted to more frail and needy individuals as other consumers regain increased levels of self-sufficiency.

UTILITY OF THE STRENGTHS MODEL IN THE CHANGING LONG-TERM CARE ENVIRONMENT

Traditionally, aging has been viewed as synonymous with disease, and a medical framework of care has been implemented to try to cure the problems associated with growing old. Traditional medical/rehabilitative models of helping remain the most prominent in most community-based, long-term care case management systems. Within this framework, older adults have been expected to be passive recipients of care. However, in the changing medical marketplace, the traditional roles of a passive patient and doctor-as-sole-decision-maker must be revised. Financial incentives for providers to reduce overutilization increases the need for patients to take the responsibility for seeing that their health care needs are met. As Medicaid and Medicare managed care plays a larger role in the aging system, treatment decisions will be closely monitored to conserve clinical and fiscal resources. Many of these plans have been attacked for reducing consumer involvement and authority to direct the course of their help. Case management that focuses on both consumer empowerment and cost consciousness is clearly needed.

Since its inception, case management has been viewed as a potentially significant mechanism for coordinating services and controlling costs to prevent premature institutionalization. In an era of limited resources, private and public payers are demanding accountability for client outcomes and cost (Quinn, 1992). Effectiveness of a case management approach has been commonly evaluated according to its ability to reduce unnecessary institutionalization. However, much less effort has been made to define and measure effectiveness of case management from a standpoint of facilitating consumer involvement and empowerment and its subsequent impact on client outcomes and cost.

The need to first articulate and then to evaluate the effectiveness of strengths-based goals, planning processes, and tasks is imperative if fiscal control becomes the driving force behind case management. Home- and community-based care have historically been embedded in the medical model delivery system where critical social, emotional, spiritual, and supportive service needs are often overlooked. The challenge for case management and home-based care becomes one of providing quality services that are acceptable to clients and effective in maintaining functioning while keeping a cost-conscious stance (Kane & Kane, 1987).

Research demonstrating the efficacy of specific case management models is still limited. Much more needs to be learned about the effectiveness of different case management models. Particular attention needs to be focused on the varying goals, tasks, processes, case manager's role, and impact upon the lives of older persons. Long-term care case managers operating strictly from a functional or broker perspective of service provision, as was the case in the Channeling Demonstration Projects, did not employ the strengths model's emphasis on mutual decision making and reciprocity, and they minimized the active pursuit and empowerment of natural helpers (Rose, 1992). Equally, the Channeling Projects failed to carry out a case management process that established a trusting relationship and a purposeful counseling approach for dealing with the emotional stresses accompanying illness and loss of functions (Amerman, Eiserberg, & Weisman, 1985). The model of case management employed influences cost effectiveness.

Although the effects of strengths case management with older persons in the long-term care delivery system have not yet been empirically tested, anecdotal evidence from Medicaid long-term care case managers trained in the use of the strengths model indicates that older adults who participate in strengths-based case management have increased levels of informal support, a more sustainable balance of formal and informal services, and fewer transitions between home and health care facilities (Fast, Chapin, & Rapp, 1994). Case management effectiveness from a strengths approach is embedded in its ability to meet case management's dual mission in long-term care—maximizing client control, dignity, and choice while containing cost.

CONCLUSION

This chapter has explored the essential practice components of the strengths model of case management with older adults in need of long-term care. This model of case management supports self-determination, maximizes consumer choice and interdependence, and can potentially help contain long-term care costs. With the growing number of elderly people in our society and the accompanying concern about health care costs, the importance of self-determination and consumer choice in creating an affordable home- and community-based long-term care system should not be overlooked. Articulation, implementation and evaluation of the strengths model of long-term care case management with older adults can help professionals focus on the capacities rather than primarily on the frailty of our elders.

DISCUSSION QUESTIONS

1. How can case managers help older consumers learn new or changed roles in decision making, and, where appropriate, relinquish old decision-making roles?
2. What can be done to engage and establish rapport to assist consumers in the development of a trusting, working relationship?
3. What are some effective strategies for helping older consumers come to believe in their own abilities, try out new behaviors, and set and accomplish personal goals?
4. In what ways can case managers involve frail, older consumers in the assessment and planning process?
5. Why is tapping into and building on the person's strengths, interests, and hopes an important function of case management?

REFERENCES

Amerman, E., Eiserberg, D., & Weisman, R. (1985). Case management and counseling: A service dilemma. In C. Austin et al. (Eds.), *Experience from the natural long-term care channeling demonstration.* Seattle, WA: Institute on Aging, University of Washington.

Applebaum, R., & Austin, C. (1990). *Long-term care case management: Design and evaluation.* New York: Springer.

Fast, B., Chapin, R., & Rapp, C. (1994). *A model for strengths-based case management with older adults: Curriculum and training program.* Unpublished manuscript, The University of Kansas at Lawrence.

Freidson, E. (1988). *Profession of medicine.* Chicago: University of Chicago Press.

Johnson, P. J., & Rubin, A. (1983). Case management in mental health: A social work domain?" *Social Work, 28,* 49–55.

Kane, R. A., & Kane, R. L. (1987). *Long-term care: Principles, programs, and policies.* New York: Springer.

Kisthardt, W. E. (1992). A strengths model of case management: The principles and functions of a helping partnership with persons with persistent mental illness. In D. Saleebey (Ed.), *The strengths perspective in social work practice.* White Plains, NY: Longman.

Kisthardt, W., & Rapp, C. A. (1991). Bridging the gap between principles and practice: Implementing a strengths perspective in case management. In S. M. Rose (Ed.), *Social work practice and case management.* White Plains, NY: Longman.

Kivnick, H. Q. (1993, Winter/Spring). Everyday mental health: A guide to assessing life strengths. *Generations,* 13–20.

Kulys, R. (1983). Future crisis and the very old: Implications for discharge planning. *Health & Social Work, 8,* 182–195.

Lustbader, W., & Hooyman, N. (1994). *Taking care of aging family members.* New York: The Free Press.

Motenko, A. K., & Greenberg, S. (1995). Reframing dependence in old age: A positive transition for families. *Social Work, 40*(3), 382–389.

Poertner, J., & Ronnau, J. (1990). A strengths approach to children with emotional disabilities. In D. Saleebey (Ed.), *The strengths perspective in social work practice.* White Plains, NY: Longman.

Perkins, K., & Tice, C. (1995). A strengths perspective in practice: Older people and mental health challenges. *Journal of Gerontological Social Work, 23*(3/4), 83–98.

Pray, J. E. (1992). Maximizing the patient's uniqueness and strengths: A challenge for home health care. *Social Work in Health Care, 17*(3), 71–79.

Quinn, J. (1992). Case management: As diverse as its clients. *Journal of Case Management, 1*(2), 38.

Rapp, C. A. (1992). The strengths perspective of case management with persons suffering from severe mental illness. In D. Saleebey (Ed.), *The strengths perspective in social work practice.* White Plains, NY: Longman.

Rapp, R. C., Siegal, H. A., Fisher, J. H., & Wagner, J. H. (1992). A strengths-based model of case management/advocacy: Adapting a mental health model to practice work with persons who have substance abuse problems. In R. Ashery (Ed.), *Progress and issues in case management* (Research Monograph no. 127, pp. 79–91). Rockville, MD: National Institute on Drug Abuse.

Rose, S. M. (1992). *Case management social work practice.* White Plains, NY: Longman.

Smith, V., & Eggleston, R. (1989). Long-term care: The medical model versus the social model. *Public Welfare, 47,* 27–29.

Sullivan, W. P., & Fisher, B. J. (1994). Intervening for success: Strengths-based case management and successful aging. *Journal of Gerontological Social Work, 22*(1/2), 61–74.

U.S. Bureau of the Census. (1991). *Statistical abstract of the United States.* Washington, D.C.: U.S. Government Printing Office.

chapter 9

Hidden Treasures: Unlocking Strengths in the Public Social Services

Mary Bricker-Jenkins[1]

In January 1964, fresh out of college with a B.A. in English, I began my social work career as a social investigator with the New York Department of Welfare. At that time, we were implementing the 1962 Defined Service Amendments to the Social Security Act. The plan was to "casework" everybody out of poverty—or at least those who were "willing to help themselves." We were to emphasize the social rather than the investigative part of our roles. Having just completed my mandatory training week, I made an appointment with Matilda Jones for her quarterly recertification visit.

MATILDA

Matilda had four children. Two were literally lost in the foster care system. Following agency advice, Matilda had voluntarily placed her children during a time of family crisis. Also at our urging, she had not visited them for a long time; the practice wisdom of the time suggested that Matilda should not visit in order to give everyone "time to adjust." Now we were unable to locate the children in the labyrinthine maze of contract agencies to whom we had entrusted their care. Matilda's third child had already been labeled "high risk" at his school—a school he attended when Matilda was able to get him there, which was not very often. Matilda had just brought her newborn home from the hospital; he had several congenital conditions that reflected poor prenatal care and marginal obstetrical services.

These were the days before the programmatic separation of income maintenance and services, so I went prepared by my training to recertify the family's

[1] The author would like to thank Dennis Saleebey for his assistance in preparing this chapter.

eligibility for AFDC as well as to proffer social services. I could see Matilda in
the window of her tenement as I turned off Broadway and walked cautiously
through the rubble of the West Side Urban Renewal District. From her observation post at the front end of her railroad apartment, she signaled to the men
hanging out on the street below to give me safe passage. It was 10:00 A.M. and
she was having her breakfast: a piece of toast and a can of beer.

Matilda had learned the system when I was still in grade school. She was
ready for me. She had her rent receipt, her electric bill, her clothing inventory,
her list of clothing and furniture needs for the baby, and the baby's health department card. She was prepared to discuss the baby's paternity. I made the
requisite notes in my little caseworker's book, then closed it and invoked my
training. I said, "Mrs. Jones, you know all of this paperwork is very important,
but there are other important things we could do together. I really want to work
with you on problems and issues and concerns that are important to you. Now
I'm going to leave my book closed, and I'd really like to talk with you, just talk
about stuff together, and about things we could do together that'll result in better things happening in your life."

Matilda studied me for a very long moment before she leaned into the space
between us and said, "Look, white girl, I wanna tell you something. I got to
document my life to you—because I'm poor. I got to show you all my papers,
prove I paid my bills, take my baby to your pig doctor, and show you this card
that says I take care of my baby—all because I'm poor. I even have to talk
about my sex life with you—because I'm poor. I gotta do all that—but I don't
have to take your social workin'.

"Now I'm gonna tell you three things about your social workin'," she continued. "Number one, it ain't got nothin' to do with my life. Number two, I can't
eat it. And number three, it don't dull the pain like my Pabst Blue Ribbon. Now
you get along, white girl—and you think about that."

I have thought about that for 30 years. One of the results has been my participation in efforts to build a strengths-oriented practice in the public social services.
Two components of that effort in which I have been involved included designing a
statewide competency-based training program and conducting field research on the
characteristics and activities of effective workers in that state. This chapter will describe the ways our strengths orientation expanded our conceptual framework for
the former, and how it was validated by the results of the latter.

COMPETENCY-BASED PRACTICE:
PROSPECTS AND PROBLEMS

In Tennessee the effort to improve worker effectiveness and retention through competency-based training began in the 1980s with front-line staff in Adult Protective
Services, Child Protective Services, Foster Care and Adoptions. Job prerequisites for
these positions (titled social counselors) included a bachelor's degree, a civil service
examination, and an interview with a field-based social services supervisor. About

20 percent of the social counselors held B.S.W. degrees. Beginning in 1988, completion of the certification program—a combination of centralized residential training and structured on-the-job training—was followed by a rigorous certification examination. A passing grade on this examination and a satisfactory performance evaluation by the supervisor were required for retention in the program.

Models, Methods, and Practice Systems

While such a competency-based approach is found now in many states, and advocated by professional organizations such as the National Association of Social Workers, the American Public Welfare Association, and the Child Welfare League of America, there are problems with it, both technological (practice theory and method) and ideological. First, competency-based approaches presuppose that we really know what to do, that we know what methods actually work with Matilda Jones and others like and unlike her in her situation. However, most of the models and methods of practice have been developed in other settings for radically different types of clients. Models developed, for example, for populations voluntarily seeking services from highly trained social workers with professional credentials do not necessarily directly apply to the world of the public social service agency. To ensure effective practice in these agencies, practice models and methods must be suitable for work with a diverse group of involuntary clients by a largely noncredentialed staff of a bureaucracy perceived as primarily performing a social control function.

Second, practice should incorporate what we *do* know. We have considerable anecdotal evidence and some research suggesting that much of what works for Matilda Jones and her sisters is not integrated into our practice at all. We know of the power of mutual aid and self-help groups, for example, but few of us teach our workers to find and develop such groups or to work with them effectively (Powell, 1986; Gutierrez & Nurius, 1994). Even when methods and techniques are developed in or successfully adapted for public social services, we often fail to integrate them into a coherent, internally consistent practice approach. Risk assessment procedures, for instance, have becoming increasingly refined and predictive. To some degree, however, that predictive power is achieved by focusing narrowly on individual and family dysfunction. After analyzing and thoroughly documenting dysfunction, workers are then expected to refocus and ally themselves with family strengths to achieve casework goals. While they may be encouraged to work with individual and family strengths, they have the methods of neither assessment nor helping that would show them how to do that. Competency-based approaches should be built not only from "what is" (task analyses), but also from "what works" in the lives of our clients. And these practice components must be integrated into the practice system.

A well-integrated practice system—one that educates, trains, and supports competent workers and meets the lifeworld of clients fully and respectfully—also depends on the structure and process of the organization. What happens at the office invariably affects the client as well as the worker. I agree with proponents of the functional school of social work who argue that the social service organization itself is an integral part of any practice orientation and system (Smalley, 1965). Unlike the functionalists, however, I believe that an organization must adapt structure and process to the life spaces of clients and workers, not the other way around. Our failure to incorporate the organizational dimension with our practice system profoundly limits our ability to implement even the most appropriate and effective direct practice approaches. Often we are thwarted because the inherent values and assumptions of a given direct practice model are not sustained and supported by the organization's culture, structure, and process. To implement and sustain a strengths-based approach requires that agency values and practices are also formed around supporting and enhancing the assets of workers and clients on a daily basis. A call to strengths-oriented practice simply will not be heard in an agency that implicitly focuses on the deficits of clients and its staff in its supervisory, management, and personnel practices.

Several years ago, for example, Tennessee administrators undertook to introduce the task-centered practice model (Epstein, 1988; Reid & Epstein, 1977) into the public social services system statewide. We trained both workers and supervisors, demonstrating how the methods could be integrated into existing policies and procedures. Training evaluations indicated that both the model and the training were perceived as highly effective. However, the model was soon abandoned in practice. Evaluating this failed attempt, we learned that few supervisors felt comfortable allowing the client to set so much of the agenda—a critical component of the model. They could not reconcile this service imperative with their perceived management directive to control workloads and avoid publicity-generating risk taking. Moreover, workers who liked the model told us that they wished their supervisors would work with them the way they were expected to work with clients. This lack of consonance between the direct practice model and supervision and management models generated conflict and confused workers, and it confounded their best practice efforts.

In sum, the core idea of competency-based training is a good one. But too often we have derived the meaning of competency without any evidence of what actually works with clients and families in the public settings in which we work with them. We tend to exclude from our practice some very powerful methods, techniques, and processes that extend from naturally occurring, health-promoting processes in our clients and their worlds as well as in ourselves. Finally, elements of our practice are often inherently inconsistent, contradictory, and incompatible with a strengths approach. These limitations do not suggest poor practice as much as incomplete *theory* for practice.

Theory for Practice

In the process of building and articulating theory for practice, we have often excluded certain elements from the mix: the strengths and assets in clients and their environments, and the characteristics and methods of effective workers. These attributes incorporated into practice theories could well be keys to effective helping and healing, but they are beyond the conceptual frameworks of most practice theories and/or their applications.

To illustrate, one of the most influential bodies of research and theory building in the area of child neglect comes form Norman Polansky and his associates (1972; 1981). While Polansky has an abiding concern about effective practice and the welfare of children, and while he emphatically states that his focus on the personalistic should not obscure economic and ecological dimensions, the message that permeates his work and, as a consequence, much of the field of practice, is reflected in the following:

> The major findings of the Appalachian study were substantially supported in the Philadelphia replication. The mother's maturity or degree of infantilism was again underscored as was its expression in the forms of apathyfutility or impulsivity. The assumption that, among white low-income families, the mother's personality plays a major role in how well the children are protected proved justified. (p.117)

This important but incomplete piece of information is the centerpiece of virtually all current training and practice models of child neglect. The problem, of course, is that practice based solely on personalistic (and sexist) theory inevitably will be focused on changing the person (mother). Moreover, if we look at neglect (or any other phenomenon) through a lens ground in psychopathological theory, we surely are going to find pathology. Polansky's instruments and conceptual framework constitute a convex pathological lens—one that narrows the focus to the person and filters out most of her nonpathological characteristics and her sustaining environmental factors. When we view the world of child neglect through this lens, the practice implications become obvious: To save the children, treat the sick mom.

Fortunately, no lens can completely filter out all the rest of the phenomenological world. In a brief discussion of other findings, Polansky describes as "unexpected strengths" the characteristics of members of his control group: "A close look at the life histories of our non-neglectful parents reveals us, once again, as a generation short on miracles but not lacking altogether in happy accidents" (1981, p. 158). What Polansky was seeing may not have been a happy accident at all but the sign of people's innate, compelling potential for growth and health converging with opportunities and support for the unfolding of that potential. If we are, then, to develop models of practice that engage the inherent strengths of individuals and families, practice that joins those strengths with opportunities and support for people to satisfy their needs for safety, growth, and health, then our practice theory must be derived from study and appreciation of those phenomena. We can see those phenomena when we replace our convex pathological lens with a concave health-oriented lens that enables us to focus on strengths and the broad spectrum of environmental resources and opportunities that client and worker have or can create together. Our theory might then direct us to do strengths assessments as rigorously and religiously as we do risk assessments.

Like life itself, practice theory must be open and organic, tentative and evolving. It must arise from and support a view of the world that incorporates the countless adaptive, creative, dynamic, and multidimensional potentials of people like Matilda Jones and her workers. That kind of theory will undergird a practice that has those same qualities, a practice that engages clients and workers in a collaborative search for and creation of another set of truths.

Ideology in Practice

Practice is more than stringing together techniques and methods around a theoretical framework; it is also the reflection and promotion of values and beliefs. In other words, every practice model has an ideological core. The core contains a set of existential and normative postulates—beliefs about "what is" and "what ought to be." These inform practice processes, the ways in which we develop practice knowledge, and the ultimate purpose served by the practice endeavor (Goldstein, 1986). In short, ideology is the glue that holds a practice system together and binds it to human conditions, institutions, and practices. And we don't think about it very much (Schön, 1983).

An illustration from work on the development of the Tennessee Social Counselor Certification Program will help highlight the importance of ideology. The curriculum had three major components: interpersonal helping skills, assessment, and case planning. A review of the literature conducted during the curriculum development phase revealed notable differences in the approaches researchers and curriculum developers took to these basic components. The differences seemed to fall along a continuum. In the three curriculum areas, the extremes of the continuum were using interpersonal helping skills to manipulate people versus using techniques to explore meanings and build consensus; assessment models and methods used to categorize and label pathology versus those employed to identify strengths and contextualize risk factors; and case planning designed to control versus case planning aimed at mobilizing strengths and resources around mutually derived goals. Where a particular author stood on the continuum was sometimes explicit and stated; more often, the ideology was discernible only through careful scrutiny of the text's language, metaphors, and case examples. Always, the implications for practice directives were remarkable.

The point here is that similar competencies or methods do not necessarily result in similar practice. Consider two workers trained in the same set of skills derived from the same knowledge base. One manipulates, labels, and controls; the other engages, explores, makes alliances, and empowers. What accounts for the difference? The easy answer is attitudes and values. While these are important, they put the spotlight on the worker. What we really need is to examine the practice model itself and its ideological core. Is the ideology hospitable to our values and our purposes as individual professionals and as social agencies? Is it hospitable to our clients' needs and interests? Ideologies are not competencies, but they determine the competencies for which we strive. Ideologies are, I believe, the very soul of practice. Matilda Jones was speaking to my soul, not my skills. We need a practice that will respond from that place.

AN ALTERNATIVE APPROACH TO PRACTICE DEVELOPMENT: CRITERIA FOR A MODEL OF PRACTICE IN PUBLIC SOCIAL SERVICES

Based on this analysis of the strengths and limitations of competency-based approaches, a team from the University of Tennessee College of Social Work and the state's Department of Human Services initiated a project to construct a model of practice specifically for our setting. The project was conceived to move beyond the competency-based approach by going back to the beginning—the client's experience—and reweaving the practice system around that. The principles and assumptions that would guide us were clear:

- A practice model should be constructed from and grounded in the client's experience of what works. Clients are considered the primary experts in this area and are regarded as consultants in the development and implementation of the helping model.
- Practice should be culturally contextualized; that is, the culture of the clients, the organization, and the community are incorporated as actual components of practice. We need to know what works with a particular group of clients in a particular community through a particular agency.
- The purpose of practice is to secure basic needs, including the need for safety. Public welfare practice should begin with an exploration of basic client needs, how the client has attempted, successfully and not, to meet them for herself and her family, and what opportunities for growth and development she perceives and pursues.
- The model's primary focus and technological base—its requisite knowledge and skills—should relate to strengths and resources, with an emphasis on identifying, engaging, developing, and mobilizing those that already exist in the client's life.
- The design of programs of the agency, its technological base, the organizational structure and process, the organizational culture, and its supervisory and management models should all mirror the principles and assumptions of the practice model. For example, workers and supervisors should be seen as the experts on what works for them, their strengths are assumed and sought, and these become the basis of supervision and management systems.

In 1990, we conducted the direct practice phase of our Practice System Development Project[2] a field study of (1) what effective practitioners do—the processes by which they engage and work with clients daily and the attributes they bring to that work which enhance it; (2) how they work with the strengths and resources of the clients and their environments; and (3) what clients perceived as effective. Our

---

[2] This project was funded in part by USDHEW/OHDS/ACFY Grant No. 90CW0941.

primary method was grounded theory, an approach developed by Glaser and Strauss to build conceptual bridges between dynamic and evolving real-world phenomena and substantive theory (Glaser, 1978; Glaser & Strauss, 1967; Strauss, 1986).

For several months, we[3] observed and analyzed the characteristics, practice processes, and environments of workers who had been identified as "effective" by a consensus of clients, coworkers, supervisors, and administrators. We "shadowed," interviewed, and read the case records of 22 workers across the state; we also interviewed their supervisors, colleagues, representatives of other agencies, and clients. The initial list of workers was provided by administrators, supervisors, and colleagues. We then developed a purposive sample stratified on the basis of geography, race, and ethnicity. We believed that the data we gathered would provide a measure for the best that was possible within the system, provide a fund of knowledge for the training of existing staff, and help us develop more sharply focused and relevant guidelines for the selection of new staff.

The interviews and observations were relatively unstructured, but, as grounded theory suggests, certain themes and patterns emerged and the later interviews became more focused around some of these themes. A total of 193 interviews and observations was completed. Thirty interviews and observations with the workers themselves were done (some were interviewed and observed twice—in different roles). The workers were Adult Protective Service, Child Protective Service, and Foster Care and Adoption Service workers, seven in each category, and one worker who worked in two service components.

THE EFFECTIVE PUBLIC SERVICE PRACTITIONER: SUPPORTING THE LIFEWORLD AND STRENGTHS OF THE CLIENT

What follows is a profile of the characteristics and processes of the effective workers, organized around four domains of primary significance to them: the worker with the client, the worker in the community, the worker in the workplace, and the worker in him- or herself (interior life).

The Worker with the Client

Comments about, interviews with, and observations of effective workers coalesced around a variety of attributes, behaviors, traits, and processes. These workers were clearly seen to have a commitment to the clients' rights to direct their own lives; their right to choose and to have choices; and their right to the least restrictive, most natural milieu for daily living. This, in essence, is the basis of empowerment (Pinderhughes, 1994).

---

[3] The author would like to thank her consultants, Patricia Lockett and Eloise Rathbone-McCuan, for their invaluable assistance in designing and carrying out the study. In addition, Department of Human Services staff, Hazel Arthur, Nancy Blanton, and Marilyn Whalen, provided much needed consultation and technical support.

These workers were *effective communicators,* creating a lively, conversational, intimate form of relating ("just good conversation," said one client). They did not act only as agents of the department, speaking as "The Department"; typically, they owned up to their own views and expressed themselves by making "I" statements. Metaphorically and physically, these workers were expressive, responsive, and "therapeutic." They created a *participatory* framework by listening and "envisioning"—inviting clients to imagine and think about what they wanted, what should be done, and what the future might look like. Questions were asked not just for information but towards understanding. In short, the competent worker was *fascinated with the lives of the people* with whom he or she worked.

Clients and colleagues perceived a willingness to *"go the extra mile"* in these workers. As one worker said, "There is nothing I won't do, from hanging curtains to going for coffee." If it was in the best interests of the client and of forging an alliance with client strengths and hopes, it was done: "I move with the need of the client." All of what these workers did was clearly in the service of building client and network strengths, forging alliances with the larger community and its resources, and keeping clients engaged with living and doing as well as possible.

MRS. T

As I pulled up in Mrs. T's driveway on this date I saw the elderly lady and her big yellow cat on the front stoop. She was poking her walking cane at something just off the stoop. As I approached the house, I saw a large, black, spotted snake. I was afraid Mrs. T. would fall off the stoop trying to poke at it. I explained to her that it was not a poisonous snake, but she said it would have to be killed as she could not rest knowing it was in her yard. I went to her car shed, got a rake, killed the snake, and dragged him to the edge of the yard out of her sight.

The competent workers were adept at discovering and *using the social networks* of clients and their families, whether the network was composed of relatives, friends, fellow churchgoers, or other clients. The idea was to see the individuals and families through the widest possible lens, to be client centered and network focused. If life is lived in context, help must be rendered in that same context. Networks were regarded, then, as important sources of support, knowledge, and respite. The workers who engaged networks skillfully had two competencies that were essential: They were *"culturally competent"* knowing how to get "inside the skin" of a culture not familiar to them; and they *used the oral histories* of clients to assess their strengths and understand their systems of meaning. Thus they were able to place clients not only in time and situation but in their ethnic and class medium as well. These workers were able to assume, with patience and sensitivity, the "standpoint" of their clients. This knowledge was used as a basis for understanding what the client and the network could and could not do and deciding what the worker would and would not do. One worker regularly took several clients to the county fair to help them get to know each other in a nonthreatening environment. Each year, new friendships resulted. Particularly important to clients was the workers' being *accessible, available,* and *reliable* ("She wasn't always a phone call away, but was always just a phone message away"). Clients frequently said that what made their workers effective was *"good manners."* Building on that foundation, being willing to *persevere* and persist in *advocacy* proved their *acceptance* and contributed to strengthening the network of support and encouragement.

Effective workers were skilled at creating a helping environment oriented around tasks and accomplishments and movement toward client goals. Helping clients take *small attainable steps* toward their aims, and assisting them in *recognizing the progress* they made was important to clients. In service of this, workers also consciously *modeled* skills, attributes, and abilities in such a way that clients were able to make them a part of their own repertoire. Workers also were able to make *contracts,* verbal and written, with clients so that, at the end of each session, and at the end of each phase of work together, clients clearly knew what gains they had made, what skills they had developed, and what capacities they had strengthened.

In spite of the attention to task and detail, effective workers believed, as one said, "In the end, it's the journey that matters." The *process* of working together toward a goal was a goal in itself. While the reduction of risk and stress was the first immediate objective, the setting of a general direction to travel with everybody in the system was an essential next step. Analytically, these workers were also *a step ahead,* scanning for other options and directions that might subsequently be taken. One described the process as "something like a game of checkers". . . moving to get pieces in order to have more options and opportunities that could be seized or created later on.

Finally, with their clients, in their daily lives, these workers were truly *reflective practitioners* (Schön, 1983). They could explain why they did what they did—perhaps without reference to a formal theory or model, but with reference to their beliefs, intuitions, and appreciations. They also were *able to see patterns* and think on their feet—skills that often brought clients unanticipated rewards.

MARY

Mary had been working with various workers in the Child Protective Service unit for several years. Martha began working with Mary when her children were returned to her from foster care. For over a year, their work focused on stabilizing and strengthening family relations and reducing the likelihood that there would be any future neglect of her two daughters. Mary had come a long way. She had discovered strengths that were helping her become a more energetic, interested, and vital parent. The worker was confident that Mary's case could be closed. But every time Martha came close to discontinuing contact, a crisis or chaos would erupt in the family, requiring continued support and guidance to reduce the risk of abuse. Finally, Martha asked Mary if she might be afraid of something around the "closing of the case." After some thought, Mary said that she was terrified that something bad would happen if the worker were not available to monitor her; she also felt she was losing a significant relationship. With Mary, the worker hit on a possibility. Believing that Mary really was capable of carrying on, the worker suggested arranging a support group for her and other mothers who were about to "graduate" from the child welfare system. The support group, which culminated in a graduation ceremony, was a huge success. Mary and the other mothers were able to build a network among themselves and to ritually, symbolically, and really acknowledge their progress and to affirm their transition to a new stage of their lives.

The Worker in the Community

Effective workers regarded the community as the developmental milieu for their efforts and not simply a collage of agencies and institutions. They knew the importance of *being a "presence"* in the community, of making oneself known to both formal and informal associations, institutions, and resources. Though not necessarily "of" the community, they were most definitely "in" the community.

Perhaps one of the most important attributes of skilled workers was their ability to develop, curry, and *mobilize resources, both formal and informal,* within the community. While one would certainly not downplay the effect of the helping relationship on the client's or family's well-being, connecting resources and clients was seen as the centerpiece of building strengths and employing assets in the "system." Mobilizing networks of support by making clear the needs of clients, assuring the potential source of help that they could meet the needs, and enabling the connection were elements of this developmental strategy. The workers' relationships with community agencies, institutions, and associations were not formal and instrumental as much as they were *reciprocal and affective.* The capacity to "befriend" agencies and individuals provided the basis of much of their perceived effectiveness and presence in the community. To that end, they did not "pass on"' their clients to other agencies, but carefully prescreened referrals and they knew well the functions of other agencies. They saw their role as resource manager or, with other agencies now involved, as *team member.*

Effective workers did not rely only on the formal service system. They made use of *"mediating structures"* like churches, schools, volunteer organizations, service clubs, neighborhood groups and associations. Everything in a community was regarded, until proven otherwise, as a resource. They were also *resource developers.* Workers were able to recruit volunteers, encourage donations of in-kind services, and manage exchanges of assets, talents, and commodities as needed. One worker who covered several rural, impoverished counties was able to maintain many clients in their beloved but deteriorating homes by organizing a network of supplies and services donors: lumber yards, carpenters, termite services, plumbers, roofers, and the like.

These workers were described by one of the community respondents as *"ambassadors."* They did not just represent an agency (the Department of Human Services), they represented the "people," their clientele. Furthermore, they maintained solid, respectful, and working relationships with other service providers in the community, giving attention to their requests, and carefully screening and assessing their needs for information, assistance, and service. They knew the functions of other agencies and had established personal relationships with many of the workers in those agencies. Very importantly, they *followed through* on requests for assistance and information from other members of the community and its agencies.

The Worker in the Workplace

The single most important characteristic of highly effective workers in a public service setting was that they were almost always seen as *team players*. They were always ready to give help and support, and they were able to ask for assistance and advice when they needed it. Helping to create and sustain the workplace as a *"learning environment"* was a significant element of their teamwork. They often were involved in peer consultation and supervision, even teaching. All of these workers were or had been involved in a project to improve policy, worker relationships, or work conditions; they expanded their jobs to *change the contexts* of their casework.

These workers clearly understood that the nature and character of the work environment would, ultimately, have an effect on clients. A thorough *knowledge of the laws and policies* that governed their work also contributed to this understanding and awareness. This was a part of a larger, more general appreciation they had—understanding the public roots of private pain. This sensibility undoubtedly laid some of the foundation for their empathic tie to people whose lives were often laced with chaos, violence, loss, and trauma.

In terms of their *management of the enormous amount of work* demanded of agency workers, effective workers typically did their *paperwork "on the fly"*—waiting for appointments, in coffee shops, in their cars—whenever they had a moment. And while their office environment may not have looked like it, in fact they did have *orderly, if idiosyncratic,* methods for keeping records, resource lists, and files. Likewise, they had workable *systems* for the retrieval and transmission of information and data. One worker had about a half-dozen blotters on her desk, each containing scores of telephone numbers; she could retrieve an agency contact's name and number faster than most computers could.

Many of these individuals remarked on the importance of a *sense of humor* in the workplace as well as in relationships with their clients. Sarcasm, put-downs, or gallows humor were avoided, however. Rather, humor was conceived as the ability to take a felicitous perspective on serious matters; to laugh at one's foibles, not take oneself too seriously; to see the absurd in challenging and difficult moments. Too, effective workers avoided the inevitable office gossip, complaints, pejorative stereotyping of clients and client groups, declining to join cliques of disaffected peers. They rarely complained and did not see themselves in competition for scarce economic and interpersonal resources on the job. To those who knew them, then, these individuals were regarded as joys to work with, and as positive influences in the work environment.

We asked the effective workers about the kind of supervision they found supportive of their practice. Two very different structures were described. Some supervisors used *peer-based supervision,* encouraging workers to support and educate each other, to cover for each other when needed, and to create a team approach to work. Their role was to help workers help each other. The other model was more *conventional:* The supervisor served as case consultant but also demonstrated direct practice skill by following through on a worker's case when the worker was absent or unable to continue.

Whichever model the supervisor chose, the capable ones *identified what each worker did best* and supported that. They regarded themselves as supervising *a team* and not a collection of unrelated individuals. However, that did not prevent them from individualizing workers, understanding their strengths, skills, as well as their needs and gaps in their knowledge. Supervisory expectations were based on this understanding of the individual.

These supervisors did three consequential things for their staff. First, they *helped workers to "let go"* when no more could be done to help a client or family. Second, they reduced unnecessary competition and *increased cooperation* by identifying, playing to, and building on the strengths of each worker. This, in turn, became a model of worker relationships with their clients (demonstrating, at the least, that building on strengths is doable). Finally, supervisors worked hard to *defend and protect* their workers from administration, other agencies, community entities, and disgruntled clients when demands or stresses were clearly out of place or inappropriate.

The Worker Him- or Herself

To appreciate and work with the strengths of clients who often are in dire straits or under extraordinary pressure requires positive self-regard and a well-rounded lifestyle. The effective workers exhibited *balance*—attending to many dimensions of their personhood—intellectual, social, emotional, physical, spiritual, and cultural/ethnic. They also knew which domains of their lives were most important. For many, a profound spiritual dimension enhanced the tenor and energy of their work. Not necessarily tied to a specific religion, this appreciation allowed them to remain "centered" and to *see their work in the much larger context* of human striving, struggle, and hope. This perspective seemed to mediate any tendency to create dependency in their clients or an inappropriate effort to meet needs through controlling others—peers and clients alike.

The workers had a significant and healthy *identification with the client.* Several described the connectedness they felt as deriving from understanding that there "but for the grace of God, go I." The human condition was defined as having, generically, moments of turmoil and catastrophe as well as moments of redemption and rebound. Contingency, circumstance, and luck affect all human beings—even those who work at the Department of Human Services—their attitude seemed to say. This belief was accompanied by a sense of *humility;* one-sided "expertise," distance, and power plays within the helping relationship were seen as antithetical to genuine service. These workers learned from everybody, including clients. They worked *with* and not *on* individuals and families, and they had a deep *respect* for those who became their clients. Nonetheless, these workers were *self-confident.* They knew and trusted their own capacities. They also recognized that, in the words of one worker, "We *all* do the best we can."

Their sense of "wholeness" was often manifest in the sources of knowledge, information, and direction they selected. While their professional knowing and doing certainly included methods, techniques, and models gleaned in their education and through experience, consultation, and training, they also *trusted nonrational, intuitive, tacit sources of knowledge,* decision making, and action. One worker, for example, said that in difficult situations he sometimes found direction, often in symbolic or metaphorical forms, from certain dreams.

Very importantly, these capable workers were motivated by the *values* that drive the profession of social work. Altruism, social justice, and regard for the inherent dignity of human beings were at the core of their belief systems. For some workers, these were values that were rooted and grew in their religion; for others, these values were formed in the family; and, for still others, professional education was the source. Whatever their source, these values were a significant part of the dynamic of effective, inventive, and adroit work.

Finally, to have *strong social and/or family ties* outside the Department of Social Services was essential to the vitality of the work these individuals did. That is to say, they found great succor, surcease, and knowledge in networks of caring individuals—the very same thing they often sought for their clients. So once again, there is a parallel seen and sought between the worker as human being in multiple contexts and the client as human being in multiple contexts.

THE EFFECTIVE WORKER IN PUBLIC
SOCIAL SERVICES—REPRISE

The orientation of these workers, the reasons they were identified as effective included: (1) They did the work and more; (2) they believed in, and developed access to, the strengths of clients and the resources in their environment; (3) they got into the lifeworld of their clients, the daily round of relationships, conversations, demands, child-rearing, work, and play; and (4) they saw themselves as human beings with the same capacities, dreams, foibles, and challenges as their clients might very well have. In addition, there are dimensions and processes that typify most of these workers.

In their work—with clients, as peers, in the community, in the work environment—some themes appear, in slightly different forms, repeatedly. There was a *spiritual dimension* to their approach to work, a sense of the importance of this work and its character as a kind of devotion or calling. A firm *belief in the values* that inform the work, a sense of the relationship between private troubles and public issues that lead them away from finding fault in the individual or family, but toward finding prospects in the individual, family, and community. While they had doubts now and then, they *believed deeply in what they did,* in their clients, and in themselves.

These effective workers understood the importance of *connection:* connecting families and individuals with the formal and informal resources in the community; connecting resources in the community with each other; connecting peers with each other; and most importantly, connecting with their clients in a deeply felt, personal relationship. They understood as well that their work always depends on relationships, whether they be the transactions they enjoyed with clients, peers, or other members of the community made no difference. *The relationship is the medium.* A commitment to clients, their need for options and their right to choose among them, to help move individuals and families closer to their hopes is the basis for *empowerment,* as these workers attempted to realize it in their practice.

Finally, for most of these individuals, there was little or no discrepancy between how they practiced their profession and how they lived their lives. The principles, beliefs, and values that guided them, the actions they took in support of those beliefs characterized all dimensions of their lives. As citizen, partner, parent, colleague, professional, there was a sense of a seamless whole about the way they approached every aspect of living.

TIM AND MISS FANNY MAE C.

This was our first worker observation and I was more nervous than Tim, the worker we were studying. He was doing just what we asked him to do: go on with his work as if we were not there shadowing him and interviewing everybody he works with.

We were on our way to see how Miss Fanny Mae C. was doing, but we had to stop by the Food Bank first to pick up a box for the family. Tim was talking about the way he sets boundaries for his clients so he doesn't get burned out. I really wanted to know about that because everyone we had interviewed said that Tim was "always there" and "accessible."

"I tell the folks what I can do and what I can't," he explained. "Then, after I get to know them a bit, I tell them what I will do and what I won't. I make it a policy never to do anything for clients that they can do for themselves. That's what they teach you in school, but the trick is to figure out what your clients can do and where they really need your help. I make myself really available, then I take my cues from the client about how close to get. They'll let you know what they need you for. But I make it my business to find out from them what they've done for themselves in the past and I look at the changes to see what they can do now. I can get pretty firm and direct. But I also stay very humble and listen very carefully."

At the Food Bank I watched Tim chat with a few of his clients and do two sidewalk consultations with a member of the agency board. Each walked away with some follow-up to do. "I will follow through immediately," Tim said as we drove toward Fannie Mae's. "In this job you never get everything done, so you have to set priorities. Keeping my word, following through on commitments I make to clients and these community agency people—that's something I always do. That's how I build trust. And the agency people will really extend themselves for my clients."

Fannie Mae, aged 72, had Alzheimer's disease. Often incontinent and usually bedridden, she was only intermittently able to recognize people and express her needs and wants. She was Medicaid eligible for a nursing home placement but her only daughter, Jolene, insisted that she could and would provide the necessary care for her mother. Although Jolene was tender and attentive to her mother, Tim explained, her life was so chaotic that Fannie Mae was at risk.

Two months previously, Jolene, along with her mother and two boys, aged 10 and 2, had been evicted from their dilapidated rental house for creating "dangerous and unsanitary conditions." A report was made to DHS on this family, now homeless and out of cash, but with enough property resources in Fannie Mae's name that they were ineligible for cash assistance. Tim had opened a case to provide both Adult Protective Services and Child Protective Services, and he had gone to churches for help on the family's behalf. Funded by a series of 3-day donations, the family had moved from motel to motel until Jolene found one willing to barter a room for cleaning services. The family moved into a dark, leaky room with one double bed.

As Tim was working with the family on housing, entitlements, emergency food, and home health assistance, the father of the 10-year-old had sought and obtained custody of his son through the court. Confused and angry about his brother's sudden disappearance, the toddler had begun to have tantrums. During one of these, he had severely beaten his bedridden grandmother. Tim felt it was necessary to place Fannie Mae in a health care facility, at least temporarily, over Jolene's objections. He had told Jolene of his decision and had initiated the necessary legal proceedings; meanwhile he was stopping by the motel daily.

"That lady is from the university," Tim explained to Jolene, nodding toward the car. "They are following me around for a research study. They want to know about my job. Yesterday they met some of my clients that always agree with me. You and I have not always agreed and we've had some hard times finding ways to work together. I thought it would be important for them to see that too." Tim explained the consent form, obtained her signature, and asked Jolene if she wanted me to wait outside until the visit was over. Jolene gestured for me to come in.

Tim retrieved the Food Bank box from the car, greeted the toddler, and quietly approached Fannie Mae, who was asleep on the sheetless bed. She had fresh bruises on her face and upper torso. Jolene did not know how she got them. Her son was still having tantrums, but she was watching him very carefully. The nurse was coming this afternoon. No, she would not sign to put her mother in the nursing home. "I know you are trying to get the judge to sign the papers. I'm going to fight you. I have to. She belongs with me." Jolene looked at me. "I'm going to fight him. He's going to do his job, and I understand that, but I'll fight to keep her with me." As we talked about the bleak history of her family with institutional care, Jolene cried in Tim's presence for the first time. He provided a long, gentle silence.

Then, after a discussion on housing plans, the home health services, working with the toddler's anger and anxiety, arranging visitation with the older boy, and finances, Tim reviewed what each had agreed to do next. "And you will be sure your son isn't alone with her. And you know that I will be seeing our attorney in the morning to get her into the nursing home. I know you don't want me to. I am really sorry that I have to go against you. And I will see about transportation to get you there every day."

"Yeah, I know what you're going to do, and you know that I'm still going to try to stop you. But I'll think about what you said. And the boy will not be alone with her." She turned to me. "He's just doing his job. He's good."

"What makes him good?"

"His job is to watch out for my momma and the kids, but he cares about me too. He cares about all of us. Look over there. He don't mind bringing the food when he knows I can't get it. But he respects me. He's very honest with me. He always tells me what he's going to do and why. He never goes behind my back. If he disagrees, he just tells me. He visits with me, talks with me. My friends don't come by much anymore because of my momma. He knows about my life. And he's not afraid of it."

DISCUSSION QUESTIONS

1. In your experience, what are the hallmarks of an effective practitioner? What could we do to educate such practitioners more capably?
2. What attributes of the effective practitioner in public welfare did you see in Tim's dealings with Fannie Mae, Jolene, and the boys?
3. What do you think is the trouble with some of the models and techniques of practice that we use in public social services?
4. Do you regard yourself as an effective practitioner? If so, what attributes do you bring to the helping situation that make you competent?

REFERENCES

Epstein, L. (1988) *Helping people: The task-centered approach*. Columbus, OH: Charles Merrill.

Glaser, B. G. (1978). *Theoretical sensitivity: Advances in the methodology of grounded theory*. Mill Valley, CA: The Sociology Press.

Glaser, B. G., & Strauss, A. (1967). *The discovery of grounded theory*. New York: Aldine.

Goldstein, H. (1986). Toward the integration of theory and practice. *Social Work, 31*, 322–327.

Gutierrez, L., & Nurius, P. (Eds.). (1994). *Education and research for empowerment practice*. Seattle, WA: University of Washington School of Social Work, Center for Policy and Practice Research.

Pinderhughes, E. (1994). Empowerment as an intervention goal: Early ideas. In L. Gutierrez & P. Nurius, (Eds.), *Education and research for empowerment practice* (pp. 17–30). Seattle,

WA: University of Washington, School of Social Work, Center for Policy and Practice Research.

Polansky, N., Borgman, R. D., & DeSaix, V. (1972). *Roots of futility*. San Francisco: Jossey-Bass.

Polansky, N., Chalmers, M., Buttenweiser, E., & Williams, D. (1981). *Damaged parents: An anatomy of child neglect*. Chicago: University of Chicago Press.

Powell, D. R. (1986). Parent education and support programs. *Young Children, 41,* 47–52.

Reid, W. J., & Epstein, L. (1977). *Task-centered practice*. New York: Columbia University Press.

Schön, D. A. (1983). *The reflective practitioner*. New York: Basic Books.

Smalley, R. (1965). *Theory for social work*. New York: Columbia University Press.

Strauss, A. L. (1986). *Qualitative analysis*. Cambridge, UK: Cambridge University Press.

chapter **10**

The Strengths Perspective and the Politics of Clienthood

Gary E. Holmes

This chapter provides an overview of some of the critical issues that arise in trying to understand the rudiments, the application, and the ethics of the strengths perspective in contemporary social work practice. Professionals in any discipline must feel psychologically comfortable with the tools of their trade and with their beliefs about the work they do. In short, practitioners want to know not only the "what," but also the "why" of their profession.

Toward these ends, what follows is a discussion of the strengths perspective compared to the older practice model that emphasizes client deficits and pathologies. An admitted bias in what follows is the notion that the older model in social work practice (and in other human services) has not worked so well in terms of promoting client self-determination. In some instances, actual harm has been done to clients. In other instances, client outcomes have been only marginally effective. These will be discussed in terms of the differing politics of clienthood.

THE NOTION OF CLIENTHOOD

As explained below, the older paradigm has helped perpetuate *clienthood* as a sociopolitical status in which clients are devalued, marginalized, and left powerless. The power imbalance inherent in paternalistic forms of professional practice has reduced *clienthood* to a form of deviancy in which clients are viewed as globally weak and lacking capacity. Among other things, the strengths perspective seeks to unseat this perception of clienthood by encouraging a brand of social work practice that sees clients as human beings who possess the innate strengths and powers necessary to survive and flourish.

Social workers who want to lay claim to the strengths perspective as a new basis for professional practice face a formidable task. At first glance, the new perspective seems to concern itself mainly with client characteristics. In reality, however, the strengths perspective first focuses upon the practitioner's ability and willingness to see the world in a new way.

Several notions implied by this new perspective may even seem threatening to some. The strengths perspective calls for far-reaching changes in how social workers are educated, in how they interact with clients, and even in how they see themselves as professionals. Perhaps the first step in this understanding is to appraise the roots of the older viewpoint (herein called the deficit/pathology model), and to acknowledge that the practice of any human service constitutes *political action* within the context of clients' lives and within society as a whole.

All theories and practices of helping are value laden and politically biased but some are biased in such a way that helping professionals have functioned as agents for social control of clients. The idea here is that understanding the need for a strengths perspective paradigm depends in part on social workers' understanding of the ethical and political implications of an older practice model centered on weaknesses, deficits, and pathologies.

Social workers should keep in mind that much is at stake in the process of a new model overthrowing an older one. Because of its position among human services, what the social work profession does in the way of practice will have an influence on what other professions do as well. To the degree that social workers operate from a strengths perspective, other professions may follow. Already, ideas about client strengths have been voiced in psychology (Wright & Fletcher, 1982), rehabilitation counseling (Holmes & Saleebey, 1993), therapy (Miller & Berg, 1995), and school counseling (Stalling, 1994). However, to date only social work has produced actual theories and methods to sustain or to lead the way into a strengths-based approach.

Social workers, like all human service professionals, wield certain powers that affect clients for good or ill. The strengths perspective is an orientation to practice that seeks to transform this political action and power into practice methods that are consistently beneficial to clients. Ideal outcomes are viewed as the natural consequences of client strengths and professional strengths alike.

The main purpose of this chapter is to illustrate *how* the two perspectives described above may affect clients differently. Two client groups—those with culturally different backgrounds and those with disabilities—are discussed as examples in which the deficit/pathology model has had a particularly virulent impact.

Simply stated, the following discussion will illustrate that the disempowering nature of the deficit/pathology model hinges upon the practitioner's *power* to rewrite the *meaning* of the client's life story so that the "facts" fit assumptions, policies, and prejudices arrived at long before the client seeks services.

How We Make Clients from People

Clients typically arrive with stories about their lives and situations. The social work practitioner must find some way to understand these stories before helping is possible. Client stories are often seen as mere subjectivity based on faulty perception, cognition, or behavior. The subjectivity is suspected of hiding or disguising some hidden truth that must be discovered. The practitioner may disregard the subjective story by gleaning only the "facts" that seem objectively true. Such a process may seem logical and wise to professionals who do the sifting without understanding that they already have exercised political power over the client by deciding which facts are true and which are spurious (subjective). If the professional believes that clients embody only weaknesses and pathologies, only the facts that seem to prove deficiencies are likely to be recognized, recorded, and taken into account. The rest of the stories may fall away and be forgotten.

Yet an obvious problem arises. The client's story as lived depends on context for its being understood. The deficit-minded professional ignores context and derails understanding by excerpting the "facts" of the client's life for the purpose of rewriting client meaning into an "official" story of deficits. Thus, client strengths remain in the background and meaningless.

Romanyshyn (1982) noted that story, not fact, characterizes the psychological life of humans. Similarly, Steenbarger (1991) and Saleebey (1994) have described the importance of the practitioner's understanding of the client's constructed, contextual world. Ignoring the client's contextual world, world view, or constructed reality leaves the professional with a distorted view of clients' lives.

Some professionals who provide therapeutic services may come to believe that the *act* of coming for therapy is proof in itself of pathology or incompetence in the client. For them, the process of rewriting the meaning of the client's story may be as simple a task as assigning a diagnostic code, fitting the objective facts into a taxonomy or collection of prewritten official deficit stories.

Another important issue arises here. If the practitioner begins the helping process by using official power to rewrite and perhaps to invalidate the client's own story, how does he or she enforce the new story with the client during subsequent encounters? Typically, subtle enforcement methods encourage the client to conform and accept the official story as valid and as "more true" than the personal story originally told by the client. These methods may include the following:

- The professional refuses to discuss any topic outside the parameters of the official deficit story.
- The client is encouraged to see his or her shortcomings as problems that require professional solutions.
- The professional interacts in such a way as to convey the idea that the client possesses no strengths or that existing strengths are inappropriate for resolving the current problem.

- The professional encourages the client to use language consistent with the deficit/pathology model in discussing issues and solutions.
- The professional encourages the client to believe that only the professional has sufficient power and knowledge to attach meaning to life events and behaviors.
- The professional frames all potential solutions to be consistent with the professional's view of reality.
- The professional enlists the aid of other professionals who will agree with the official story and will help reinforce its validity with the client.

Story and Meaning

Over time, these enforcement methods may have other effects on the client besides the intended ones. Saleebey (1994) has noted that meanings in personal narratives usually account for the expected events in life, but not for the unexpected. In seeing the professional rewrite the meaning of the unexpected (the "problem"), the client may come to doubt his or her own ability to assign meaning even to the expected events in life. The client's faith in his or her own competency may be eroded to the point that the client reaches no conclusions, attaches no meanings, and avoids any personal attempts to understand his or her world. Increased paternalism by the professional may encourage the client to experience increased dependency and increased helplessness.

There may be other far-reaching psychological and existential ramifications as well. Personal stories or narratives contain symbolic meanings that help each of us understand the world at large (Bruner, 1990). In a real sense, a story only becomes a story once it is told to someone else. It seems as if people have a need not only to understand the world, but also to tell their stories to others so that their understanding can be appreciated, validated, and shared.

Some researchers, for example, have stipulated that people "work through" unexpected life events by the essential act of confiding their stories about "causes" to others (Weber, Harvey, & Orbuch, 1992). These same studies indicated that under certain circumstances stories (accounts) may translate life complexities into forms of self-introduction as in, "As you can see from my story, I understand these things" (p. 268). Personal stories are social accounts of cause and effect, and of understanding. It is important that a story be accepted as valid by others (social honoring); even the way it is told may be shaped by the desire to have others accept it as "true" (Read, 1992).

Given the facts that humans "give" world meaning through stories, that they want to tell the stories to others, and that they want their stories to be accepted by others, it would seem that the storytelling process is an important one. Such personal issues as self-esteem, dignity, competency, identity, autonomy, and social acceptance may be clarified, explained, or resolved in part from storytelling episodes. If professional practitioners routinely react to storytelling by rewriting and changing meaning, what will be the long-term impact on the client? For one, the client may not be able to complete the storytelling or to gain satisfaction from the telling. If the professional rewrites the meaning and continually reinterprets the client's role in the story as evidence of pathology instead of as understanding its contextual roots, the client's sense of efficacy and future hopes may suffer accordingly.

For another, rewriting client stories preemptively may serve to isolate the client from his or her natural community. The client may become a specimen of professional designation set adrift from life context (Holmes & Saleebey, 1993). Personal stories are usually taken as "true" because they contain human meaning, but may (particularly in therapy) center upon "intentions gone awry" (Parry & Doan, 1994, p. 3).

Finally, the potential harm to clients in the rewriting of meaning into an official story lies in the effect of using the clients' own stories against them. The client who is taken as without resource or resourcefulness, and whose story of intentions gone awry is rewarded with a diagnostic label might perceive the situation as one in which his or her coping attempts are nothing but symptoms of pathology and incompetency.

In day-to-day social encounters, the meaning of a story is usually arrived at through social negotiation. The negotiating for meaning revolves around turn-taking (Boden, 1990), in which each person gets a chance to speak and to listen. However, something of the spirit of this exchange may be altered in the encounter between client and professional. If the professional operates from the deficit/pathology model the client's talk may be taken as the source of pathology more than as one side of a negotiated and shared meaning.

Listening for proof of pathology over meaning affects the basic helping relationship. Most human service professionals are taught to interact with clients through empathic understanding. Empathy requires that the listener experience the feelings of the speaker to some degree (Goldman, 1993). If the professional listens only for indications of deficits/pathology, it is doubtful that the client's feelings will be shared experientially. In turn, the client telling his or her story may come to realize that the listener has an agenda other than empathic understanding and sharing. In such circumstances, clients often know that their stories are not being honored by the listener and that the listener has the power to subvert meaning.

The difference between the older paradigm and the strengths perspective is that proponents of the strengths perspective listen to stories and hear reason to celebrate the client's strengths. Helping focuses on the client's discovering or recognizing his or her own strengths as abilities to be used in the processes of growth, change, and development.

Organizational Culture

Even those who practice from the deficit/pathology model do not do so in a vacuum. They work in agencies offering a variety of human services. Many such agencies continue the tradition of the deficit/pathology model merely because they have always operated that way. Paradoxically, social workers and other professionals are usually inculcated with ethics that promote client welfare and assert altruistic ends. Yet many learn quickly to conform on the job to the deficit/pathology model of service delivery when organizational culture encourages it.

One might reasonably ask how this could be. Many bureaucratic organizations are extremely slow to change, while maintaining strict rules about employee conformity. The pressures are great for the employee to conform to the usual way of doing business. In some organizations managers believe that questioning the rules is unthinkable (Ladd, 1970/1989). Organizations may seek to hire only those who are "like-minded," while rejecting others on the claim that they lack appropriate work competencies (Murphy, 1988). The motives of those who seek change may be interpreted as malevolence by others in the organization (Baron, 1990).

Policies and politics also play a role in organizational culture. Allocation of agency resources may provoke conflict related to efficient use versus fair use (Elster, 1992). Policies do not always have the effect of bringing people together. One researcher has even argued that governmental regulation has replaced free land in America as the main vehicle of keeping people isolated and separated from one another (Kemmis, 1990). When policies and regulations conflict with client life-context, they form a barrier between client and professional.

Human service agencies or organizations that maintain the deficit/pathology model can easily translate client stories into official stories of deviancy and failure. The process requires no mention of client strengths and leaves the client powerless to "out run" the deviancy label. An obvious advantage of the deficit/pathology model to organizations is that it provides a large group of "sick" clients that the organization must "help." Additionally, the model may provide the following benefits to the organization:

- Handling client issues is easier if the clients are considered incompetent or helpless.
- Client problems can be reduced to a few basic types (with rewritten stories) that are easily quantified.
- Power to define client outcomes is retained by the organization.
- Case failures are more easily attributed to client deficits or personal failures.
- Services are more easily prescribed when organization members do not have to recognize clients as possessing strengths conducive to self-determination.

The professional social worker desiring to adopt the strengths perspective for everyday practice may first have to deal with an organizational culture that retains a vested interest in the deficit/pathology model of services. The social worker should keep in mind, however, that organizations may use the same control methods with employees that it does with clients. Nonconformity may be interpreted as deviancy against organizational norms or rules.

CLIENTHOOD AND GROUP
MEMBERSHIP: TWO EXAMPLES

As a social status, clienthood is bestowed as much from political ideology as from theories of helping. Two client groups are discussed below because their relationship to the helping professions illustrates well the flaws of the dominant deficit/pathology model. Also, the groups' experiences point to issues of social justice and to the viability of the strengths perspective for social work practice. Individual and group differences are typically seen as liabilities or deficits in the older model of services and as strengths in the new perspective. It should be noted that the example groups, people with different cultural backgrounds and people with disabilities, have been portrayed stereotypically in society as a whole as well as in human service fields. In the context of the preceding discussion about rewriting the meaning of client stories, it should also be acknowledged that stereotypes represent prewritten stories. At its worst, the deficit/pathology model merely rewrites the individual story to fit the stereotype of deviancy, deficiency, or pathology.

The Culturally Different

As often as the word culture is used in conversation one might think that all Americans are practicing anthropologists. Yet we lay claim to a respect for cultural diversity while continuing traditional efforts to exclude some people from social participation. It seems as if the two things we do not know about culture are how to define it and what to do about it. Rosaldo (1989) observed that Americans think of themselves as having *psychology* and of others as having *culture.* The term *culturally different* is often used as more than a descriptive phrase—it may be used to convey subtle ideas about race, ethnicity, and values, or may imply labels of weakness or deviance. In some ways, culturally different serves as a code-phrase used by the dominant culture to imply inferiority, undesirability, and the need for social distancing. Rosaldo's (1989) observation noted above takes on new meaning here—those with psychology are "normal" and those with culture are not. Having culture (being different) makes one suspect.

The deficit/pathology model is one of absolutes. One is either sick and incompetent or well and functional. In the context of cultural differences, this absolutism precludes appreciation for that aspect of cultural assimilation that allows people to move competently from one group to another. Being different may be viewed as inherent weakness with no regard for an enhanced repertoire of social skills derived from social contact and assimilation. So abilities that would be considered advantageous in the strengths perspective may be defined as shortcomings in the deficit/pathology model.

Part of the personal cost of cultural assimilation may be the difficulty of keeping two ways of life sacred when the original is defined as inferior in negative social messages. Rodriguez (1989) offered an excellent glimpse into the difficulties of self-identity during assimilation and acculturation. He also noted that economic differences may be a greater force in social mobility for people of different cultural backgrounds. If labeling as deviant people with cultural differences leads to social control, that control may restrict economic as well as social participation, thus reinforcing some stereotypes.

Economic issues embedded in society's views about culture and differences may be strongly linked to human service philosophies of practice. If economic segregation is maintained under the guise of cultural differences, the process is augmented by notions of culture-as-pathology. Free use of deviancy labels on people who are ethnically (if not strictly culturally) different has the effect of limiting even more opportunities for socioeconomic participation. If people who are poor or who have darker skin are more readily categorized as lacking the abilities of self-determination and autonomy, it is because they have the least social power to oppose negative labeling. Wagner (1994) has shown that the nonworking poor in America have traditionally been considered pathological because they fail the standards of the dominant work ethic and the normative definitions of "work," no matter how the job market fails them.

Cultural values run deep, so professionals may not even recognize that their world view can harm others. Some behaviors become unconscious and automatic. Here is an example relayed by a human service professional (personal communication, 1992): A few years ago a school teacher in the midwest routinely washed her hands in the classroom sink. She was startled to learn that this behavior immediately followed any physical contact she had with African-American students. The message she conveyed with the behavior was one of difference-as-unclean, a form of deficit.

Diagnostic processes are often vague enough to allow cultural or personal differences to be rewritten as stories of pathologies. For example, Rosewater (1985) illustrated the difficulty some diagnosticians have in distinguishing schizophrenia and other forms of mental illness from behavioral responses to spouse abuse. In other words, the reaction of women who are physically abused may be translated into a story of personal pathology from an account that speaks of coping, resisting, and courage.

A social worker related to the author (personal communication, 1995) the following example of culture taken as pathology: A woman was apprehended by the police in a midwestern state. The woman did not seem to be able to communicate coherently. Eventually she was diagnosed with mental illness and placed in a mental institution. Some years later, a social worker took an interest in the woman's situation. As it turned out, the woman spoke a rural Indian dialect found only in Mexico. In time an interpreter was found and the woman was released from the institution to return to her home in Mexico. She had no mental illness, but she was culturally different. An important point here is that the social worker looked beyond the deficit/pathology model and facilitated true freedom for a client. It had not occurred to others that the client was competent.

People with Disabilities

In some ways, people with disabilities have been treated like people with cultural differences. However, the impact of the deficit/pathology model may be more easily seen with this group because the model has been applied more blatantly and overtly. The label of *disability* has generally been one of social devaluation. Cultural attitudes about disability no doubt influence the ease with which this has happened.

Some negative notions about disability originate in religious teachings (Weinberg & Sebian, 1980). Myths about disability-related incompetencies are common (DeLoach & Greer, 1981) and may become institutionalized into some agencies (Holmes & Karst, 1990). The deficit/pathology model has been so ubiquitous in rehabilitation (Holmes, 1993) that even the professional literature has helped perpetuate stereotypes of people with disabilities (Fine & Asch, 1988).

Historically, Americans with disabilities have been viewed as children (Perin, 1988), deviants, subhuman, and diseased (Wolfensberger, 1972). These extant ideas help create a way of thinking in rehabilitation that disability is something existing only "inside" the person (Berkowitz, 1989). In an outstanding work, Scott (1969) explained in detail how one group of people with disabilities (blindness) are urged to conform. He noted that, "For blind workers, one key indicator of the success of a rehabilitation endeavor is the degree to which the client has come to understand himself [sic] and his problems from the workers' perspective" (p. 19).

Thus, not only is the client's story rewritten to focus on weaknesses and pathologies, the client is encouraged to conform to this rendition of the self. Client strengths are not as important as conformity. Here are some other examples known to the author:

- A client with carpal tunnel syndrome was found to have no vocational potential because he spoke Spanish instead of English.
- A teenage boy spent 17 years in a mental institution because his father could not deal with him. After years of drug treatment and therapy, the client was found to have no mental illness. A client advocate discovered that a valid diagnosis had never been made (personal communication, 1993).
- A young man whose brain aneurysm had been surgically repaired was told by his counselor that he would require rehabilitation for cognitive deficits and could not return to his craft of electronics repair. During the rehabilitation process, he secretly worked on a part-time basis for his old employer doing the same kind of repair work as before.

These few examples illustrate that the deficit/pathology model applied to people with disabilities discourages self-determination in favor of paternalistic prescription. In the examples, issues of forced conformity, negative labeling, and devalued status are apparent. Professional power that has the effect of oppressing people with disabilities or limiting their opportunities to secure resources is neither helpful nor encouraging. But it *is* political in that self-serving organizational values and personal prejudices are superimposed on clients to foster the devalued social role of clienthood.

STRENGTHS TO BUILD ON

Once one understands the essential nature of the deficit/pathology model, the strengths perspective may seem an attractive alternative for ethical practice. Although practice is no less of a political endeavor with the strengths perspective, its political and ideological goals are markedly distinct from those of the older model. Social justice, human caring, and quality of life for the client are the primary political goals. Clienthood is redefined as an acceptable, situational, and transitional status in which clients participate in the political process instead of falling victim to it.

Other chapters in this book (6–9, 11–13) describe the practice ideas and methods that have emerged from social work experience with the strengths perspective. In addition, however, there are a few important issues related to the actual launching of a practice based on the strengths perspective. Because it constitutes a new paradigm that influences even the most routine aspects of everyday social work practice, the strengths perspective requires careful thought to guarantee consistency of its applied philosophy. The remainder of this chapter is devoted to the three main practice elements in which this philosophy is put to work—organizational issues, professional issues, and client issues.

Organizational Culture

The first step in implementing social work practice from the strengths perspective within an organization is to recognize the need for comprehensive planning. All staff members should be invited to participate. Depending on organizational resources, discussion groups and focus groups may be utilized, but their conclusions or recommendations should be shared with all other staff members. Discussions may first focus upon agency mission to illustrate the fact that the deficit/pathology model is not a necessary vehicle for mission achievement.

Concise agency goals supporting the overall mission should be developed and worded in such a way that the emphasis on client strengths is clear. Goal statements will reflect the overt values of the organization. If the organization is attempting to change from the deficit/pathology model it is vital that free discussions be conducted about covert organizational values. The covert or hidden values are the ones most likely to undermine the strengths perspective.

In the planning phase, identify values that promote health, autonomy, and competence and those organizational values that do not help members understand which values are to be abandoned and which are to be fostered in support of the strengths perspective. If case files are to be maintained, the planning needs to provide a method by which the files can be written to describe and emphasize client strengths, without simply ignoring authentic problem areas. Diagnostic information should be included if it is well documented. However, case plans must be built on actual or potential client strengths, so strengths must be described in detail in individual case files.

Public policies and regulations applicable to the organization must be analyzed to determine ways to adapt the strengths perspective. In the past, practitioners using the deficit/pathology model developed ways to interpret policies and regulations to support their political orientation. Some clients were taught to fill the socially defined sick role even when it was inappropriate (Bickenbach, 1993). On the whole, public policies affecting most human services do not contain inherent requirements to use the deficit/pathology model. More often, organizational cultural values encourage that policies be interpreted as mandates for the older model.

Staff training, too, is an important issue. Most agencies and programs have access to internal or external training opportunities. Internal trainers can plan appropriate training on the strengths perspective by first gathering relevant professional publications that describe practice under the strengths paradigm. Training sessions can be tailored to local requirements by emphasizing appropriate recommendations from the literature.

Professional Issues

Self-awareness and concentration help professionals learn to listen for information about client strengths. For the person educated and experienced in the deficit/pathology model, this process may be difficult at first. He or she may continue to listen for hints of pathology and failure. However, client stories contain information about strengths for coping, enduring, and understanding the world as well as hopes and visions for the future. When the professional listens for them, they can be heard. By listening to the client's entire story, the professional begins to understand the life-context where certain attitudes, affects, and behaviors are relevant strengths.

Because clients may be unclear about the direction the strengths perspective is "supposed" to take, the professional may choose to explain the perspective and its goals. In this way the client gets a sharper vision about directions and may become more interested in discovering and discussing personal strengths. Traditional, professional jargon should be avoided in such discussions. If clients have a history of clienthood under the deficit/pathology model, they will certainly understand that technical jargon has most often been used to describe failures, pathologies, and shortcomings. Everyday language usually serves best.

There is another advantage to nontechnical language. Client stories often contain meaning in metaphoric expressions whose language tends to be that of the everyday lifeworld of that individual. The professional's sensitivity to this kind of language can help him or her recognize metaphoric meaning. Where there is metaphor, there is understanding and strength. Metaphoric language reveals something about world view and about how the storyteller perceives his or her role in that world.

The strengths perspective in social work practice has a special connection to client storytelling. Holding no interest in rewriting the personal meaning of the client's story, the client is free to tell it without misgivings. People seem to derive from storytelling a sense of closure, a sense of personal history, and some sense about the "why" of the world (Weber, Harvey, & Orbuch, 1992). By honoring such stories, social workers using the strengths perspective get a sense of the client's life-situation. The client may derive "therapeutic" value from the telling when the listener respects storytelling itself.

Client Issues

Clients who have been subjected over time to professional helping that focused on weaknesses, may bring with them certain habits and expectations about the nature of being helped. Some may have grown used to dependency, helplessness, and avoidance of self-determination. These are not faults, but adaptations to lessons of clienthood from the past. For such clients, the professional should discuss openly the difference between the old paradigm and the new. Open discussions help the client understand the professional's role as well as his or her own. The client can then perceive what strengths-based clienthood requires in the way of expectations and possibilities.

A word of caution is warranted here. If the client has a long history with the deficit/pathology model, he or she, too, may want to use the jargon of pathology learned in the past. Deficit labels may have taught some clients to think of themselves as characterized by pathology, sickness, and failure. If use of the supporting jargon continues, they may have difficulty in thinking of themselves as humans with actual strengths. The client's life-context, as the source of both meaning and strength, must be respected during the helping process. So social workers of the strengths perspective recognize that solutions, too, must have resonance with this life-context. For such reasons, clients set their own goals and make their own decisions about changes to be made. In political equality with the professional, the client is free to continue his or her life story, to write the next chapter, or to rewrite previous chapters. The strengths perspective professional is there to understand their meaning and their virtues, not to edit the storyline.

CONCLUSION

The preceding discussion offers at least a brief view of the relationship among human stories, social justice, political power, and meaningful professional helping. The strengths perspective as a new paradigm for social work practice is, in the language of this chapter, attempting to write a story of a different sort on a different scale. Human service disciplines in general have endorsed the deficit/pathology model for many years now. The strengths perspective in social work represents a serious but singular challenge to the older paradigm.

To date, the strengths perspective has shown itself to be sound in concept and robust in application. It constitutes a constructed reality just as client stories do. Its scale differs, however, in that it has the potential to affect the lives of many clients and professionals alike. The "flavor" of the helping process may change with the strengths perspective, so that clients become more comfortable, less defensive, and more open to help.

Ironically—and this is true for all human service fields—much of what we know about clients' responses to the helping process may, in fact, be only their situational reactions to a deficit/pathology model of interaction and involvement that leaves them powerless. As the strengths perspective becomes more prevalent in social work practice, practitioners and researchers may find that clients have an abundance of strengths to be discovered. It may simply be the case that no one has ever asked clients about their own strengths.

The individual social worker will play the key role in such future explorations because it is at the one-to-one level of encounter that the strengths perspective comes into its own. It may also be that social workers, too, will discover new strengths of their own with the new way of thinking. In their willingness to celebrate the client's story without feeling the need for political alterations or power-editing, social workers may lead the way for other helping disciplines.

Strengths exist in humans at least as much as pathologies do. By emphasizing the one over the other, the nature of the enterprise is changed. A concluding story illustrates the profundity of that change (personal communication, 1993): A few years ago, a single parent with three children became a "welfare" client. In time, she worked as a janitor and attended school at night. Upon graduating, she went to work for a human service agency. Today, she manages a program in adult services. The story is remarkable for this reason—the woman served as client, janitor, social worker, and manager in the same agency and in the same building. In the final analysis, all human stories are about human strengths. No rewriting is necessary.

DISCUSSION QUESTIONS

1. Why do you think society is so preoccupied with labels of pathology?
2. Which personal traits or characteristics do you believe would be most beneficial to a social worker who uses the strengths perspective in his or her practice?
3. Which values in organizational culture do you think would be most conducive to the strengths perspective?
4. What role do you think social work managers or supervisors should play in supporting a strengths perspective approach to service delivery?
5. How would you best explain the strengths perspective to a new client?

REFERENCES

Berkowitz, E. D. (1989). *Disabled policy: America's programs for the handicapped.* New York: Cambridge University Press.

Bickenbach, J. E. (1993). *Physical disability and social policy.* Toronto: University of Toronto Press.

Boden, D. (1990). People are talking: Conversation analysis and symbolic interaction. In H. S. Becker & M. McCall (Eds.), *Symbolic interaction and cultural studies* (pp. 244–274). Chicago: University of Chicago Press.

Bruner, J. (1990). *Acts of meaning.* Cambridge, MA: Harvard University Press.

DeLoach, C., & Greer, B. G. (1981). *Adjustments to severe physical disability: A metamorphosis.* New York: McGraw-Hill.

Elster, J. (1992). *Local justice: How institutions allocate scarce goods and necessary burdens.* New York: Russell Sage Foundation.

Fine, M., & Asch, A. (1988). Disability beyond stigma: Social interaction, discrimination, and activism. *Journal of Social Issues, 44*(1), 3–21.

Goldman, A. I. (1993). Ethics and cognitive science. *Ethics, 103*(2), 337–360.

Holmes, G. E. (1993). The historical roots of the empowerment dilemma in vocational rehabilitation. *Journal of Disability Policy Studies, 4*(1), 1–20.

Holmes, G. E., & Karst, R. H. (1990). The institutionalization of disability myths: Impact on
vocational rehabilitation services. *Journal of Rehabilitation, 56*(1), 20–27.

Holmes, G. E., & Saleebey, D. (1993). Empowerment, the medical model, and the politics of
clienthood. *Journal of Progressive Human Services, 4*(1), 61–78.

Kemmis, D. (1990). *Community and the politics of place.* Norman, OK: University of Okla-
homa Press.

Ladd, J. (1989). Corporate goals and individual values. In P. Y. Windt, P. C. Appleby, L. P.
Francis, & B. M. Landesman (Eds.), *Ethical issues in the professions* (pp. 256–264). Englewood Cliffs, NJ: Prentice Hall.

Miller, S. D., & Berg, I. K. (1995). *The miracle method.* New York: Norton.

Murphy, R. (1988). *Social closure: The theory of monopolization and exclusion.* New York:
Oxford University Press (Clarendon).

Parry, A., & Doan, R. E. (1994). *Story re-visions: Narrative therapy in the postmodern world.*
New York: Guilford.

Perin, C. (1988). *Belonging in America: Reading between the lines.* Madison, WI: University
of Wisconsin Press.

Read, S. J. (1992). Constructing accounts: The role of explanatory coherence. In M. L.
McLaughlin, M. J. Cody, & S. J. Read (Eds.), *Explaining one's self to others: Reason-giving
in a social context* (pp. 3–19). Hillsdale, NJ: Erlbaum.

Rodriguez, R. (1989). An American writer. In W. Sollors (Ed.), *The invention of ethnicity* (pp.
3–13). New York: Oxford University Press.

Romanyshyn, R. D. (1982). *Psychological life: From science to metaphor.* Austin, TX: University of Texas Press.

Rosaldo, R. (1989). *Culture and truth: The remaking of social analysis.* Boston: Beacon Press.

Rosewater, L. B. (1985). Schizophrenia, borderline, or battered? In L. B. Rosewater & L. E. A.
Walker (Eds.), *Handbook of feminist therapy: Women's issues in psychotherapy* (pp. 215–
225). New York: Springer.

Saleebey, D. (1994). Culture, theory, and narrative: The intersection of meanings in practice.
Social Work, 39(4), 351–359.

Scott, R. A. (1969). *The making of blind men.* New York: Russell Sage Foundation.

Stalling, J. E. (1994). *Toward a strengths perspective in counseling* (Rep. No. CG 025 882).
Hays, KS: Fort Hays State University, Department of Administration, Counseling and Educational Studies. (ERIC Document Reproduction Service No. ED 378 483)

Steenbarger, B. N. (1991). All the world is not a stage: Emerging contextualist themes in
counseling and development. *Journal of Counseling and Development, 70,* 288–296.

Wagner, D. (1994). Beyond the pathologizing of nonwork: Alternative activities in a street
community. *Social Work, 39*(6), 718–227.

Weber, A. L., Harvey, J. H., & Orbuch, T. L. (1992). What went wrong: Communicating accounts
of relationship conflict. In M. L. McLaughlin, M. J. Cody, & S. J. Read (Eds.), *Explaining one's
self to others: Reason-giving in social context* (pp. 261–279). Hillsdale, NJ: Erlbaum.

Weinberg, N., & Sebian, C. (1980). The bible and disability. *Rehabilitation Counseling Bulletin, 23,* 273–281.

Wolfensberger, W. (1972). *The principle of normalization in human services.* Toronto: National Institute on Mental Retardation.

Wright, B. A., & Fletcher, B. L. (1982). Uncovering hidden resources: A challenge in assessment. *Professional Psychology, 13,* 229–235.

part IV

The Strengths Approach in the Environment: Groups and Community Development

chapter **11**

Fostering Resiliency in Children and Youth: Promoting Protective Factors in the School[1]

Bonnie Benard

The field of prevention, both research and practice, came a long way in the 1980s: from short-term, individual-focused interventions in the school classroom to a growing awareness and beginning implementation of long-term, comprehensive interventions expanding beyond the school to include the community. Furthermore, in the mid-1980s the research and literature on prevention highlighted strategies and programs based on identified risk factors for problems such as alcohol and other drug abuse, teen pregnancy, delinquency and gangs, and dropping out (Freiberg, 1994). Clearly a giant step in the right direction, the identification of risks does not necessarily provide a clear sense of just what strategies will reduce the risks. More recently, preventionists are discussing "protective factors," building "resiliency" in youth, basing strategies on what research has told us about the environmental factors that facilitate the development of youth who do not get involved in life-compromising problems (Benard, 1994; McLaughlin, Irby, & Langman, 1994). What clearly becomes the challenge for practitioners, administrators, and legislators is the implementation of prevention strategies that strengthen protective factors in our families, schools, and communities—and not only protective factors, but also generative factors; those unbidden, and fortuitous elements of life that dramatically increase learning, resolve, resource acquisition, and hardiness. After a brief overview of the protective factor research, I will discuss the major factors that research has identified as contributing to the development of resiliency in youth and the implications of this for building effective prevention programs.

---

[1] This is a revised and edited version of B. Bernard, *Fostering resiliency in kids: Protective factors in the family, school, and community.* Portland, OR: Western Regional Center for Drug-Free Schools; Northwest Regional Educational Laboratory.

PROTECTIVE FACTORS

As has been argued throughout this book, the social and behavioral sciences have followed a problem-focused approach to studying human and social development. This retrospective model of research traditionally examines problems, disease, illness, maladaptation, incompetence, and deviance. The emphasis has been placed on identifying the risk factors of various disorders like alcoholism, schizophrenia and other mental illnesses, criminality, and delinquency, among others. The data yielded from such research studies have ultimately been of only limited value to the prevention field, concerned as it is with building health-promoting, not health-compromising, behaviors and with facilitating the development of social competence in children and youth.

Investigators studying risks for the development of "problem behaviors" were stymied by the issue of whether the abnormalities observed in people diagnosed as schizophrenic, criminal, or alcoholic were cause or consequence. With the exception of some earlier studies, beginning in the late 1950s and on into the 1960s and 1970s, a few researchers decided to circumvent this dilemma by studying individuals postulated to be at high risk for developing certain disorders—children growing up under conditions of great stress and adversity such as neonatal stress, poverty, neglect, abuse, physical handicaps, war, and parental schizophrenia, depression, alcoholism and criminality. This risk research used a prospective research design, developmental and longitudinal, assessing children at various times during the course of their development in order to better understand the nature of the risk factors that result in the development of a disorder.

As the children studied in these various longitudinal projects grew into adolescence and adulthood, a consistent—and amazing—finding emerged: While a certain percentage of these high-risk children developed various problems (a percentage higher than in the normal population), a greater percentage of the children became healthy, competent young adults. The Wolins (1993), for example, found that in contrast to the conventional wisdom, in their study, children, now adults, from families where one or both parents engaged in serious alcoholic drinking and often chaotic, abusive behavior managed to surmount this adversity often with great dignity and aplomb. Rather than becoming alcoholic or psychiatric casualties themselves, these children developed a set of competencies and personal traits that have stood them in good stead in their adult lives. The bottom line? According to the Wolins and others (Peele & Brodsky, 1991), most children of alcoholics do not become alcoholic. Anywhere from 70 to 92 percent (depending on the study samples) do not! Likewise, Manfred Bleuler found that 75 percent of the children of schizophrenic parents developed into healthy adults with "remarkable evidence of strength, courage, and health in the midst of disaster and adversity" (Watt, 1984, p. 525). Similarly, Michael Rutter's research on children growing up in poverty found "that half of the children living under conditions of disadvantage do not repeat that pattern in their own adult lives" (Garmezy, 1991, p. 419). In the 1980s, researchers in the collaborative, international, interdisciplinary Risk Reduction Consortium reported the same phenomenon in their ongoing prospective, longitudinal research—

children who somehow become "invulnerable," "stress-resistant," "hardy," "ego-re-silient," "invincible," and, the most current popularly used term, "resilient," in spite of severe stress and adversity.

Increasing theoretical acceptance in the child development field of the transac-tional-ecological model of human development in which people are viewed as self-righting organisms engaged in active, ongoing adaptation to their environment (Werner & Smith, 1992), has resulted in a growing research interest in moving be-yond the identification of risk factors for the development of a problem behavior to an examination of those traits, capacities, and personal and environmental re-sources that propel individuals in the direction of health, stability, and growth (Mas-ten, 1994). The importance of this research to the prevention field is obvious: If we can determine the personal and environmental sources of social competence and wellness, we can better plan preventive and ameliorative interventions focused on creating and enhancing the personal and environmental attributes that serve as the key to healthy development.

While researchers have commonly categorized protective factors according to those falling within the domains of individual personality attributes or dispositions, family characteristics, and environmental influences, the discussion here will begin with a profile of the resilient child and then will examine the protective factors con-sistently found in the family, the school, and the community. In order to avoid fall-ing into the pathology paradigm and "blaming the victim" syndrome with its con-comitant focus on "fixing kids," my perspective is that personality and individual outcomes are the result of a transactional process between self, agency, and envi-ronmental influences. To be successful, prevention interventions must focus on en-hancing and creating positive environmental contexts—families, schools, and com-munities that, in turn, reinforce positive behaviors.

Profile of the Resilient Child

While there is disagreement about precisely what they may be, there is agreement among researchers and practitioners that the many children and youth who turn out to be resilient and resourceful do develop a number of traits and competencies, perhaps forged in the face of adversity, that ultimately stand them in good stead over the trajectory of their development.

Social Competence.   This commonly identified attribute of resilient children usu-ally includes the qualities of responsiveness, flexibility, empathy and caring, com-munication skills, a sense of humor, and any other prosocial behavior. Resilient chil-dren are considerably more responsive (and can elicit more positive responses from others), more active, and more flexible and adaptable even in infancy. Furthermore, a great number of resilient children have a sense of humor. That is, they have the ability to generate comic relief and find alternative ways of looking at things as well as the ability to laugh at themselves and ridiculous situations. As a result, resilient children—from early childhood on—tend to establish more positive relationships with others, including friendships with their peers (Higgins, 1994; Masten, 1994; Werner & Smith, 1992; Wolin & Wolin, 1993).

Problem-Solving Skills.   These skills include the ability to think abstractly, reflectively, and flexibly and to be able to attempt alternative solutions for both cognitive and social problems. For example, Rutter (1984) found especially prevalent in the population of abused and neglected girls who later became healthy adults the presence of planning skills that resulted in their planning marriages to nondeviant men. The literature on "street" children growing up in the slums of the United States and other countries provides an extreme example of the role these skills play in the development of resiliency as these children must continually successfully negotiate the demands of their environment or not survive (Felsman, 1989).

Autonomy.   Different researchers have used different terms to refer to autonomy: a strong sense of independence; an internal locus of control and sense of power; self-esteem and self-efficacy (Anthony & Cohler, 1987; Garmezy, 1994; Rutter, 1984; Werner & Smith, 1992). Essentially, the protective factor researchers are talking about is a sense of one's own identity and an ability to set boundaries, to act independently, and to exert some control over one's environment. Several researchers have also identified the ability to separate oneself from a dysfunctional family environment—to maintain a compassionate distance—as the major characteristic of resilient children growing up in families with alcoholism and mental illness (Anthony & Cohler, 1987). According to Berlin and Davis (1989), "In our work with children and families of alcoholics we have begun to view the crucial task that they must master, if they are to cope successfully with the dilemmas of alcoholism, as the task of adaptive distancing" (p. 95).

Such adaptive distancing, according to Wallerstein (1983) in her study of children who dealt successfully with their parents' conflict and divorce, involves two challenges: (1) to disengage enough from the centrifugal pull of parental distress to maintain pursuits and satisfactions in the outside world of peers, school, and community; and (2) to remove the imposing symbolism, imagery, and language of the family's problems from its central place in the child's thinking.

Sense of Purpose and Future.   Related to a sense of autonomy and self-efficacy and the belief that one can have some degree of control over one's environment is another characteristic of resilient children—a sense of purpose and future. Within this category fall several related attributes invariably identified in the protective factor literature: healthy expectancies, goal directedness, success orientation, achievement motivation, educational aspirations, persistence, optimism, hopefulness, hardiness, belief in a bright future, a sense of anticipation, a sense of a compelling future, and a sense of coherence. This sense of purpose and future appears to be a most powerful predictor of positive outcome.

According to Brook, Nomura, and Cohen's (1989) research on risk and protective factors for adolescent alcohol and drug use, high-achievement orientation appeared to have a protective influence that even offset the effects of alcohol consumption by peers, the most commonly identified influential risk factor. Furthermore, Newcomb and Bentler (1986) found that educational aspirations were an even more powerful predictor of high school graduation than actual academic achievement. Werner and Smith (1982) also validate the power of this attribute. This sense of coherence, of purpose and meaning and optimism lies in direct contrast to the "learned helplessness" that Seligman (1975) and others have consistently found present in individuals experiencing mental and social problems.

Resilience, however, is not a trait or even a set of traits. It is, instead, the accumulating matrix of capacities, resources, talents, strengths, knowledge, and adaptive skills that continues to grow over time. Resilience is not a constitutional/genetically contrived set of capabilities that only a few "superkids" possess. Lifespan studies demonstrate over and over that all human beings, even those who are developmentally compromised, have the potential for self-righting over the course of the life-cycle. Finally, resilience and the development of strengths and resources occurs in interaction with the surrounding environment, notably families, schools, and neighborhoods. Those environments that foster resilience and build strength all have similar attributes. I will discuss these primarily in terms of the school system.

PROTECTIVE FACTORS WITHIN THE SCHOOL

The evidence demonstrating that a school can serve as a protective environment to help children weather the many demands and challenges of a stressful world continues to grow. The literature on inner-city schools that have remarkable successes from their students (Edmonds, 1986; McLaughlin, Irby, & Langman, 1994; Mills, 1995) and the rich body of ethnographic research in which youth, families, and teachers explain their successes and failures corroborates the research on resiliency. Both protective factor research and research on effective schools clearly identify the characteristics of schools that provide this source of protection for youth. And, lo and behold, they parallel the protective factors found in the family environments of resilient youth!

Caring and Support

Given the incredible stresses that many urban families and communities face, even in the inner city, for many youth and children the school is a refuge. School serves as "a protective shield to help children withstand the multiple vicissitudes that they can expect of a stressful world" (Garmezy, 1991, p. 427). Garbarino's (1980) inquiry into the fate of children growing up in what he calls "war zones" in the United States and elsewhere led him to this conclusion: "Despite the overwhelming pressures in the environment, 75–80% of the children can use school activities as a support for healthy adjustment and achievement when the schools are sensitive to them and their burdens" (p. 121).

In their research Werner and Smith (1982) found that "among the most frequently encountered positive role models in the lives of the children of Kauai, outside of the family circle, was a favorite teacher. For the resilient youngster a special teacher was not just an instructor for academic skills, but also a confidante and positive model for personal identification" (p. 162). Noddings (1988) concluded the following from her research into the power of caring relationships at school to effect positive outcomes for children:

> At a time when the traditional structures of caring have deteriorated, schools must become places where teachers and students live together, talk with each other, take delight in each other's company. My guess is that when schools focus on what really matters in life, the cognitive ends we now pursue so painfully and artificially will be achieved somewhat more naturally. It is obvious that children will work harder and do things—even odd things like adding fractions—for people they love and trust. (p. 32)

Based on his research into effective schools, James Coleman (1987) similarly speculates that if we were to "reinstitute the school as an agent of families," with the primary emphasis on caring for the child—on providing the "attention, personal interest, and intensity of involvement, some persistence and continuity over time, and a certain degree of intimacy—children would develop the necessary attitudes, effort, and conception of self that they need to succeed in school and as adults" (p. 33).

CARRIE

Carrie is 6, the daughter of a white mother and a black father. She, too, is a child of poverty—the oldest of three, whose mother has been hospitalized twice for a serious illness. Carrie lives with her mother and two siblings in a subsidized rental apartment. Her mother has lost her part-time clerical job at a local company due to chronic illness, and the family is struggling on welfare. Carrie's kindergarten teacher, Mrs. Juno, describes the family as being "in constant crisis" and expresses her concern about Carrie's two younger siblings, who are waiting to be accepted into Head Start, though all the available slots are filled. Carrie, according to Mrs. Juno, has problems, "but what child wouldn't after all she's gone through?"

When Carrie has conflicts with other children, she often frowns and clenches her teeth, and her eyes fill with tears. Mrs. Juno handles her aggressive behavior toward other children by removing her from the situation and giving her time to calm down without punishment. She then uses a conflict-resolution approach to help the children recognize each other's feelings. It is difficult for the other kids to recognize Carrie's, for they often become the unprovoked targets of her anger. But Mrs. Juno tells them, "Carrie is worried about her mommy, and sometimes she feels sad or mad because she's going through a hard time and we all need to help her." Consequently, some children are very solicitous of Carrie and take care of her in class, while others reject or avoid her. Mrs. Juno worries that the other children will notice her special treatment of Carrie and feel it is unfair, although she tells them, "Anyone in this class can always ask for a special time with me if they feel sad." Over a period of 3 months, I observe noticeable changes in Carrie. She begins to participate more willingly in large-group activities and becomes excited about her growing mastery of reading. . . . The flexibility in the room allows options that work particularly well for a stressed child like Carrie. . . . It is clear that a child such as Carrie does not fit easily into a classroom environment, but with a sensitive teacher, accepting of her needs, Carrie gradually becomes a nontargeted participant in the classroom. In many other classrooms, Carrie might already have been classified as emotionally impaired. . . . Carrie has found a place in the classroom— her presence, while problematic, is valued and she matters. As she nears the end of her kindergarten year, there are questions, seeded with meaning, that hover above her: Whose eyes will see Carrie next year? Will she be given the space for promise? Or will she, too, become another casualty, another child at risk? (Polakow, 1993)

While the importance of the teacher as caregiver cannot be overemphasized, a factor often overlooked that has definitely emerged from protective factor research is the role of caring peers and friends in the school and community environments (Kohn, 1991). Research into the resiliency of "street gamins" clearly identifies peer support as critical to the survival of these youth (Felsman, 1989). Similarly, Werner and Smith (1982) found caring friends to be a major factor in the development of resiliency in their disadvantaged population. James Coleman (1987) also cites the positive outcomes for youth who have lived with their peers in boarding schools when their families were no longer able to be supportive. Convincing evidence for the role of peers in reducing alcohol and drug use are the findings of two meta-analyses (comparing the effects of more than 200 studies): These studies concluded that peer programs (including cooperative learning strategies) are the single most effective school-based approach for reducing alcohol and drug use in youth (Bangert-Drowns, 1988; Tobler, 1986).

Obviously, resilient youth are those youth who have and take the opportunity to fulfill the basic human need for social support, caring, and love. If this is not available to them in their immediate family environments, it is imperative that the school provide the opportunities to develop caring relationships with both adults and other youth. The positive outcomes of prevention programs—including reduced levels of alcohol and drug use—which have focused on increasing the amount of social support available to youth in their schools by facilitating the development of teacher and peer relationships (Eggert & Herting, 1991) or the numerous forms of peer helping programs which exponentially increase the caregiving resources available to a youth unequivocally demonstrate that a caregiving environment in the school serves as that "protective shield" (Benard, 1990).

Creating an ethos of caring in a school means that teachers and other professionals like social workers, too, must be involved in mutual support and aid to each other. Clearly collegial support is the key to sustaining positive change in school and it has a measurable effect on increasing student achievement and satisfaction. The ethic of caring is not a prefabricated program per se; rather, it is a way of being, of relating, of seeing that is based on genuine compassion, interest, respect, trust, and acceptance (Benard, 1994).

High Expectations

As with the family environment, research has identified that schools that establish high expectations for all kids—and give them the support necessary to achieve them—have incredibly high rates of academic success (Brook, Nomura, & Cohen, 1989; Edmonds, 1986; Rutter, 1979). Probably the most powerful research supporting a school "ethos" of high expectations as a protective shield is that reported by Michael Rutter and colleagues in their book Fifteen Thousand Hours (Rutter et al., 1979). As Garmezy (1991) put it, this work "stands forth as a possible beacon for illuminating the role of schools as a strategic force in fostering the well-being of disadvantaged children" (p. 425). Rutter found that even within the same poverty-stricken areas of London, some schools showed considerable differences in rates of delinquency, behavioral disturbance, attendance, and academic attainment (even after controlling for family risk factors). The successful schools, moreover, appeared to share certain characteristics: academic emphasis, teachers' clear expectations and regulations, high level of student participation, and many, varied alternative resources—library facilities, vocational work opportunities, art, music, and extracurricular activities. A major critical finding was that the relationships between a school's characteristics and student behavior increased over time; that is, the number of problem behaviors experienced by a youth decreased over time in the successful schools and increased in the unsuccessful schools. Rutter (Rutter et al., 1979) concluded that schools that nourish high and doable expectations for their students show not only high achievement levels but a clear reduction in the incidence of behavioral and emotional disorders. The incredible power of a schoolwide ethos of high expectations has also been borne out in the protective factor research of Judith Brook (Brook, Nomura, & Cohen, 1989) and her colleagues, who found that this factor, in conjunction with a school value of student participation and autonomy, was even able to mitigate against the most powerful risk factor for adolescent alcohol and drug use—substance-using peers.

During the last several years, research on successful programs for youth at risk for academic failure has clearly demonstrated that a schoolwide climate of high expectations is a critical factor in reducing academic failure and increasing the number of college-bound youth. For example, according to Phyllis Hart (California Department of Education, 1990) of the Achievement Council, a California-based advocacy group, the establishment of a college core curriculum in an inner-city, disadvantaged community resulted in over 65 percent of its graduates going on to higher education (up from 15 percent before the program began). Several students participating in this program stated a major factor in their decision to attend college was "having one person who believed I could do it!" (California Department of Education, 1990). Similarly, Henry Levin's (1988) Accelerated Schools Program and Robert Slavin's (Slavin, Karweit, & Madden, 1989) Success for All project have clearly demonstrated that engaging students at risk for school failure in a challenging, speeded-up as opposed to a slowed-down curriculum has positive academic and social outcomes. These findings are in direct contrast to the dismal outcomes of children who are labeled as slow learners and tracked into low-ability classes (Oakes, 1985). Hart (California Department of Education, 1990) claims that low expectations do not help anyone and that no one is immune to the power of high and positive expectancies. In *Among School Children,* Kidder (1990) describes the powers that teachers have to motivate children: "For children who are used to thinking of themselves as stupid or not worth talking to or deserving rape and beatings, a good teacher can be an astonishing revelation. A good teacher can give a child at least a chance to feel, 'She thinks I'm worth something; maybe I am'" (p. 3).

There are many ways that schools can convey low or negative expectations, implicitly or explicitly: administering standardized tests that are too narrow in the skills and attributes they target; offering a rote and parochial curriculum; focusing on a small range of learning styles; ignoring the realities of other cultures and other ways of being; grouping students according to "ability"; and relying exclusively on a constricted range of extrinsic rewards.

"Schools that are especially successful in promoting resiliency build on students' intrinsic motivation. These schools actively engage students in a variety of rich and experiential curricula that connect to their own interests, strengths, and real world activities" (Benard, 1994, p. 15). Furthermore, they provide opportunities for real and active participation in the civic, intellectual, and social life of the school, thus making kids more responsible and providing a degree of ownership of elements of the school—curriculum, governance, and recreation, for example.

JOHN P. AND JOHN T.

Several years ago students identified by the district as promising young leaders were invited to spend an all-expenses-paid weekend at Notre Dame University, participating in a youth leadership training program. One year there were two students whose names were very similar—John P. Williams and John T. Williams. John T. was a member of the National Honor Society and had an outstanding curricular and extracurricular record during his first 2 years of high school. John P., on the other hand, was categorically defined as learning disabled. Although he attended school regularly, he did not excel academically and never participated in extracurricular activities.

Through a clerical error, John P. Williams received the written invitation to the leadership program and he decided to attend. (The error was not noticed until after the students returned from the program.) Several weeks later, the building principal complimented his staff, particularly on the selection of John Williams. He had been advised by Notre Dame that John showed the leadership qualities that those conducting the workshop truly admired. I am confident that John P. Williams responded at Notre Dame according to his understanding of their collective perception of what they thought he was. In fact, they created a new reality for John P.

Reprinted from *The Power of Participation,* by R. J. Golarz and M. J. Golarz (1995), p. 25. National Training Associates, Sebastopol, CA. Reprinted with permission.

Youth Participation and Involvement

Participating in decisions about one's circumstances and future is a basic human need, closely tied to the need to have power over the direction and course of one's life. And providing youth with the opportunities for meaningful involvement in the intellectual and civic life of the school and community is a natural outcome in schools having high expectations for their students. Implanting the occasions for participation into the life of the classroom, school, or community doesn't require any special augmented programs but "requires adults to let go of the role of the 'sage on the stage' to become the 'guide on the side,' to see youth as a valuable resource, to willingly share power with youth, to create a system based on reciprocity and collaboration rather than on control and competition; in other words, to create a democratic community" (Benard, 1994, p. 16).

Carta's (1991) primary finding from her research analyzing instructional factors in inner-city classrooms was that the students were not actively challenged and involved by their teachers and by the curriculum. Furthermore, Carta (1991) identified the "opportunity to respond" as the key variable for differentiating classrooms that were effective or not effective. In their examination of inner-city schools that promoted resilience, Wang, Haertel, and Walberg (1994) found that effective teaching was characterized by: articulation and organization of the curriculum so that there were ties to student's everyday life and concerns; high expectations, opportunities to respond and reflect; a high degree of engagement in classroom activities; student participation in setting goals and making decisions about learning experiences; and involvement in cooperative learning. The key words were "involvement," "engagement," and "belonging" (pp. 51–52).

Asking questions that encourage critical and reflective thinking; making learning more relevant to youths' daily life concerns, interests, and passions, as well as making it more experiential; giving youth a genuine role to play in curriculum and program planning; allowing students to evaluate curriculum and programs; practicing cooperative learning through activities such as peer helping and tutoring, cross-age mentoring, and performing community service are all strategies that not only heighten learning and responsibility but encourage youth to give back their resources to the larger community (Benard, 1994).

Michael Rutter's research on successful schools unequivocally documents the protective nature of youth participation (1984). According to Rutter, in the schools with low levels of problems such as delinquency, children were given and took on considerable responsibility. They were active participants in almost every phase of school life. They were expected to be responsible and mature—and they were. These schools created a variety of opportunities to ensure that all students found something they were interested in and could succeed in.

The power of creating chances for vigorous involvement from an early age was vividly demonstrated in the High/Scope Educational Research Foundation's 15-year follow-up study, the Perry Preschool Project. When children from an impoverished inner-city environment were given the opportunities to plan and make decisions in their preschool environment, they were at the age of 19 significantly less (as much as 50 percent less!) involved in drug use, delinquency, teen pregnancy, and school failure (Berrueta-Clement et al., 1984; Schweinhart & Weikart, 1986).

Once again, the operating dynamic reflects the fundamental human need to bond—to participate, to belong, to have some power or control over one's life. When schools ignore these basic human needs—of children and adults—they become ineffective, alienating places. Seymour Sarason (1990) says it well: "When one has no stake in the way things are, when one's needs or opinions are provided no forum, when one sees oneself as the object of unilateral actions, it takes no particular wisdom to suggest that one would rather be elsewhere" (p. 83).

Summing up his literature review of resiliency in the face of poverty, Norman Garmezy's eloquent statement validates the power of the school to promote positive developmental outcomes: "What is apparently needed by school personnel is the proud awareness that by putting forth the best effort in their classrooms and schools, they are engaged in the most worthy of societal enterprises—the enhancement of competence in their children and their tailoring, in part, of a protective shield to help children withstand the multiple vicissitudes that they can expect of a stressful world" (1991, p. 427).

OASIS HIGH SCHOOL

The students who enter Oasis High School typically have a history of trouble, failure, hurt, and/or violence. But Oasis High is a story about success. An alternative school, it helps the students beat the odds. On leaving Oasis, students are primed for success. Recently, a survey found that 36 percent of the graduates (1987–1992) were attending college, 5 percent were at home with young children, 5 percent were in the armed forces, 51 percent were employed, only 3 percent were out of work. They practice individualized love at Oasis High, staff involving themselves at an emotional level to nurture and strengthen students' growth. They believe in the power of love, often missing from their students' lives, to right the course of students' development. But there are other factors too: a variety of teaching methods including individualized instruction, mastery learning, experiential learning, outdoor education, and cooperative learning; emphasis on "whole person" learning—all school interdisciplinary units and discussion based on students' knowledge, interest, and background; a noncoercive discipline policy—few suspensions and no vandalism; and student *ownership* of the school.

CAPITALIZING ON PROTECTIVE FACTORS

The development of human resiliency is none other than the process of healthy human development—a dynamic process in which personality and environmental influences interact in a reciprocal, transactional relationship. The range of outcomes, according to Werner (Werner & Smith, 1982), is determined by the balance between risk factors, stressful life events, and protective factors. Furthermore, this balance is not determined only on the basis of the number of risk and protective factors present in the life of an individual but on their respective frequency, duration, and severity, as well as the developmental stage at which they occur. According to Werner (1990), "As long as [this] balance between stressful life events and protective factors is favorable, successful adaptation is possible. However, when stressful life events outweigh the protective factors, even the most resilient child can develop problems" (p. 98).

No one is invulnerable; every person has a "threshold" beyond which he or she can "succumb" (Rutter, 1979). Nonetheless, Werner and Smith (1992) argue that "[o]ur findings and those by other American and European investigators with a life-span perspective suggest that these buffers [protective factors] make a more profound impact on the life course of children who grow up under adverse conditions than do specific risk factors or stressful life events" (p. 202). Thus, effective interventions and prevention efforts must reinforce in every arena—community, school, and family—the natural social bonds that exist. These efforts "between young and old, between siblings, between friends, that give meaning to one's life and a reason for commitment" (Werner & Smith, 1982, p. 163) must be directed toward building connectedness—this sense of belonging—by encouraging and guiding families, schools and communities to become "psychological homes," wherein youth can find mutually caring, and respectful relationships and opportunities for meaningful involvement.

WHAT ROLE CAN SOCIAL WORKERS PLAY?

Shifting the balance or tipping the scales from vulnerability to resilience may happen as a result of one person or one opportunity. As we have seen in this review, individuals who have succeeded in spite of adverse environmental conditions in their families, schools, and/or communities have often done so because of the presence of environmental support in the form of one family member, one teacher, one social worker, one school, one community person who encouraged their success and welcomed their participation and relationship. As protective factor researcher, David Offord (1991) concludes: "A compensating good experience, good programs in the schools, or one good relationship can make a difference in the child's life" (p. 3). A social worker can be that person or, more importantly, assure that each child teetering between risk and possibility can find a person who is steadfast, expectant, and caring, or can help the school define and arrange experiences, in the classroom and after school, that are affirming, challenging, and that capitalize on nascent strengths in children and youth.

While tipping the scales toward resiliency through individual, serendipitous relationships or events are certainly important, the increasing number of children and families that are experiencing growing numbers of risks in their lives due to environmental deprivation necessitate that social workers and other youth workers take the attitude of preventionists and assume a systems perspective intervening with planned environmental strategies to build protection into the lives of all children and families. From this perspective, a major underlying cause of the development of social problems such as school failure, alcohol and drug abuse, teen pregnancy, child abuse, etc. can be traced back to the gradual destruction of naturally occurring social networks in the community. The social, economic, and technological changes since the late 1940s have created a fragmentation of community life, resulting in breaks in the naturally occurring networks and linkages between individuals, families, schools, and other social systems within a community that traditionally have provided the protection, the "social capital"—that is, the social supports and opportunities for participation and involvement necessary for healthy human development (McKnight, 1995). As is discussed in other chapters (12, 13, 14), any environment is full of resources and assets, protective factors, many lying fallow or untapped, even unimagined. What is clear is the need for social workers, and other involved professionals, to build networks and intersystem linkages in which the profound capacities of the people, families, and institutions in a community are employed in the service of both youth and community-building. While it is certainly true that as a society America seems not to value nor invest much in its children, even when community resources do exist they are often so fragmented they become ineffectual at dealing with the root causes of risk and, thus, fall short of building a protective shield or "safety net" for children. As Sid Gardner (1989), a national expert in children's policy, states, "In fact, we are ultimately failing our children, not only because we haven't invested in them, but also because as communities we have failed to work together to hold ourselves accountable for the substantial resources we do invest—and for the outcomes of our most vulnerable clients" (p. 19).

To ensure that all children have the opportunities to build resiliency—to develop social competencies (like caring and responsiveness), problem-solving skills, autonomy, and a sense of purpose and future, social workers must build linkages between families and schools and schools and communities. It is only at this intersystem level—and only through intersystem collaboration within our communities—that we can build a broad enough, intense enough network of protection for all children and families. One of the legacies of social work as well as one of its professional charges is to work, whether through case management or community organization and development, to cement these bonds and to forge alliances among community members and organizations in the service of helping children and youth realize their inherent capacities. John McKnight says, "Those who seek a community vision . . . see a society where those who were once labeled, exiled, treated, counseled, advised, and protected are, instead, incorporated into community, where their contributions, capacities, gifts, and fallibilities will allow a network of relationships involving work, recreation, friendship, support, and the political power of being a citizen" (1995, p. 169).

Building community and creating belonging is the essence of fostering resiliency. This presents both personal and political challenges. Personally, fostering resiliency is an inside-out, deep-structure process of changing our belief systems. It calls upon social workers, teachers, and other human service providers to see resilience and not risk, strengths instead of deficits, resources and not problems in children and youth, their families, their cultures, and their communities. It requires, as Polakow (1993) says, "an ethic of caring—a change of heart and a change in our ways of seeing" (p. 182). It demands the fundamental belief in every person's innate mental health and wisdom and the willingness to share power with others, to create systems based on reciprocity and sharing rather than on adult or professional control.

Furthermore, fostering resiliency compels us to work politically for educational, social, and economic justice. Studies of resilience document that, just as a phoenix rises from the ashes, so do human beings have the capacity to transform suffering into joy, anger into forgiveness, and scarcity into abundance. However, as educator and social reformer Jonathon Kozol stated recently, "Society cannot be built on miracles; it must be built on justice" (1996). Social workers working from a strengths perspective have the power—the knowledge, beliefs, and skills—to one-by-one, school-by-school, and community-by-community begin to build the critical mass of concern and commitment that will ultimately create a just and caring democracy in this nation.

DISCUSSION QUESTIONS

1. In your experience, what are the elements in the school, community, or family that serve as "protective factors" for children and youth? How, as a social worker, might you work to assure that these are strengthened and more widely available to all children?

2. What are the key differences between taking an approach to prevention or intervention that is based on the idea of resilience as opposed to one based exclusively on problems, deficit, or risk?

3. What are the characteristics of resilient children? their families? their communities? Are all children potentially resilient? Why or why not? If so, how can individual social workers help in such a way as to increase the likelihood of resilience in the face of adversity?

REFERENCES

Anthony, E. J., & Cohler, B. (Eds.). (1987). *The invulnerable child.* New York: Guilford Press.

Bangert-Drowns, R. (1988). The effects of school-based substance abuse education. *Journal of Drug Education, 18,* 243–264.

Benard, B. (December, 1990). *The case for peers.* Portland, OR: Western Center for Drug-Free Schools and Communities.

Benard, B. (1994, December). *Applications of resilience.* Paper presented at a conference on the Role of Resilience in Drug Abuse, Alcohol Abuse, and Mental Illness. Washington, D.C.: National Institute on Drug Abuse.

Berlin, R., & Davis, R. (1989). Children from alcoholic families: Vulnerability and resilience. In T. Dugan & R. Coles, (Eds.), *The child in our times.* New York: Brunner/Mazel (pp. 81–105).

Berrueta-Clement, J., Schweinhart, L., Barnett, W., Epstein, A., & Weikart, D. (1984). *Changed lives: The effects of the Perry Preschool Program on youths through age 19.* Ypsilanti, MI: High/Scope Press.

Brook, J. (1986). Onset of adolescent drinking: A longitudinal study of intrapersonal and interpersonal antecedents. *Advances in Alcohol and Substance Abuse, 5,* 91–110.

Brook, J., Nomura, C., & Cohen, P. (1989). A network of influences on adolescent drug involvement: Neighborhood, school, peer, and family. *Genetic, Social and General Psychology Monographs, 115,* 303–321.

California Department of Education. (1990). *Enhancing opportunities for higher education among underrepresented students.* Sacramento, CA.

Carta, J. (1991). Inner-city children's education. *American Behavioral Scientist, 34,* 441–453.

Coleman, J. (1987). Families and schools. *Educational Researcher, 16,* 32–38.

Coleman, J., & Hoffer, T. (1987). *Public and private high schools: The impact of communities.* New York: Basic Books.

Dugan, T., & Coles, R. (1989). *The child in our times: Studies in the development of resiliency.* New York: Brunner-Mazel.

Edmonds, R. (1986). Characteristics of effective schools. In U. Neisser (Ed.), *The school achievement of minority children: New perspectives* (pp. 93–104). Hillsdale, NJ: Erlbaum.

Eggert, L., & Herting, J. (1991). Preventing teenage drug abuse: Exploratory effects of network social support. *Youth and Society, 22,* 482–524.

Felsman, J. K. (1989). Risk and resiliency in childhood: The lives of street children. In T. Dugan and R. Coles (Eds.), *The child in our times* (pp. 56–80). New York: Brunner/Mazel.

Freiberg, H. J. (1994). Understanding resilience: Implications for inner-city schools and their near and far communities. In M. C. Wang & E. W. Gordon (Eds.), *Educational resilience in inner-city America: Challenges and prospects.* Hillsdale, NJ: Erlbaum.

Garbarino, J. (1980). Preventing child maltreatment. In R. Price (Ed.), *Prevention in mental health: Research, policy, and practice* (pp. 63–108). Newbury Park, CA: Sage.

Gardner, S. (1989, Fall). Failure by fragmentation. *California Tomorrow,* 18–25.

Garmezy, N. (1991). Resiliency and vulnerability to adverse developmental outcomes associated with poverty. *American Behavioral Scientist, 34*(4), 416–430.

Garmezy, N. (1994). Reflections and commentary on risk, resilience, and development. In R. J. Haggerty, L. R. Sherrod, N. Garmezy, & M. Rutter (Eds.), *Stress, risk, and resilience in children and adolescents: Processes, mechanisms, and interventions* (pp. 1–18). Cambridge, UK: Cambridge University Press.

Golarz, R. J., & Golarz, M. J. (1995). *The power of participation: Improving schools in a democratic society.* Sebastopol, CA: National Training Associates.

Higgins, G. O. (1994). *Resilient adults: Overcoming a cruel past.* San Francisco: Jossey-Bass.

Kidder, T. (1990). *Among school children.* New York: Avon.

Kohn, A. (1991). Caring kids: The role of the schools. *Phi Delta Kappan, 72,* 497–506.

Kozol, J. (1996, February 5). Interview. Berkeley, CA: KPFA Radio

Levin, H. (1988). Accelerated schools for disadvantaged students. *Educational Leadership, 44,* 19–21.

Masten, A. S. (1994). Resilience in individual development: Successful adaptation despite risk and adversity. In M. C. Wang & E. W. Gordon (Eds.), *Educational resilience in inner city America: Challenges and prospects.* Hillsdale, NJ: Erlbaum.

McKnight, J. (1995). *The careless society: Community and its counterfeits.* New York: Basic Books.

McLaughlin, M., Irby, M., & Langman, J. (1994). *Urban sanctuaries: Neighborhood organizations in the lives and futures of inner city youth.* San Francisco: Jossey-Bass.

Mills, R. (1995). *Realizing mental health.* New York: Sulzburger & Graham.

Meixner, C. (1994). Teaching with love at Oasis High. *Educational Leadership, 52,* 32.

Newcomb, M., & Bentler, P. (1986). Drug use, educational aspirations, and workforce involvement: The transition from adolescence to young adulthood. *American Journal of Community Psychology, 14,* 303–321.

Noddings, N. (1988, December 7). Schools face crisis in caring. *Education Week.*

Oakes, J. (1985). *Keeping track: How schools structure inequality.* New Haven, CT: Yale University Press.

Offord, D. (1991, February). *Research and Training Center for Children's Mental Health of the Florida Mental Health Institute.* Conference summary, Tampa, FL: University of South Florida.

Peele, S., & Brodsky, A. (1991). *The truth about addiction and recovery.* New York: Simon & Schuster.

Polakow, V. (1993). *Lives on the edge: Single mothers and their children in the other America.* Chicago: University of Chicago Press (excerpted in *Teacher Magazine,* March 1993).

Rutter, M. (1979). Protective factors in children's responses to stress and disadvantage. In M. W. Kent & J. E. Rolf (Eds.), *Primary prevention of psychopathology, Vol. 3: Social competence in children.* (pp. 49–74). Hanover, NH: University Press of New England.

Rutter, M. (1984, March). Resilient children. *Psychology Today,* 57–65.

Rutter, M., Maugham, B., Mortimore, P., Ouston, J., & Smith, A. (1979). *Fifteen thousand hours.* Cambridge, MA: Harvard University Press.

Saleebey, D. (Ed.). (1992). *The strengths perspective in social work practice.* White Plains, NY: Longman.

Sarason, S. (1990). *The predictable failure of educational reform.* San Francisco: Jossey-Bass.

Schweinhart, L., & Weikart, D. P. (1986). *A report on the High/Scope Preschool Curriculum Comparison Study: Consequences of three preschool curriculum models through age 15.* Ypsilanti, MI: High/Scope Educational Research Foundation.

Seligman, M. (1975). *Helplessness: On depression, development, and death.* San Francisco: Freeman.

Slavin, R., Karweit, N., & Madden, N. (1989). *Effective programs for students at risk.* Needham Heights, MD: Allyn and Bacon.

Tobler, N. (1986). Meta-analysis of 143 adolescent drug prevention programs: Quantitative outcome results of program participants compared to a control or comparison group. *Journal of Drug Issues, 16,* 537–567.

Wallerstein, J. (1983). Children of divorce: The psychological tasks of the child. *American Journal of Orthopsychiatry, 53,* 230–243.

Wang, M. C., Haertel, G. D., & Walberg, H. J. (1994). Educational resilience in inner cities. In M. C. Wang & E. W. Gordon (Eds.), *Educational resilience in inner-city America: Challenges and prospects* (pp. 45–72). Hillsdale, NJ: Erlbaum.

Watt, N., et al. (1984). *Children at-risk for schizophrenia: A longitudinal perspective.* New York: Cambridge University Press.

Werner, E. (1989). High-risk children in young adulthood: A longitudinal study from birth to 32 years. *American Journal of Orthopsychiatry, 59,* 72–81.

Werner, E. (1990). Protective factors and individual resilience. In S. Meisels & J. Shonkoff (Eds.), *Handbook of early childhood intervention.* New York: Cambridge University Press.

Werner, E., & Smith, R. S. (1982). *Vulnerable but invincible: A longitudinal study of resilient children and youth.* New York: McGraw-Hill.

Werner, E., & Smith, R. S. (1992). *Overcoming the odds.* Ithaca, NY: Cornell University Press.

Wolin, S. J., & Wolin, S. (1993). *The resilient self: How survivors of troubled families rise above adversity.* New York: Villard.

chapter **12**

On Strengths, Niches, and Recovery from Serious Mental Illness

W. Patrick Sullivan

In the past few years, the term "recovery," once reserved for substance abuse treatment, has entered the lexicon of those primarily concerned with serious and persistent mental illnesses (Anthony, 1993; Sullivan, 1994a). In many respects, a focus on recovery requires fundamental shifts in (a) the manner in which the course of illnesses like schizophrenia are understood, (b) the design and delivery of professional interventions, and (c) the mission of specialty mental health services. While recovery is still an imprecise term, Anthony (1993) notes that recovery "is a way of living a satisfying, hopeful, and contributing life even with the limitations caused by illness" (p. 15).

Research on the recovery process among those with severe mental illness is at a nascent stage. However, preliminary explorations illustrate how strengths-based approaches to social work practice can aid the recovery process. Consistent with the basic tenants of social work, it is also clear that recovery must be understood as an interactive phenomenon, one that calls into play the efforts of the individual, the actions of the professional, and the marshaling of community forces and opportunities.

This chapter will examine the relevance of strengths-based approaches to the recovery process. In the first half of the chapter, the author offers insights of consumer-informants on the recovery process, as well as some intriguing findings from cross-cultural research on mental illness. Following is a discussion of the concept of "social niches" as developed by Taylor (1996, chapter 14, this volume). Finally, the implications for strengths-based social work practice, particularly in the design and delivery of mental health programs, are addressed.

RECOVERY: INDIVIDUAL, COMMUNITY, AND CULTURAL DIMENSIONS

There is little question that severe mental illnesses, such as schizophrenia and bipolar disorders, are the result of biophysical catastrophe. However, even at this point in history our knowledge of the etiology of these illnesses is incomplete and evolving. New techniques to study the brain are providing important information that help us understand and manage these conditions. Given the state of our knowledge, it is important to recognize that the long-term course of mental illnesses may simply reflect biophysical processes that cannot be detected at this time. In a similar fashion, cultural differences in outcomes may also be confounded by the same variables. Nonetheless, it is also clear that individual and cultural forces influence the understanding and response to disease and illness and exert some influence on the course of all disorders (Kleinman, 1980; Marsella, 1988). Accordingly, if recovery is to become a viable construct that guides practice and offers hope to those with severe mental illness, it behooves us to uncover the relevant personal and cultural variables that affect long-term prognoses.

A strengths model for social work practice should also call forth fresh research questions and agendas. A focus on recovery should elicit a similar response from mental health researchers. One simple way to decipher key variables in the recovery process is to learn from those who have successfully surmounted the challenges presented by neurobiological disorders. Such research elevates informants from the role of subject to expert, a basic premise that is consistent with the strengths perspective. Additionally, an exploration of the success experienced by this population counters the more common examination of relapse and rehospitalization rates.

The Recovery Process: Observations from Key Informants

In an early attempt to decipher key elements of the recovery process, 46 current and former consumers of mental health services were asked to identify, through semi-structured interviews, those activities, attitudes, and behaviors, initiated by self and others, that are essential to their success. All interviews were transcribed verbatim and analyzed using elements of Spradley's (1979) ethnographic interviewing method. These respondents could be characterized as facing severe and persistent mental illness and having extensive hospitalization histories. However, this sample had avoided psychiatric hospitalization for the past 2 years, were living in at least a semi-independent setting, and were engaged in some form of vocational activity (Sullivan, 1994a).

While there was an attempt to understand commonalties in the stories of these informants, by using the ethnographic interview method it was understood that each individual deals with the challenges presented by severe mental illness differently. Indeed, it has been argued that strengths-based interventions, particularly when driven by the development of an individualized care plan, affirm the uniqueness of each consumer. The data in Table 12.1 present the most commonly identi-

TABLE 12.1 Factors associated with success (*N* = 46)

Medication	72%
Community support service/Case management	67%
Self-will, self-monitoring	63%
Vocational activity (including school)	46%
Spirituality	43%
Knowledge about the illness/acceptance of the illness	35%
Mutual aid groups—supportive friends	33%
Significant others	30%

SOURCE: From Sullivan, W. P. (1994). A long and winding road: The process of recovery from mental illness. *Innovations and Research, 3*(3), 20. Reproduced with permission.

fied areas (listed as the percentage of respondents who identified this specific domain) noted by informants as important to their success.

Before taking a more specific look at some of these areas, it is useful to view them in totality. In many respects, these factors mirror the evolution of mental health services from institutional care to community-based services, and more recent efforts at normalization and full integration. It may be that professional services are now catching up with the needs of the consumer. Even the key elements of our language have changed, such as the movement away from the label "chronically mentally ill" as well as the more individual-specific progression from "patient," to "client," to "consumer," and perhaps finally, to "citizen."

The factors generated from the informants represent their acknowledgment of the challenge of mental illness, the identification of helpful services, a recognition of personal responsibility, and a proclamation of desire to participate in the normal activities of adulthood. Viewing the factors from a systems perspective, we see they extend from the inner self, through family, the community, and beyond. The task for social workers is to provide assistance that can help align these layered systems in a fashion that supports the recovery process.

Medication.   The use of medication, the most universally noted factor for success, represents the one area of standard medical treatment of mental illness highlighted by these individuals. One informant noted, "If I stay on my medicine I can live in the community just like anyone else." Even here, however, many consumers discussed difficulty in communicating with doctors about medication. Some described periods where dosages seemed to be extraordinarily high or particular medications did not agree with them. Practicing from a strengths-based approach requires that we take our cues from consumers, beginning with the assumption that they can inform us about what is needed to improve their life. This does not preclude the importance of dialogue or even deny that disagreements are likely—but beginning from the premise that consumers should be afforded the opportunity to make choices about their lives provides an important contextual backdrop for the recovery process to become activated.

Community Support Service/Case Management.   When we review the second highest factor identified by consumers as critical to their success, case management and community support services, similar themes also emerge. For it was not the technical facility of the case managers or the specific programming offered by community-based programs that the consumers identified as important; rather it was the strength of the relationships and the caring atmosphere and protection these programs and persons offered. Case managers were valued for their friendship and companionship, and for the fact that they looked after their charges while providing constant encouragement. These professionals also helped with basic problems in living and the daily hassles of life that become magnified for those facing severe mental illness. The programs offered basic safety and shelter and also made people feel welcome and wanted. These same programs helped provide structure and activities.

Self-Will, Self-Monitoring.   Some of the identified factors for success fell into a far more personal range. The notion that the actual behaviors of consumers, or the more illusive concept of self-will, affects the course of mental illness has received scant attention in professional literature. Indeed, as our understanding of biophysical processes has progressed, the appreciation of personal and cultural determinants in the illness/healing process has withered. These informants described the arduous process of recovery using phrases like "fighting spirit" and described periods where they had to "grit it out."

These same individuals also recognized their idiosyncratic signs of impending difficulty and learned to take proactive steps to cope and manage. Some of these actions were fairly traditional, such as calling their doctor to explore a possible medication adjustment. Others managed in their own unique way by listening to music, praying, or challenging their voices. In other cases, consumers chose to manage their stress by restricting some activities or being more mindful of their diet and sleeping habits. Thus, they were actively engaged in the process of managing a serious illness. It is important to note that by successfully surmounting crises, or by just dealing with day-to-day stress, consumers experienced a greater sense of personal power and an enhanced belief in their ability to exert control over their lives. This is in direct contrast to helping activities that essentially require consumers to hand over their lives to others. Helpers operating from a strengths approach explore and validate the consumers' personal experience of the illness and work with them to devise strategies to manage crisis and daily life hassles.

Spirituality.   Perhaps nothing is more personal than one's religious or spiritual beliefs. The postulated relationship between spirituality and mental illness takes a number of divergent paths. Certainly helpers have witnessed religious themes in the delusional systems of consumers. On the other hand, the efficacy of pastoral counselors, particularly in institutional settings, has an equally long history. Participation in formal religious activities, or even a deeply held set of spiritual convictions, is a central aspect of daily life for many individuals. Some people would feel vacant and rootless in the absence of such beliefs or the ability to exercise their faith. Respondents in this study, while often recognizing times where they became overindulgent in their beliefs and behaviors, spoke clearly of the importance of spirituality in their recovery.

The power of spirituality takes many forms. At the most basic level, some respondents experienced the instrumental and emotional support of a congregation. Others described moments in which they felt that their beliefs offered solace in the times of deepest despair. Prayer was often mentioned as important in times of crisis. It seems wise to consider spirituality as an important aspect of social support, and these reports suggest that the locus of this support does not rest solely in people or animate objects but may emanate from nonmaterial sources.

Mutual Aid Groups—Supportive Friends. There are, however, more observable sources of support that are identified as important to the recovery process. Mutual aid groups have become increasingly popular for a variety of human conditions and have become important aspects of the total system of care for those facing mental illness. In recent years, we have seen an explosion of consumer-focused and -managed support groups. The ability to learn and share with those in similar situations, to actually offer help to others, and to acquire relevant information, are key aspects of good support networks. It is also important to note that informal support appears to be critical to the recovery process. Among this sample of respondents, some had developed their own check-in and response system within an apartment complex. For many of these respondents, the ability to participate in a formal support group or simply to live among those who seemed to take a genuine interest in their lives was their first adult experience of being in a community.

Significant Others. In a similar vein, many of the consumers mention the power of their personal relationships—and here we are talking most specifically about romantic involvements not the support offered by family. The lack of attention to relationship building and sexuality among those with severe mental illnesses, as evidenced by the dearth of discussion in professional literature, is striking. Given the nature of severe mental illness, and the reality that difficulties often begin in late adolescence or early adulthood, it is not surprising that so many lead lonely lives. In fact, the ability to develop the confidence and skills needed to forge a relationship is an obvious sign of recovery. Once these relationships have been established, they also provide a level of support, stability, and strength that continues to fire the drive to do better. As one respondent noted: "When I met [my wife] she introduced me to the idea that I was somebody that someone else could get enjoyment from and I made quantum leaps after that because my self-image was poor." The sensitive professional provides basic information, helps with the actual skills of communication and relationships, and deals with the individual's feelings with concern and compassion. Thus, support is offered, not discouragement. The practitioner must be committed to the proposition that the consumer has the right to assume adult roles and responsibilities and must offer the necessary support to assist this progress.

Vocational Activity. Another key step in the normalization and recovery process is vocational activity. Vocational services have been a keystone of rehabilitation throughout the history of treatment services. In this study, vocational activity included such items as volunteer work, school, and maintaining a home. Nearly one-half of the respondents mentioned one of these activities as central to their recovery. Work provided needed structure, and remaining occupied kept attention off personal difficulties. More common, however, was an expressed desire to make a contribution to others. Waters (1992), offering the consumer perspective, notes that

> work puts us in a unique relationship with other human beings so that the opportunity to form meaningful relationships is readily available to us. Work also allows us to feel a common bond with the larger community and gives us a better picture of what our lives will be in the future. All people benefit from work . . . but in many ways, given the isolation and confusion that so often accompanies mental illness, people with psychiatric disorders may benefit most of all. (p. 40)

The percentage of those with severe and persistent mental illness who work is abysmally low. This is, in part, an interaction effect between the disability, the professional, and the workplace. Operating from a strengths perspective requires maneuvering around such boundaries and impediments while matching the inherent strengths of people with nurturing aspects of the community—an area that will be explored in-depth later in the chapter.

These respondents recognized the challenges they faced and have learned how to effectively manage the illness process. Yet, they have also displayed a desire to accomplish individual goals and participate in regular community discourse. This is not to suggest that these individuals are symptom-free or that there are guarantees that they will never face a significant setback. However, drawing from Anthony's (1993) tentative definition of recovery, these persons are enjoying satisfying and hopeful lives. Recovery is a distinctive lived experience, and certainly the contributing factors discussed here should in no way be construed as a recipe for success. However, these data, and the insights gained from cross-cultural studies, may point to those attitudes, behaviors, services, and systems that can support recovery.

Sociocultural Forces and Recovery

One of the most intriguing aspects of severe mental illness is that it affects people in a similar fashion, at similar points in the life span, and at similar rates throughout the world. Indeed, this universality (unlike many illnesses) implicates biophysical processes as prime suspects in the search for causative agents of severe mental illness. As noted above, *any* effort to understand the progression of these disorders must accept the role of currently undetectable forces in the biophysical realm. Yet, it is nearly fatalistic to assume that the affected individual exerts no influence, that professional interventions offer no tangible benefit, and that there are no cultural modifiers that *influence* the impact of such illnesses. There are, of course, many personal and empirical reports that support the relationship between behavior and attitudes on the disease process. In a similar fashion, cross-cultural studies are also suggesting the action of environmental/cultural forces on the course of illnesses like schizophrenia (Sullivan, 1994b).

The majority of cross-cultural studies that have examined the outcomes associated with severe mental illness have produced counterintuitive results. Specifically, such explorations have indicated that the prognosis for severe mental illness is much better in the developing world than in developed nations—this in spite of the range of professional services and interventions available in more developed nations. These findings, coupled with generally comparable incidence rates worldwide, point to the power of environmental forces in the recovery process even if merely indicative of a greater willingness to accommodate and support those with serious mental illnesses.

While some may doubt the robustness of this cross-cultural research, Warner (1992) notes that "the differences in the recovery rates in schizophrenia between the Third World and the West is so great that it must compensate for minor concerns about methodology" (p. 85). Taking this one step further, Lin and Kleinman (1988) suggest that the differences in outcomes uncovered in cross-cultural research have the most consistent support and may be the most significant finding among studies of this genre. Therefore, cross-cultural studies may provide further clues about recovery and suggest personal or professional actions that support the goal of recovery for those with severe and persistent mental illnesses. What follows is a short review of the range of theories and suppositions offered to account for disparities in outcomes cross-culturally.

In Western society the concept of the self is preeminent, and many of our helping endeavors deal with such phenomena as self-esteem, feelings of inadequacy or, on the other end of the spectrum, narcissism or grandiosity. There is a sense of firm boundaries between the self and others, and we embrace rugged individualism as a basic orientation. Severe mental illness and other disabling conditions are particularly traumatic in such a context. In the extreme, such persons are viewed as less than a total person. In this view, the individual is seen as changed in such a fundamental way that in many respects a different person exists as a result. Estroff (1989) has suggested that schizophrenia becomes an "I am" disease and becomes synonymous with one's sense of self.

In contrast, in much of the developing world, the sense of self is seen as permeable and malleable. More specifically, the self is often viewed as subject to influence from external forces and the spirit world. This paradigm provides a functional understanding of mental illness that reflects a belief that the resultant changes in personality and behavior are transient and subject to reversal. In many respects, this view of mental illness is hospitable to the vision of recovery. To embrace recovery as a mission for community care, and to practice from the strengths perspective, requires that hard dichotomies between health and illness be suspended. For example, many professionals resist interventions aimed at normalization because troublesome symptoms, or other manifestations of illness, are still present. This is the antithesis of the strengths approach, as demonstrated in case management practice for over 15 years and best practices in community care, where consumers' strengths, interests, and aspirations are accentuated and natural community supports are cultivated.

It has also been noted that the developing world often embraces a sociocentric orientation. In such settings, social relationships and group cohesiveness are valued more than individual achievement, consistent with differences in the concept of the self described above. The idea of permeable boundaries of the self paves the way for an organic view of family and community. In this scenario, disease, illness, and healing are community concerns. When community and self are merged, there is less impetus to exclude members. Lefley (1990) suggests that a world view that values interdependence reduces the internal and external stress a person with schizophrenia experiences. Recovery in such a setting "is very much a communal phenomenon, tending not only to reintegrate the deviant individual into the group but also to reaffirm the solidarity of the community" (Warner, 1983, p. 209).

In the developed world, the basic orientation can be characterized as egocentric, with emphasis placed on individual achievement and autonomy. This is reflected in the Western rehabilitation approach, where we strive to build social support networks but goals are clearly focused on individual accomplishment and independence. There certainly is nothing inherently wrong with such goals—but the ability to accomplish them requires input from the larger community, particularly in the form of supports and opportunities.

To illustrate, the previous section offered the observations of former and current consumers of mental health services. One of the key variables of the recovery process identified by this group was vocational activity. Unfortunately, in spite of a desire to contribute in a meaningful way, the percentage of those with severe mental illness participating in the work force is extremely low. The history of employment programs in the United States also reflects the adoption of a strengths/normalization paradigm as we have progressed from the sheltered workshop model to supported employment. However, this progress has required public education to reduce stigma, the creation of fiscal incentives to employers, and policy decisions to provide the allocation of funds needed to support such programs.

In contrast, Warner (1992) has noted that in the developing world people are allowed and needed to contribute at whatever level they can. Such a contribution is seen as central to the collective good of the community, and there is built-in flexibility to accommodate the individual. Not only does this allow the person to engage in activity that is seen, in a Western context, as therapeutic, but it is one more way that the person remains tied to the community.

Regardless of any desire to engage in romantic musing about a return to simpler times, the reality is that the basic organization of industrial and postindustrial society has reduced a collective sense of responsibility for others. Life and work are compartmentalized and the mobility of citizens has diminished the sense of community. It has also become increasingly difficult for people to care for their own given the multiple roles that must be played by members in a nuclear family. In the developing world, the presence of extended family and the collectivist orientation described above create a structure where burden can be shared. Yet, it is also clear that the burden experienced by families, particularly among the poor, is a universal problem (Yellowe-Martyns, 1992).

In spite of the caveats offered above, studies comparing families in the developing and the developed world reveal some interesting differences. One provocative area of study has been in expressed emotion (EE), a controversial subject in the psychosocial rehabilitation field. Expressed emotion, usually a measure of the regularity of negative and critical comments directed at family members with mental illness, has been identified as a predictor of subsequent relapse (see Lefley, 1992, for a review of the EE literature). Research has indicated that families in the developing world generally score lower on EE scales, indicating lower levels of EE, thus offering another hypothesis to explain cross-cultural differences in recovery (Lefley, 1990). Since expressed emotion may simply reflect the stress of caring for a family member with mental illness, the availability of supports may be an important confounding variable.

Another important consideration has been touched on above; that is, the basic cultural framework by which mental illness is understood and how care is delivered. In Western culture, birth and death, for example, are treated as medical conditions, and care has progressively moved to specialized facilities staffed with professionals. In most respects, mental health has adopted the same model.

It has been observed among some families, including Hispanic families in the United States, that the use of indigenous labels to describe mental illness reduces stigma, promotes a sense of optimism, and provides a framework that helps the coping process (Guarnaccia, Parra, Deschamps, Milstein, & Argiles, 1992; Swerdlow, 1992). Robinson (1993), in a similar vein, notes that families often cope with chronic illnesses by developing a normalization story. She suggests that professionals often disrupt this process by offering a problem-saturated perspective as opposed to providing the basic help and information one needs for "getting on with your life" (p. 20).

Kleinman (1980) sees important differences between the concepts of disease and illness. Disease is "the malfunctioning of biological and/or pathological processes" (p. 73). Studies of brain structure, information-processing capabilities, and biochemistry represent the modern search for the cause of the disease we label schizophrenia. Illness, on the other hand, is psychosocial in nature, and reflects the impact and context of this disease process. Thus, illness is an interactive process that must be understood within the individual/cultural transaction. In the West, a reductionist biotechnical approach is relied on. Yet healing, or recovery, is not only an interpersonal episode between an individual and a healer *but also a cultural phenomenon*, for as Kleinman (1980) notes, "the system as a whole, not just the healer, heals" (p. 72). Indeed, a significant failure of the mental health system to help those with severe illness, using Kleinman's terms, has been the lack of attention to the idea of illness.

The strengths model of case management and subsequent applications of the strengths paradigm in a number of fields offer a different approach to helping. Frequently our attempt to explain troubling conditions has forced us to blame the person or environment and stimulated efforts to correct the source of the malady. Unfortunately, so many of the conditions that cause human suffering are beyond cure or remediation—and in Kleinman's terms, the illness remains. The strengths model, consistent with the person-in-environment perspective adopted by social work, looks to capitalize on both individual and environmental strengths and, in the case of severe mental illness, support the recovery process.

Recovery and the Enriched Social Niche

The accounts of those successfully surmounting severe mental illness illustrate key elements of the tentative definition of recovery offered by Anthony (1993). These persons have persevered in their efforts to live in the community and perform the roles and functions germane to adulthood. Cross-cultural studies point to the important role of the community, or environment, in the recovery process, particularly in the areas of acceptance, opportunities, support, and accommodation.

Social work has long been guided by environmental/ecological models. Students are taught early on to consider the influence of both individual and environmental factors on human behavior, and to draw on this information in direct practice at all levels. Interventions are commonly designed to ameliorate individual or environmental factors thought to be the source of difficulty experienced by self or others. Strengths and competence models, in contrast, have focused on efforts to release or stimulate the capacities of people and the environment in order to maximize human potential. If the ecological framework is to guide social work practice and strengths-based models, then we should explore key elements of this paradigm to assess how it can guide our understanding of human needs, problems, and solutions (Brower, 1988; Taylor, 1996, chapter 14, this volume).

Brower (1988) has observed that human beings forge an accommodation with their environment—a task marked by action, decision making, goal setting, and perceptions of past and future experiences. Through this accommodation process the person comes to occupy a niche: "the unique place in which one 'fits' into the environment, the workplace or community. It is a special place within which one feels comfortable " (p. 412). Taylor (see chapter 14) has also explored the usefulness of this concept for human services. Taylor has defined the social niche as

> the places and conditions in which are found a specific category of persons, including the settings typically utilized by those persons, the source of resources available to those persons, the resources typically used by those persons, and other categories of people commonly found in association with those persons. (p. 219)

Taylor posits two ideal types of niches at polar extremes: entrapping and enabling.

It is far too common for those struggling with severe mental illness to occupy an entrapping niche. Entrapping niches are highly stigmatized, and people who occupy them are defined by their social category, or in this case, their illness. Because of stigma and the lack of opportunities, people must turn to others in like situations, and ultimately their social world becomes highly constricted. In the most

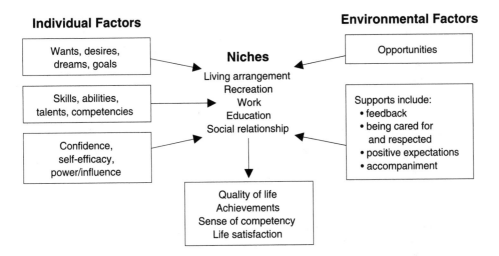

FIGURE 12.1 The creation of niches

SOURCE: From Sullivan, W. P., & Rapp, C. (1994). Breaking away: The potential and promise of a strengths-based approach to social work practice. In R. Meinert, J. T. Pardeck, and W. P. Sullivan (Eds.), *Issues in social work: A critical analysis* (p. 101). Westport, CT: Auburn House. Reproduced with permission of Greenwich Publishing Group, Inc., Westport, CT.

dire situations, the individual is segregated to such a degree that there is little reality feedback, and this limits the opportunity to learn from real-life experiences. Over time there is little expectation, on the part of self or others, that growth and change will occur.

Enabling niches, in contrast, offer a range of opportunities and experiences that facilitate growth and achievement. Setting long-term goals is expected and rewarded, and corrective feedback loops are omnipresent. Access to resources and opportunities increases the ability to have meaningful interaction with others who bring different perspectives and expand one's social world. In this environment, growth and development are both expected and encouraged.

The niche one occupies is the product of a host of individual and environmental forces. Figure 12.1 is a graphic representation of those forces that impact the kind of niche one occupies. Note that both individual and environmental factors are highlighted, and it is posited that the outcome of these inputs directly impacts quality of life and overall life satisfaction (see Sullivan & Rapp, 1994).

In the personal accounts offered by the respondents, opportunities and supports were obviously critical to success, as were innate talents and a heightened sense of confidence and self-efficacy. In the United States, community support programs (and one could argue all social services) attempt to provide emotional and functional support that may be naturally provided in some parts of the world. As community-based care for those with severe mental illness has evolved, there has been increased emphasis on normalization. Figure 12.2 presents a simple table highlighting the contrasting idealized niches described above and variables labeled natural and created. Each quadrant in this table will be described below.

	Natural	**Created**
Entrapping niche	**Natural exclusionary processes** Stigma Labeling Homelessness	**Institutionalization** Psychiatric hospitalization Sheltered workshops Group/board & care homes
Enabling niche	**Natural inclusionary processes** Work opportunities Family involvement Affiliation with community	**Normalization** Supported employment Supported housing Consumer programming Self-help

FIGURE 12.2 Natural and created niches

SOURCE: From Sullivan, W. P. (1994). Recover from schizophrenia: What we can learn from the developing nations. *Innovations and Research, 3*(2), 13. Reprinted with permission.

The social fabric, in some parts of the developing world, supports natural inclusionary processes and spawns natural enabling niches. The world view and cultural underpinnings of such settings create a context in which those with severe mental illnesses are assimilated in activities of daily life. There are opportunities for work and continued involvement with family and community, and illness is not fused with personal identity.

In the developed world these same individuals may occupy a naturally occurring entrapped niche—suggesting the presence of forces that tend to label and ostracize those defined as deviant. The ideology of rugged individualism, the focus on individual achievement, and other social factors, including the impact of an industrial or postindustrial economy and mobility, have reduced a sense of collective responsibility. In the rawest form, abject poverty and homelessness are the results of such forces. Individuals become disaffiliated from family and community and become objects in a netherworld recognized by some but ignored or avoided by many.

In the developed world, the traditional active response to those who face particularly troublesome problems, like severe mental illness, have created entrapping niches. Psychiatric institutions, sheltered workshops, and similar specialized programs fall into this category. This is not to suggest that these efforts are void of the humanitarian impulse. However, the end result of these programs is that they keep people physically, emotionally, and economically segregated from the mainstream. People are forced to live and work in such environments because it is believed that their illnesses make it impossible for them to do otherwise. In time, these people become defined by the illness, and their social world becomes constricted to a few select family members, others in similar situations, and professionals. Eventually there is a shared belief that specialized care or environments are necessary for a lifetime. This is the essence of entrapment.

The final quadrant in this scheme is the created inclusionary niche. While it is impossible, and perhaps even undesirable, to turn back the clock to simpler times, it is wise to remember that economic development and social development are not synonymous. In many respects, the United States is underdeveloped socially. The evolution of community-based services for those with severe and persistent mental illness reflects the adoption of the normalization perspective. The focus here is one of inclusiveness and civil rights. From this standpoint, social work practice with those facing severe mental illness should result in citizenship, not consumership. Strengths-based practice in mental health is consistent with this vision. It would appear that those social services that have the greatest opportunity to support recovery are those that can create a community-based context that mimics naturally occurring niches.

Strengths-based case management, for example, activates both individual and community factors that may have positive impact on life satisfaction. Beginning with assessment, this model seeks to identify areas of competence and invigorates the desire to maximize potential. The relationship that develops between case managers and consumers in community settings is not marked by distance but by collaboration and respect. The personal accounts offered above, for example, exposed those attributes of case managers that were valued—and the thrust of the strengths model of case management is consistent with these reports. In addition, the long-standing assumptions of the strengths model, that behavior is, in part, a function of the resources available to people and that equal access to these resources is a social value call forth nurturing qualities in the social environment (Rapp, 1992).

Vocational opportunities have been highlighted in both the individual recovery stories and the exploration of cross-cultural studies. While vocational rehabilitation has been a centerpiece of mental health treatment, the prevailing viewpoint can be described as "train then place." This model has proven to be particularly poor for those facing mental illnesses. The supported employment (SE) method, consistent with strengths-based practice, is based on the choose, get, and keep model of helping. Anthony and Blanch (1988), detailing a central premise of supported employment, assert that "all people—regardless of the severity of their disability—can do meaningful, productive work, in normal settings, if that is what they chose to do, and if they are given the necessary supports" (p. 7).

The choose-get-keep model has also been employed in other important areas. For example, so often housing has been viewed as a part of the treatment enterprise. Supported housing (SH), however, is based on the premise that people need a home, not a program. In traditional mental health services, people are often grouped on the basis of their disability. Those who are severely disabled reside in hospitals, and movement to less restrictive settings, from any place on the continuum, is contingent on changes in symptomatology or behavior. In a peculiar way, the disabled person must prove that she or he is ready for the next step toward independence and normalization. In the SH method, the primary focus is on two areas—choice and support. Again, it is believed that all consumers can live in the environment of their choice if offered necessary supports. In these models, it is believed that the failure to provide necessary support and accommodation, not the illness, leads to unsuccessful placements.

Returning to Figure 12.1, choose-get-keep models and strengths-based helping match key elements of the proposed scheme. Operating from the strengths method the practitioner begins by exploring the *wants, desires, dreams, and goals* of the individual. For many of those facing severe mental illness, it has been years since someone has asked these kinds of questions. Early work may involve honing or relearning old *skills and abilities,* or even perhaps learning new skills (and supported education models also exist). *Opportunities* may be the result of professional advocacy, but when normalization models are in place, access difficulties are reduced. Needed *support* may come from family, case managers, and job coaches, but it is hoped that over time natural supports will develop. Coworkers, members of a congregation, or a basketball team begin to take on the functions once only served by professional helpers. Finally, the ability to experience success can increase a sense of personal *competence and self-efficacy.* One respondent offering his success story noted, "When I got that chance to be stable and grab a few classes, getting the grades—it didn't take very long before that's what I wanted to do more than go manic." In short, attention to each of the areas identified in Figure 12.1 can operate synergistically to promote recovery.

Exploration of the key principles and values of strengths-based practice reveals the utility of this model in mental health services. The process of recovery from mental illness is far from linear; indeed, it is a long and winding road. Nonetheless, strengths-based models of helping make great sense when the effort is to improve the overall quality of life of those facing severe challenges. These strategies ameliorate the effects of biophysical challenge, affirm the uniqueness and dignity of the consumer, and provide individuals and families the help they need to get on with their lives. Such efforts are the heart and essence of social work practice. The reports of those who have successfully surmounted severe mental illness and the results of cross-cultural studies confirm the importance of assessing and activating individual and environmental strengths. While recovery for all who face severe mental illness may be an unreachable standard, it is the only acceptable goal for us to establish.

DISCUSSION QUESTIONS

1. What are the differences between enabling and entrapping niches? What sort of niches are provided for clients you work with? What affect do these niches have on recovery?
2. What is the difference between disease and illness (Kleinman, 1980)? In assessment, how would the idea of illness (as opposed to disease) affect your approach?
3. Why do you think there is a disparity between the way people with severe mental illness are treated in developing countries and the way they are treated in developed countries? What lessons could we learn from developing countries?

REFERENCES

Anthony, W. (1993). Recovery from mental illness: The guiding vision of the mental health system in the 1990s. *Psychosocial Rehabilitation Journal, 16*(4), 11–23.

Anthony, W., & Blanch, A. (1988). Supported employment for persons who are psychiatrically disabled: An historical and conceptual perspective. *Psychosocial Rehabilitation Journal, 11*(2), 5–23.

Brower, A. (1988). Can the ecological model guide social work practice? *Social Service Review, 62*(3), 411–429.

Estroff, S. (1989). Self, identity, and subjective experiences of schizophrenia: In search of the subject. *Hospital and Community Psychiatry, 15*(2), 189–196.

Guarnaccia, P., Parra, P., Deschamps, A., Milstein, G., & Argiles, N. (1992). *Si Dios Quiere:* Hispanic families' experience of caring for a seriously mentally ill family member. *Culture, Medicine, & Psychiatry, 16*(2), 187–215.

Kleinman, A. (1980). *Patients and healers in the context of culture.* Berkeley: University of California Press.

Lefley, H. (1990). Culture and chronic mental illness. *Hospital and Community Psychiatry, 41*(3), 591–598.

Lefley, H. (1992). Expressed emotion: Conceptual, clinical, and social policy issues. *Hospital and Community Psychiatry, 43*(6), 590–598.

Lin, M., & Kleinman, A. (1988). Psychopathology and clinical course of schizophrenia: A cross-cultural perspective. *Schizophrenia Bulletin, 14*(4), 555–567.

Marsella, A. (1988, Suppl, 344). Cross-cultural research on severe mental disorders: Issues and findings. *Acta Psychiatrica Scandinavica, 78,* 7–22.

Rapp, C. (1992). The strengths perspective of case management with persons suffering from severe mental illness. In D. Saleebey (Ed.), *The strengths perspective in social work practice* (pp. 45–58). White Plains, NY: Longman.

Robinson, C. (1993). Managing life with a chronic condition: The story of normalization. *Qualitative Health Research, 3*(1), 6–28.

Spradley, J. (1979). *The ethnographic interview.* New York: Holt, Rinehart, & Winston.

Sullivan, W. P. (1994a). A long and winding road: The process of recovery from mental illness. *Innovations and Research, 3*(3), 19–27.

Sullivan, W. P. (1994b). Recovery from schizophrenia: What we can learn from the developing nations. *Innovations and Research, 3*(2), 7–15.

Sullivan, W. P., & Rapp, C. (1994). Breaking away: The potential and promise of a strengths-based approach to social work practice. In R. Meinert, J. T. Pardeck, and W. P. Sullivan (Eds.), *Issues in social work: A critical analysis* (pp. 83–104). Westport, CT: Auburn House.

Swerdlow, M. (1992). "Chronicity," "nervios," and community care: A case study of Puerto Rican psychiatric patients in New York City. *Culture, Medicine, and Psychiatry, 16*(2), 217–235.

Taylor, J. (1996). Niches and practice: Extending the ecological perspective. Chapter 14, this volume.

Warner, R. (1983). Recovery from schizophrenia in the third world. *Culture, Medicine, and Psychiatry, 16*(1), 85–88.

Warner, R. (1992). Commentary on Cohen, prognosis for schizophrenia in the third world. *Culture, Medicine, and Psychiatry, 16*(1), 85–88.

Waters, B. (1992). The work unit: The heart of the clubhouse. *Psychosocial Rehabilitation Journal, 16*(2), 41–48.

Yellowe-Martyns, I. S. (1992). The burden of schizophrenia on the family. A study from Nigeria. *The British Journal of Psychiatry, 161,* 779–782.

chapter **13**

Community Development, Group Empowerment, and Individual Resilience

Dennis Saleebey

$\mathbf{T}$he profession of social work has gradually withdrawn much of its interest in, and emphasis on, community development and community organization as areas of practice, education, and inquiry. Some 25 years ago, nearly every school of social work had curricula, if not tracks, devoted to community organization. Today, few schools have a robust curriculum in any aspect of community, theory or practice. In this chapter, I would like to explore three interlocking, although rudimentary, developments that might have significant importance for the profession—in the restoration of theory and practice around community and the extension of the strengths perspective.

First, in a variety of fields outside of social work, there seems to be renewed interest in community phenomena, especially community development (Hanna & Robinson, 1994; Kretzmann & McKnight, 1993; Mills, 1995; Specht & Courtney, 1994). This "rediscovery" of community has brought refinements in thinking and action that have implications for the direction of the profession in the future. In addition, they provide some new language and perspectives with which to address the nettlesome problems of oppression, isolation, and marginalization that too many clients of social workers face.

Second, there has been a virtual explosion of knowledge in the field of individual, family, and community resilience (see chapters 2, 4, 11). Like the strengths perspective, these various literatures, developed somewhat independently, are founded in the idea that each individual and community has capacities, knowledge, and means that enhance revitalization. Likewise there are factors, some operating, others immanent, that elicit and sustain resilient behavior, relationships, and institutions. Furthermore, there is thought to be a complex and abiding calculus of resilience—that community and individual or group resilience are inextricably bound together (Kretzmann & McKnight, 1993; Mills, 1995).

Finally, the notion of empowerment, favored these days by so many groups from the spectrum of political beliefs and by many professions, can be put into dramatic relief by some of the ideas we will discuss. A noble ambition or sentiment, empowerment as a practice sometimes falls far short of its intention. Nonetheless, the idea of empowerment as a framework for practice is regaining considerable ground in social work (Gutierrez and Nurius, 1994; Kondrat, 1995; Lee, 1994).

Some of the concepts of the emerging approaches to community development will be discussed below and then illustrated with reference to a number of current programs that operate from a strengths- and assets-based framework.

COMMUNITY DEVELOPMENT: EMERGING IDEAS AND PRACTICES

Let us turn now to some of the emerging themes and practices around community development. A conviction that social workers have long prized but often forget in practice is that individual troubles and successes must be framed within the larger context of family, community, and society. To "decontextualize" individuals and groups as we attempt to help them is to strip away much of the essence of their identity. Community development harks us back to the time-honored belief in the importance of the person–environment interplay.

Some Basic Ideas about Community Development

A few simple ideas bespeak the basics of community development in the 1990s. Many of the conceptions of community development focus interest on making an accounting of, and using, the assets, resources, and strengths available in the community. In this view, the beginning steps in community development involve assaying what resources exist in the community; what human and physical capital underwrite community life; what competencies and resources the people who live and work there possess; what organizations and associations having roles to play contribute to community wealth (Kretzmann & McKnight, 1993). As in the strengths approach to practice with individuals, the first steps in the development process do not focus on the problems, deficits, and conflicts of the community. Rather, the emphasis is on first discovering the assets in the community.

Because practitioners are looking for and making an accounting of the resources, assets, and capacities of the community, they necessarily begin their work from within the community. External forces do exist and may even be crucial for community vitality. These factors ultimately will be addressed, but by searching for the assets, problem-solving capacities, and leadership in the community, practitioners stress the importance of locality, neighborhood, and interdependence.

Being serious about appreciating and stimulating the resources, capacities, and assets that abound in the community requires that community development workers constantly be on the lookout to build or reconfigure relationships between themselves and residents and formal resident associations (Kretzmann & McKnight, 1993; Mills, 1995; Shaffer & Anundsen, 1993). As one volunteer community developer in an inner-city program for the community's youth said, "I love it when somebody tells me, 'You can't change those kids. Those kids are no good.' They're never *our* kids, it's *those* kids. And my philosophy is that they're *our* kids. They're *my* kids and they're *our* kids, as a community" (McLaughlin, Irby, & Langman, 1994, p. 97). The fundamental principle abides that the community and its surround may have the internal resources to propel the residents to a place of increasing energy, synergy, growth, prosperity, and progress, but the vehicle is often the development of trusting, caring, and responsible relationships.

For a variety of reasons, these ideas have been devastated in the 1980s and 1990s thanks, in part, to the forces of segregation, isolation and alienation, the separation of work and residence, and, importantly, the increasing inequity in the distribution of wealth and other social resources (Lind, 1995). So "the sense of efficacy based on interdependence, the idea that people can count on their neighbors and neighborhood resources for support and strength has weakened. For community builders who are focused on assets, rebuilding [and building] . . . local relationships offers the most promising route toward successful community development" (Kretzmann & McKnight, 1993, p. 10). Regrettably, individuals and communities, especially those struggling against poverty, oppression, and isolation, often do not think of themselves as having an accessible fund of assets. Those outside the community, too often service providers as well as other institutions and individuals, act on stereotypes, myths, unquestioned assumptions about who people really are, and clearly do not regard them as having strengths and competencies. As Paula Wehniller says, "When there are walls of ignorance between people [and communities], when we don't know each other's stories, we substitute our own myth about who that person or community is. When we operate with only a myth, none of that person's or people's truth will ever be known to us" (Benard, 1994, p. 380). What assumptions, for example, do we make about the people who live in a given public housing complex? about the environment itself? and where did we acquire those suppositions? To operate as a professional seeking assets, searching out resilience, is to turn your back on stereotypic, certainly class-based, and often media-induced, misunderstanding. In community development, a strengths- and assets-based orientation can induce optimism, hope, and motivation *for both clients and workers.*

From all this, we may conclude the following about community and about community development . . . "a community is a dynamic whole that emerges when a group of people

- participate in common practices,
- depend on one another,
- make decisions together,
- identify themselves as part of something larger than the sum of their individual relationships,
- commit themselves for the long term to their own, one another's and the group's well-being" (Shaffer & Anundsen, 1993, p. 10).

In this view, community development involves helping unleash the power, vision, capacities, and talents within a (self-defined) community so that the community can strengthen its internal relationships and move closer toward performing the important functions of solidarity and support, succor and identification, and instructing and socializing. The community must also be helped to strengthen its relationship to outside institutions, associations, and organizations. These can be the lifeblood that allows the community to find its heart, solve its problems, and reach its goals. But the primary resources to be found and employed are the strengths and resiliency, the skills and talents of the residents and members of the community.

COMING TOGETHER: COMMUNITY AND INDIVIDUAL RESILIENCE

Let us review here some of the ideas and conclusions from the varied fields of resilience research. We will see, as we do, that there is a growing sense that individual and familial resilience and the characteristics of the communities in which people live are inseparable. While there is not general agreement on all of the following, there is much to think about.

- Most children who are raised in chaotic, violent, disorganized family environments do better than we would probably predict (Garmezy, 1994; Masten, 1994; Vaillant, 1993). That does not mean that they do not bear scars, suffer or even develop disorders of various kinds. They do. But they also show some remarkable, often subtle, capacities that have flowered as they struggled with adversity. As an instructive example, most children of alcoholic parents do not become alcoholic. Rather, the large majority, from 70 to 92 percent (depending on their circumstances as children), become stable, well-functioning adults, who deliberately construct and define their adult life without alcohol or drugs (Peele & Brodsky, 1991; Wolin & Wolin, 1993). In order to do this, however, there must be for them a community of interest and relationships, and a connection to that community that reinforces those values supporting a salutory lifestyle (Peele & Brodsky, 1991).

- It is not a specific group of individuals who are resilient; rather, each individual has the capacity for resilience, at least potentially. It was formerly thought that resilience was an exclusive property of certain kinds of people blessed with particular genetic/constitutional characteristics, interpersonal relationships, traits, and environments. Now the effort is to discover the processes by which anyone might rebound or regenerate following adversity or decline (Benard, 1994; Garmezy, 1994; Wolin & Wolin, 1993). Having discovered those processes, we might well think about how they can be transformed into lessons, possibilities, and directions for others who labor under the burden of trauma, abuse, and illness. It is certain, too, that resilience for many children and adults is a communal phenomenon (Benard, 1994).

- Finally, two related ideas mark the importance of these areas of inquiry: *Resilience is a process,* often developmental, and *it can only be understood in context.*

As Benard says, "The fostering of resilience operates at a deep structural, systemic, human level, at the level of relationships, beliefs, and opportunities for participation and power that are a part of every intervention, no matter what the programmatic focus" (1994, p. 7). In this regard, decades of research continue to show that resilience is a process and an effect of *connection.* In Rutter's words, "Development is a question of linkages that happen within you as a person and also in the environment in which you live. . . . Our hope lies in doing something to alter these linkages, to see that kids who start in a [difficult] environment don't continue in such environments and develop a sense of impotency'" (Benard, 1994, p. 8). To Emmy Werner and Ruth Smith, who have done the most ambitious longitudinal study of resilience and vulnerability (see chapters 11 and 15), effective interventions (including natural ones) in every arena must reinforce the natural social bonds between young and old, between siblings, between friends, "that give meaning to one's life and a reason for commitment and caring" (1982, p. 163).

The research on resilience challenges us to build this connectedness, this sense of belonging—by helping to transform families, schools, and communities to become "psychological homes" where people can find caring and support, respect, and opportunities for meaningful involvement. Everyone has the potential for self-righting, the self-correction of life course, but it doesn't operate in a vacuum; it operates when environments challenge and support, provide protective and generative factors. Mclaughlin, Irby, and Langman, after their research into the inner city and effective leaders and programs for youth, quote former gang-banger Tito as summing it up most aptly, "Kids can walk around trouble, if there is someplace to walk to, and someone to walk with" (1994, p. 219).

In a very important sense, then, fostering resilience, capitalizing on and extending strengths and capabilities is about building community and creating opportunities for belonging and participation. This is where the paths of community development and resilience cross. As social workers we know this, we certainly claim it: that we work both sides of the psychosocial street, the individual and the environment, and the transactions between them. In fact, however, our recent history suggests that we have turned away—not completely, but too frequently—from our community obligations and the contextual side of practice. "Most important, social work's objective is to strengthen the community's capacity to solve problems through the development of groups and organizations, community education, and community systems of governance and control over systems of social care" (Specht & Courtney, 1994, p. 26).

According to Kelly, "The long-term development of the 'competent community' depends on the availability of social networks within the community that can promote and sustain social cohesion within the community. . . . That is, the formal and informal networks in which individuals develop their competencies and which provide links within the community are a source of strength for the community and the individuals comprising it" (Benard, 1991, p. 15). These words bespeak the importance of *caring and support* across the lifecycle and within the community.

Another important protective, maybe even generative, factor in a community, and this seems especially relevant for youth, is the existence of normatively *high* but not inappropriate *expectations,* seeing "potential not pathology" (McLaughlin, Irby, & Langman, 1994, p. 96; see also Benard, chapter 11, this volume). "Loving agendas [sic] and positive missions with productive and healthy purposes" for youth in trouble in communities are essential (McLaughlin, Irby, & Langman, 1994, p. 97). Unfortunately, many communities see only gangs, drug abuse, delinquency, truancy, violence, and shrink from providing youth the expectations of possibility, and the connections to health-promoting people, places, and programs. The community and its membership, manifest in its face-to-face relationships, are powerful media for developing, sustaining, and enforcing expectations and norms. Those expectations that are communicated explicitly through the values, actions, and relationships within the community are the most durable and potent. Such expectations also encourage involvement in the community, imply membership, and foster the development and use of the capacities, strengths, and assets of individuals and families.

Related to the persistent communication of high expectations is the creation of *opportunities for people to be contributing members* of their community; opportunities for valued and consequential ways to be involved in family, work, school, associations, and the community at large. High expectations make no sense unless there is the prospect of becoming a collaborating community member, a real citizen with portfolio. A tragedy today in neighborhoods at all socioeconomic strata is that many people have little real chance for participation in the life of a given community whether we are talking of political concerns, economic development, or social/associational relationships. This particularly true in the case of youth.

> The unique energy and creativity of youth is often denied to the community because the young people of the neighborhood are all too often viewed only in terms of their lack of maturity and practical life experience. categorized as the product of "immature" minds, the legitimate dreams and desires of youth are frequently ignored by the older, more "responsible" members of the community. . . . Given the proper opportunities, however, youth can always make a significant contribution to the development of communities in which they live. What is needed for this to happen are specific projects that will connect youth with the community in ways that will increase their own self-esteem and level of competency while at the same time improving the quality of life of the community as a whole. (Kretzmann & McKnight, 1993, p. 29)

Finally, although not necessarily related to community per se, the resilience research strongly demonstrates, across culture and class, that "resilient youngsters . . . [have] at least one person in their lives who accept[s] them unconditionally, regardless of temperamental idiosyncrasies, physical attractiveness, or intelligence" (Werner & Smith, 1992, p. 205). In Alice Miller's words, this means the presence of someone in a child's life who acts as a "sympathetic witness" (1990, p. 50).

EXEMPLARS OF COMMUNITY DEVELOPMENT PRACTICE

What follows is a brief look at four community development programs and philosophies. Although the language is different in each of them, they are all clearly assets and strengths based. Following presentation of these programs, let us draw some lessons for social work community development practice.

Building Communities from within: The Assets-based Approach

Recognizing that many communities in the United States are either devastated physically and civically or deeply disturbed, John Kretzmann and John McKnight of the Center for Urban Affairs and Policy Research at Northwestern University have said this:

> In response to this desperate situation, well-intended people are seeking solutions by taking one of two divergent paths. The first, which begins by focusing on a community's needs, deficiencies and problems, is still by far the most traveled, and commands the vast majority of our financial and human resources. By comparison with the second path, which insists on beginning with a clear commitment to discovering a community's capacities and assets, and which is the direction [we] recommend, the first and foremost path is more like an eight-lane superhighway. (p. 1)

In the view of Kretzmann and McKnight (1993), each community has a surfeit of assets and resources, often unrecognized or underutilized. This is especially true of marginalized communities where individuals and groups have had to learn to survive under difficult and often rapidly changing conditions. These assets should be accounted for and mapped as a basis for working with and from within a community. The resources to be weighed are not just those of individuals but include local citizens' associations, those informal organizations in which citizens come together for the purpose of problem solving and/or building solidarity. More formal institutions—schools, government entities, businesses, churches, health and welfare organizations, colleges and universities—should likewise be included in the mapping of human and social capital within a community.

Three principles define this approach. First, it is *assets and strengths based.* Community workers start with what resources are present in the community and *not* with what is missing, what is wrong, or what the community needs. Second, this approach to community development is *internally focused.* That is, it is very important to know what is going on within the community, what assets are available, and what individual and group capacities exist. The role of external factors and institutions is ignored. Rather, for the time being, the focus on the inner life of the community demonstrates the centrality of local control, local capital, local vision, and local ownership. Finally, if the first two elements of the assets-based scheme are to hold, then the process must clearly be *relationship driven.*

If people are to be pulled into the life of the community and share their capacities, it will be done through the medium of relationship. A gift is given from hand to hand.

A significant part of assets-based community development occurs in the beginning with taking a capacity inventory, a strengths assessment, or a catalogue of community assets. The inventory is not a formal research tool. Its primary purpose is to gather information about, say, a specific person (it could also be family, organization, association, or institution) in order to see what they might give to a community "resource bank" and to help that person make a contribution to the community. But, this is a two-way street and that person should receive the gifts of resource and skill development, perhaps even education, income, and employment as well. What is actually done to help an individual contribute and receive the gifts of involvement, resource acquisition, and skill development? The practitioner must know how to

- assess the individual's skills and strengths, and then link them to the needs and aspirations of other residents or groups.
- add up the cumulative resources of individuals and groups in the community and, with the residents, combine them in the development of programs and resources the community genuinely wants and needs (for example, a food pantry, or a child care service).
- ensure that all those who make a contribution to the human and resource capital of the community have the opportunity, through connection with others, to move toward achieving personal and familial goals, to create or develop an enterprise, or to solve problems.
- help residents strengthen their sense of community through the development of activities that symbolically and practically cement ties between individuals and groups (for example, a street fair, a mini-grants program).
- help ensure that individual well-being and resilience are a part of all community activities; that there is real work, real responsibility, real opportunity to produce income, and genuinely positive expectations of success and accomplishment (Benard, 1991; Kretzmann & McKnight, 1993; McLaughlin, Irby, & Langman, 1994; Mills, 1995).

While the idea is to *connect* people as well as local associations and groups through the bartering of their capacities and resources, strengths, and competencies for mutual benefit, clearly none of this happens without the full involvement and direction of residents. Important, too, is the necessity to link residents with local businesses, local institutions and service providers, and other sources of capital and credit. Recognition of resident and community assets may be obscured by the shadow of labels such as "ex-con," "mentally retarded," "mentally ill," "drop-out," or in the case of associations and communities—"gang," "problem group," or "target population." But the root idea of community development is to identify local capacities and mobilize them, which involves *connecting people with capacities to other people, associations, institutions, and economic resources* (Kretzmann &

McKnight, 1993): "[E]very living person has some gift or capacity of value to others. A strong community is a place that recognizes those gifts and ensures that they are given. A weak community is a place where lots of people can't give their gifts and express their capacities" (p. 27). A true community, then, is inviting and encourages participation. The Foundation for Community Encouragement puts it this way, "A true community is inclusive, and its greatest enemy is exclusivity. Groups who exclude others because of religious, ethnic, or more subtle differences are not communities" (Shaffer & Anundsen, 1993, p. 12).

In the case of senior citizens, for example, their potential is augmented by the fact that they may have time, they have history and experience and often economic resources, and they are very likely to be a part of a larger peer group that can be mobilized. To release seniors' capacities, making an account of the resources of elders in a given community or association is essential; but then an inventory of the resources of local individuals, associations, and institutions must be either completed or, if completed, consulted. Following that, the building of strong and mutually beneficial "partnerships" between local seniors and other individuals, associations, and institutions is requisite. Finally, having established strong connections, bonds, and alliances within the community, then additional affiliations with resources outside the community may be built. Kretzmann and McKnight offer some examples:

- Seniors are involved in the Visiting Important Persons Program in which they visit less mobile elderly and try to assist with any practical problems. Seniors are trained to be able to provide CPR, to recognize drug abuse, to give bed baths and first aid, and to help with practical daily matters like budgeting and food selection and preparation. The oldest participant is an 82-year-old woman.
- Latch key kids who are feeling lonely, experiencing a crisis or just want to chat, can call on the telephone from their homes of senior citizens through the "Grandma Please" program.
- Seniors are recruited and trained to acquaint them with the local police station and other citywide departments. As a result, seniors visit other seniors in a door-to-door campaign in order to provide security evaluations and advice. (pp. 59–60)

Assets-based community development work, although not always known by that name, is occurring around the country. The West Philadelphia Improvement Corps and Atlanta Clark University's Partners in a Planned Community program are just two examples of programs that have their focus, among other things, on the capacity of the community to invigorate itself.

Health Realization/Community Empowerment

The work of Roger Mills (1995) has led quickly to broad application in a number of fields including addictions, education, community policing, community development, and public housing, among others. It began with a demonstration project in a

Dade County, Florida housing project in the 1980s, a housing project like many others beset with the results of poverty and racism—hopelessness, lack of opportunities and skills, high rates of violence, drug-dealing, domestic violence, teen pregnancy, and school failure (even though these problems did not characterize most families and individuals in the community). After three years, comparative analysis of the results of pre- and posttests of 142 families and 604 youth revealed improved parent–child relationships in 87 percent of the families; a 75 percent reduction in delinquency and school-related problem behaviors; a 65 percent decrease in drug trafficking (pp. 128–139). Mills did all the "right stuff" at the outset: fostering community ownership early on and developing collaborative relationships across many systems. A lengthy quote here will give some of the flavor of the program.

> We did everything we could to reduce sources of stress when we began our public housing programs in 1987. We helped our clients with emergency rental needs, paid utility bills, and provided supplementary food, clothing, and physical security. We offered job training and day care assistance. We worked hard to make circumstances easier for our clients. . . .
>
> At the same time, we never lost sight of the bottom line. . . . We wanted to see what could happen when people learned some practical ideas about how they could take charge of their own thinking. We hypothesized that they would begin to handle adversity with more hope and self-respect and find ways to improve their circumstances both as a community and on their own. We trusted that our clients' innate intelligence would surface as soon as they could drop their attachment to alienated or insecure patterns of thinking. We suspected and hoped that the buoyancy of the human spirit would deliver the resiliency they needed to frame their prospects and capabilities in a more hopeful light. (Mills, 1995, p. 128)

First, the principles that guided the program were consonant with some of the findings of the resilience research: the idea that resilience (the capacity to be relatively healthy despite exposure to a variety of severe risks and stresses) is *innate;* the idea that resilience is *directly accessible;* and that organismic wisdom, intelligence, and common sense inhere, to some degree, in all individuals.

Second, the goal of "health realization," according to Mills, is to "reconnect people to the health in themselves and then direct them in ways to bring forth the health in others. The result is a change in people and communities which builds up from within rather than being imposed from without" (Benard, 1994, p. 22). Again the importance of the idea of connection surfaces: For communities to make themselves more resilient, there has to be a critical mass of individuals and families who become attached to one another and committed to the community.

Third, the methods of health realization are based on the idea that people construct meaning in their lives. This meaning is expressed in thoughts, manifest in behavior, and fateful for the resilience and energy of the individual. Two sources of meaning (or thoughts) are: (a) those that are primal and indigenous—the immanent wisdom of the body/mind, the things that we appear, given a chance, to intuitively understand and know about ourselves and our world; and (b) those that are socialized—thoughts that are engendered in us over time by others, by social institutions, by media, by the very culture itself. For too many people, these latter accretions of meaning add up to assumptions of fear, inadequacy, and marginalization. These conditioned networks of thoughts weave the imagery of victimization, a symbolism of blame, and an array of negative expectations (Mills, 1995). Feelings of anger, depression, and despair are the unfortunate progeny of these constructions. Such feelings often are expressed in victimizing or abusive behavior toward the self and others.

Fourth, health realization is based on "teaching" one to listen and hear the message of health, resilience, possibility, and hope. But this teaching (which will eventually be done by residents for each other) can only be done after creating a positive, caring, collaborative, egalitarian relationship. Mills puts it this way, "Perhaps the most vital ingredient is the establishing of empowering relationships" (1993, p. 29). He refers to "being in a state of service" in which "[w]e have no personal agenda other than what's in the client's best interest" (1993, p. 30).

Fifth, once you "live" the principles with your clients and in your professional life, then community organizing principles come to the fore, such as enlisting a core group of people, creating a forum for them to meet regularly in small groups, and facilitating the establishment of collaborative relationships with other residents, service providers, government agencies, and the marketplace.

Sixth, this model builds at the grass-roots level a critical mass in each community, and then between communities, that will help create change and put pressure in the right places to move toward policy changes that support human well-being and individual and collective efficacy.

The approach to members of the community occurs individually and in groups and is educative and informative as well as "therapeutic," intending to help people discover the strength, capacity, and wisdom within. Establishing a respectful, collaborative, light-hearted relationship with residents—a relationship that sees clients as equals and as having the potential for insight, change, and growth—is essential. Furthermore, all individuals and groups are seen as potential teachers and "therapists" for other constituents of the community. Most important, it requires that helpers be in the real world of residents, in real time, and teach the power of hope. "The process of building rapport, of listening deeply to someone else's world, of assisting them learn how to use their own common sense and innate wisdom, are all part of any empowering relationship. . . . We usually have . . . permission to be a teacher, but it helps to remember always that what we really are is a facilitator. We are facilitating the other person realizing the resources they already have in them for health, insight, and wisdom" (Mills, 1995, p. 121).

University of Kansas Partners in Public Housing (KU Outreach)

Begun in 1989, this is a community-based, strengths-oriented, and family-centered program in a public housing community, recently expanded to another public housing community. The staff is primarily first-year M.S.W. students, but there is a professional project coordinator, a director to oversee the entire project, and a case manager.

The project is based on two interrelated goals: (1) helping residents move toward initiating those changes that would make the community a better place to live on the community's own terms and by the community's own definition; and (2) helping the residents find, marshal, and employ individual and collective resources, strengths, and competencies in developing creative and efficacious approaches to meeting needs, solving problems, solidifying relationships, and bringing the community together. In attempting to accomplish these goals, we worked initially with community leaders in carving out specific areas of operation. Three, in all, were settled on.

Case Management and Direct Services.   These are basic services. Many individuals and families, from time to time and under the enormous pressures of poverty, unemployment and underemployment, as well as the expected demands of child rearing and self-care, find themselves in crisis or at great risk for destabilization. All of these factors are aggravated by periodic rises in drug traffic and violence. Case management is resource and situation management, driven by the need to coordinate and achieve access to existing services, and, with clients, to ensure the relevancy and continuity of the service. But that's only half of the story. The other half is the identification and elaboration of the client's or family's own resources, talents, skills, knowledge, and strengths, as well as connecting people to the "natural resources" within and around the community. Case management means advocacy, brokerage, education, support, facilitation, and collaboration. Whether student or professional, the case manager, in essence, is the *agent* for the family or individual. Social workers, in their case manager role, are also builders of networks, assisting families and individuals to help each other through life-skill building, community program development, and a variety of collaborative activities in the community. There is a direct relationship between the strengths and capacities of individuals and families and those of the community.

Technical Assistance.   The Department of Housing and Urban Development (HUD) had the idea some years ago, under Jack Kemp's leadership, that money and resources should be directed at helping the residents move toward managing their own communities and, eventually, owning them. The latter is probably never going to happen, nor is it clear if it ever should, but the former is a good idea that requires practical support and experience. The fact is the residents, like residents of any community, have not learned how to govern and manage their community or neighborhood. So KU Outreach set out to assist the Resident Management Corporation board (a group of residents of this particular public housing complex, elected by other residents, who supervise the government and management of the community) by providing a range of educational and supportive activities that were intended to enhance the skills, and develop the resources needed to accomplish this daunting task of self-management. Students and staff helped with everything from developing goals and the tasks required to achieve them, to developing agenda and running meetings, to teaching grant writing, to doing outreach to the rest of the community to involve them in management and governance.

Community Development.   Assets and needs surveys of residents were helpful early on to guide the efforts of KU Outreach and identify resident leaders and people willing to give their talents to the community. On the basis of these surveys, the unit developed a mini-grants program. Up to $200 was made available to any resident who wrote a proposal for a program or project that a panel of students and residents determined would help develop and support some part of communal life. Some of the programs funded over the years included a girls drill team, a boys softball team, a bible study class for young mothers, an aerobics class, Saturday treks to the movies for kids, and a fishing expedition for residents. These activities were meant to encourage residents to "donate" their talents to the community, to engender positive relationships, and to strengthen some elements of community life. In the face of drug dealers and the potential for violence, it was important for residents to forge relationships with each other, to engage in "normalizing" activities, to discover their own resources, and to experience the affirmation of solidarity.

Another part of community development is launching symbolic activities that enhance and embolden the sense and reality of communal togetherness and connection. Street fairs, Kwaanza celebrations, a youth talent show, community Thanksgiving meals, Friday bingo games, a trip to the University of Kansas to see the wonderful photographic exhibit, "I Dream a World" (in which the lives of strong and remarkable African-American women were celebrated in story and picture), and many others became occasions for residents to connect, to celebrate, to relax, and to renew some long forgotten talents and hopes.

Of great importance in practice in any outreach program are the following:

- *Making an alliance with the dreams and hopes of the residents.* Most of the residents are working hard, against great odds—mental distress, the effects of physical abuse or struggle with an addiction—to achieve their dreams: to own a bed and breakfast; to make sure that children finish high school; to become an illustrator or cartoonist; to open a child-care facility, to become a carpenter's apprentice; to go to a community college; to own a home.

- *Connecting inner and outer resources and strengths to the dreams.* In developing a plan of work with residents, the steps to be taken toward achieving their goals, both grand and modest, are often marked by employing their own resources and assets. Important, too, for strengths-based work is helping to remove the institutional and interpersonal barriers that block the path to hope. Ms. Edwards paints a cartoon character mural on one of the walls of the community building. The children love it. The social worker encourages her to develop a portfolio and to show it to a local greeting card company. All the while, Ms. Edwards is grappling with a long-standing alcohol problem. But she moves forward, and as she does her motivation increases, and her drinking subsides. She knows the reality of what she is doing. The social worker (a student) talks with her about the difficulties in getting started, but also shares her deep faith in Ms. Edwards and her motivation, and discusses with her other avenues for her talent.

• *Identifying the barriers to the dream and working to surmount them.* Many obstacles are present to people accustomed to living in poverty, suffering from the oppression of marginality and discrimination. It is important to identify them, especially structural, political, and economic ones. It is likewise important to help the individual recognize the difference between real barriers and the conditioned thoughts implanted over the years that undermine self-esteem.

• *Demonstrating in the helping relationship the continuing belief in the innate resilience and wisdom of the individual.* Sometimes buried under years of neglect, obscured by years of strife, and belied by misfortune, the capacity for self-righting and regeneration waits to be tapped. The social worker's assumption that it is there, that it does sometimes manifest itself in everyday activities, and that it has a potential to revise and renew feeds into the individual's own willingness to take chances, to have the courage to pursue a dream, and to affirm oneself in the process. Our students are continually surprised by the inherent capacities of the individuals they work with.

We do recognize that life in public housing is stressful, sometimes dangerous, and too often lacks acknowledgment and support from the surrounding community. Frequently, public housing residents live under siege conditions, conditions that few of us can imagine. Certainly, we should be able to expect from politicians and policy makers the civic and physical resources that acknowledge the full citizenship of these residents and the necessity of public housing as an important social stock. But without these resources, we are obliged to work with residents in whatever way we can to bring about the kind of individual, familial, and communal life they seek.

Yachdav: Working with Mothers Whose Children's Development Is at Risk (Israel)[1]

Yachdav is an example of a kind of community development that works to help isolated and alienated people forge communal ties with each other. It is a program for mothers whose children appear to be at risk for problems in well-being and development, both physical and emotional. Most of the families are in poverty and

---

[1] The information about Yachdav is from a report prepared by JDC-Brookdale Institute describing eight programs in Israel that have successfully served families previously thought to be resistant to service. The report is entitled *Out from Under*, and was put together by Jona M. Rosenfeld, Donald A. Schön, and Israel J. Sykes. The information about Yachdav appears on pp. 37–55. (Published by JDC-Brookdale Institute of Gerontology and Human Development in Jerusalem, 1995.)

have a long history of despair, and, occasionally, abuse. These families are isolated and marginalized in their communities. Most social and health service providers have given up on them.

Yachdav has programs in 15 cities in Israel and serves over 200 mothers and their over 700 children. In spite of so-called evidence to the contrary from other service providers, the operating philosophy at Yachdav is that *every* mother wants the best for her child. The goals for the mothers include improving self-esteem, improving the skills required for parenting, learning how to use the services they need and to which they are entitled, developing patience and persistence in learning and using parenting skills, and becoming less isolated in their social world. The program operates through the development of groups of mothers who go through a process of mutual development, care, education, socialization, and help under the guidance of professionals.

The operating principles of the Yachdav are clearly consonant with a strengths approach. *Empowerment* of the mothers involves encouraging them to recognize and use the strengths they possess. As one of the professionals involved in the program said, "It was a very difficult emotional and cognitive process for the workers to make the change from a paternalistic to a cooperative relationship. . . . We learned to include the women in every decision, even in very small matters. They know what's best for themselves" (Pnina Pecker, quoted in Rosenfeld, Schön, & Sykeson, 1995, p. 38). It is also important to provide *nurturing and caring* for these mothers who often have lived without it. This consists of simple amenities and pleasures: listening, acknowledging their distinctive stories and experiences, providing support, breaking bread together. Every meeting of the group is "built on creating a common experience which allows everyone to learn and share something of themselves" (p. 39). *Self-expression through creative means* enables a "woman to talk about personal issues without feeling anxious or threatened. It paves the way for them to work through their own life experiences and start reflecting on themselves and their lives" (p. 39). This might occur through the sharing of drawings, stories, tape recordings, music, or games. As in other strengths-based approaches, *reaching out* to consumers is a critical act of faith and trust; to make contact and show authentic concern every step of the way.

> Obviously a major emphasis of the program is on teaching and sharing parenting skills but these are always accomplished in a group and on the terms relevant to the individuals own lifeworld. The success of the program is written in the diminished risk to the children in terms of health, safety, and attention. Educationally, most of the children were doing better, but, for some, there were still some problems in achieving at an appropriate level academically and, for others, there were emotional problems ostensibly related to persistently high levels of stress in some of the families. But all in all these 700 children, two years later, stood a much better chance of growing well, developmentally and educationally. For the mothers, there was decreased isolation and renewed self-esteem and self-reliance. As one of the group members related about her current situation and her experience in the group:

"First of all, lots of the girls have already come out of their shells. One of them wanted to learn administrative management, and she didn't know how to read or anything. Listen, all this makes me happy. Now she's succeeded. During the Gulf War she studied; she bought books, learned things that she didn't know, like arithmetic. Zohar, the teacher here, sat with her. She was a wonderful teacher. She gave her private lessons, sat with her at home at night. Listen, she helped her advance and it didn't take so long. She's wanted to work in administrative management for a long time, but she didn't succeed. She kept taking the tests but she always failed, and now she's succeeded." (p. 52)

And later,

[In our group] each one helps the other. In our group, we don't leave one another; there's no such thing. (p. 52)

In discussing the success of these eight programs, Rosenfeld, Schön, and Sykes (1995) argue that to become successful, these projects had to view their work as occurring in an ecological field in which both the participants and the projects themselves had to find a viable niche (or, in Taylor's words, an "enabling" niche; see chapter 14). These are projects and people with precious few resources; the women, as described above, were often isolated, without voice. So a major resource for the women was each other and the advocacy of the project staff, and for the staff members it was the willingness to "invent" a different, demanding form of practice. Among other things, this practice (also described as just good social and community work) required that workers be consistently available for families, that they believe in and act on what family members say, that they look within the individual family and the community for unseen resources and potentials, and that they work by invoking a communal, collaborative spirit and mode.

CONCLUSION

I hope I have been able to convey the excitement of some of the developments in thinking about the relationship between community and individual resilience, and putting them into practice. For our profession, these developments are affirmations of a noble and honorable legacy about which we may have become amnesic. The social work profession, over the years, has positioned itself to champion the cause of the underdog, the oppressed, and to envision and promote the idea of a world worth living in for all. We can not do it alone, obviously, but we are becoming in danger of not doing it at all. The long traditions of community organizing and activism, of liberation theology, of radical confrontational politics, of Marxist transformation, have often looked askance at community development activities that do not address the sociopolitical sources of oppression. The approaches described here might seem to some to be engaged in "selling out." But while we await the Godot of ultimate social metamorphosis, let us fortify ourselves and our communities to meet the daily struggles and challenges that life brings. John McKnight (1995) puts it this way:

> Community is about the common life that is lived in such a way that the unique creativity of each person is a contribution to the other. . . . Our goal should be clear. We are seeking nothing less than a life surrounded by the richness and diversity of community. A collective life. A common life. An everyday life. A powerful life that gains its joy from the creativity and connectedness that come when we join in association to create an inclusive world. (p. 123)

When transformation comes, we will be ready to seize the moment. We would do well to be guided by the words of sixth-century Chinese philosopher Lao-tsu:

> If there is radiance in the soul, it will abound in the family.
> If there is radiance in the family, it will be abundant in the community.
> If there is radiance in the community, it will grow in the nation
> If there is radiance in the nation, the universe will flourish.

DISCUSSION QUESTIONS

1. How would you describe the relationship between the resilience of the individual and that of the community? Can you think of an example in which a community did or did not help promote the resilience or competence of an individual? What were the key factors?
2. Which of the exemplars of community development practice provides a model that you, as a social worker, would find most compatible with your values and methods? Why?
3. How could you, as a clinical social worker, incorporate some of these ideas about community, individual resilience, and group empowerment into your day-to-day practice?

REFERENCES

Benard, B. (1991). *Fostering resiliency in kids: Protective factors in the family, school, and community*. San Francisco: Western Regional Center.

Benard, B. (1994, December). *Applications of resilience*. Paper presented at a conference on the Role of Resilience in Drug Abuse, Alcohol Abuse, and Mental Illness (December 5 and 6). Washington, D.C.: National Institute on Drug Abuse.

Garmezy, N. (1994). Reflections and commentary on risk, resilience, and development. In R. J. Haggerty, L. R. Sherrod, N. Garmezy, & M. Rutter (Eds.), *Stress, risk, and resilience in children and adolescents: Processes, mechanisms, and interventions* (pp. 1–18). New York: Cambridge University Press.

Gutierrez, L., & Nurius, P. (Eds.). (1994). *Education and research for empowerment practice*. Seattle, WA: University of Washington School of Social Work: Center for Policy and Practice Research.

Hanna, M. G., & Robinson, B. (1994). *Strategies for community empowerment: Direct-action and transformative approaches to social change practice.* Lewiston, NY: EmText.

Kelly, J. (1988). A guide to conducting prevention in the community: First steps. *Prevention in Human Services, 6,* whole issue.

Kondrat, M. E. (1995). Concept, act, and interest in professional practice: Implications of an empowerment perspective. *Social Service Review, 69,* 405–428.

Kretzmann, J. P., & McKnight, J. L. (1993). *Building communities from the inside out.* Evanston, IL: Center for Urban Affairs and Policy Research, Northwestern University.

Lee, J. A. B. (1994). *The empowerment approach to social work practice.* New York: Columbia University Press.

Lind, M. (1995). To have and have not. *Harper's, 290,* 35–47.

Masten, A. S. (1994). Resilience in individual development: Successful adaptation despite risk and adversity. In M. C. Wang & E. W. Gordon (Eds.), *Educational resilience in inner city America: Challenges and prospects.* Hillsdale, NJ: Erlbaum.

McKnight, J. (1995). *The careless society: Community and its counterfeits.* New York: Basic Books.

McLaughlin, M. W., Irby, M. A., & Langman, J. (1994). *Urban sanctuaries: Neighborhood organizations in the lives and futures of inner city youth.* San Francisco: Jossey-Bass.

Miller, A. (1990). *The untouched key: Tracing childhood trauma in creativity and destructiveness.* New York: Anchor/Doubleday.

Mills, R. (1993). *The health realization model: A community empowerment primer.* Alhambra, CA: California School of Professional Psychology.

Mills, R. (1995). *Realizing mental health.* New York: Sulzburger & Graham.

Peele, S., & Brodsky, A. (1991). *The truth about addiction and recovery.* New York: Simon & Schuster.

Rosenfeld, J., Schön, D. A., & Sykes, I. (1995). *Out from under.* Jerusalem: JDC-Brookdale Institute of Gerontology and Human Development.

Rutter, M. (1984, March). Resilient children. *Psychology Today,* 57–65.

Shaffer, C. R., & Anundsen, K. (1993). *Creating community anywhere.* New York: Tarcher/Perigree.

Specht, H., & Courtney, M. (1994). *Unfaithful angels: How social work has abandoned its mission.* New York: Free Press.

Taylor, J. (1996). *Niches and practice: Extending the ecological perspective.* Chapter 14, this volume.

Vaillant, G. E. (1993). *The wisdom of the ego.* Cambridge, MA: Harvard University Press.

Wehniller, P. (1992). When the walls come tumbling down. *Harvard Educational Review, 62,* 373–383.

Werner, E., & Smith, R. S. (1982). *Vulnerable but invincible.* New York: McGraw-Hill.

Werner, E., & Smith, R. S. (1992). *Overcoming the odds.* Ithaca, NY: Cornell University Press.

Wolin, S. J., & Wolin, S. (1993). *The resilient self: How survivors of troubled families rise above adversity.* New York: Villard.

chapter 14

Niches and Practice: Extending the Ecological Perspective

James B. Taylor

Carel Germain's "ecological perspective," first introduced in 1979 and elaborated subsequently (Germain, 1979a, 1979b, 1979c, 1981, 1987, 1991), attempts to advance social work theory by drawing an analogy with biological ecology. Since "ecology is the science that studies the relationship between organisms and their environments," it can "be used as a metaphor" for the human experience, and especially for the ways in which "people and environments influence, change, and sometimes shape each other" (Germain, 1991, p. 16). Germain draws some concepts directly from ecology—most notably the concepts of environment, adaptation, and adaptedness—and uses others as suggestive analogies. The withholding and abuse of power, for example, is said to be analogous to "social and technological pollution" (Germain, 1991, p. 17). However, the concepts Germain cites as central to the ecological perspective appear to come mainly from the social sciences. The twin notions of stress and coping come principally from psychology, as do the concepts of life course, human relatedness, competence, self-direction, and self-esteem/self-concept (Germain, 1991). For the most part, the "ecological perspective" has little to do with the biological science of ecology.

Should it? Not necessarily. We ask a "perspective" to provide a point of view, a framework for thought, and some possibilities for action. The ecological metaphor, by drawing attention to person–environment transactions, does just this. It works: It provides a way of talking about social work's central concerns, and it emphasizes holistic thinking and interactive processes. Since it works, there is no inherent reason to delve further into biology.

One wonders, however: Could more be done with biological ecology? General perspectives are all very well and good, but social work also needs more specific concepts. Biological ecology is rich with causal models that might, with careful thought, shed new light on human predicaments. There are striking parallels between biological and social ecosystems. Some organizational theorists have successfully used ecological models to shed light on the evolution and distribution of human organizations (Hannan, 1989; Hannan & Freeman, 1977; see also Singh and Lumsden, 1990; Sosin, 1985). A similar approach, in social work hands, might help clarify aspects of social and individual strengths and dysfunctions.

This chapter uses ideas drawn directly from biological ecology in order to develop some concepts and action principles for social work. It focuses upon the concept of "ecological niche," and shows how this concept, suitably modified to fit the social world, can lead to new insights and to new practice principles consonant with understanding sources of strength in the environment.

DEFINING AND DESCRIBING "NICHE"

Biologists have defined the "ecological niche" in different ways, depending on the aspect of niche with which they are most concerned. Strickberger defines it as "[t]he environmental habitat of a population or species, including the resources it utilizes and its association with other organisms" (1990, p. 518). Alternatively, it may be defined as, "The resources and conditions needed if a species population is to maintain itself over time without in-migration" (p. 518). By both definitions, a niche exists as something in the environment. Its description requires details about the place and conditions where the species is found, the resources that allow the species to maintain itself over time, and the relationships of that species with other species.

This biological definition needs revision if we are to describe niches in human social systems. One biological species inhabits at most a few niches over a lifetime, but we want a concept that allows us to describe an infinite variety of social niches filled by a single species, *Homo sapiens.* Unlike a biological ecosystem, a social system contains symbols and meanings and social forms. In all other species, it is the genes that transmit information across the generations, and biological evolution proceeds slowly as the gene pool shifts. In humans, it is mainly language that transmits information across generations, allowing social evolution to proceed with astonishing speed. The biologist's "ecological niche" at best provides a framework, an analogue, for the concept of "social niche."

The idea of "species" is central to the biologist's notion of ecological niche. Species inhabit a niche. Is there anything equivalent to "species" for "social niches"? In talking about niches in the social world, it seems natural to refer to different categories of persons. Instead of Bay-breasted warblers and Myrtle warblers, we have niches filled by "welfare mothers" and "welders" and "college professors"—all with their own environmental habitats and their typical resources. Thus by analogy, we could replace the idea of "species" with the idea of "categories of persons." But not just any category will do. We might categorize a person as red-headed, plump, shy, an introvert, a democrat, etc., but these particular categorizations are probably irrelevant to the niche; they have little to do with habitat or with resource acquisition. Welfare mothers, welders, college professors, prison inmates, "bag ladies," CEOs—these are the kinds of categories that correspond to the "species" distinction in biology, as these social categories reflect patterns of resource acquisition. "Species" of persons are commonly found in association with other categories of persons: teachers with students, physicians with patients, pimps with prostitutes, politicians with lobbyists, etc. These complementary categories often act either as resources or as competitors for resources. Such resource-linked associations help define the niche.

The idea of "habitat" includes the "place and conditions in which an organism normally lives" (Strickberger, 1990, p. 518). Places are easily described: They include residences, stores, shopping malls, saloons, McDonalds, etc. The term "community" captures some of this, as does the idea of "settings" in Roger Barker's (1968) ecological psychology. A species' habitat is set by the availability within it of the resources needed for it to maintain itself; by the same token, a human habitat is set by the availability within it of the resources needed for particular categories of people to maintain themselves.

In humans, the idea of "resource" becomes a bit complicated. For an animal, a "resource" may be an optimal temperature range, the presence (or absence) of water, the availability of food or prey, the presence of soil suited for burrowing. . . . The list can be long, but it generally will refer to tangible things. For humans, tangible resources are mainly acquired by money or barter, so for our culture and time we include "money" and access to sources of money (jobs, transfer payments, investments, etc.) as resources, and this has no analogue in the animal kingdom.

Since human beings are a social species, and distinctively information-using, their important resources are as much social as tangible. They need social support, help in the construction of social norms and social skills, aid in setting socially meaningful goals, group feedback to establish and maintain consensus on social reality, and reciprocal ties of mutual aid. The variety and need for such social and intangible resources is uniquely human.

Putting this all together, we may define a social niche most simply as, "[t]he environmental habitat of a category of persons, including the resources they utilize and the other categories of persons they associate with." The habitat conditions include the range of communities, settings, and domiciles in which these persons are usually found, the sources and ranges of income available to these persons, the range of social resources and supports typically used by those persons, and the other categories of people commonly found in association with those persons. With this definition, the biological analogy leads us, I believe, to something beyond metaphor: It results in a specification of the elements needed in a careful description of any social niche.

Note that this definition preserves the original notion of niche as a slot or space in the environment that can be filled by some object. Some impressionistic discussions of niche in the social work literature abandon this notion, so that the concept becomes very fuzzy. For example, Brower (1988) defines "niche" in cognitive/ emotional terms:

It is the special place within which one feels comfortable; one has made it "one's own.". . . Once established, the niche is said to have attained a state of "homeostasis," or "dynamic equilibrium." Barring abrupt changes in either the person or the environment that would threaten the survival of the whole, the niche maintains itself by adjusting to the continual fluctuations of everyday life. . . . The niche is the smallest and most reasonable "unit" with which to work in practice. (pp. 412-413)

Brower is not here talking about ecological niches. Ecological niches have little to do with homeostasis or dynamic equilibrium. Ecological niches do not have motives that would lead them to "maintain themselves" or "adjust"; and ecological niches have nothing to do with comfort. In fact, the kinds of niches discussed in the next section are seldom comfortable, and given a choice few people would make them "one's own."

Niche Entrapment

A theory is no good unless it results in new insights and possibilities. In the following sections, I discuss two generic types of niches: "entrapping" niches and "enabling" niches. Their characteristics are described, and their implications for pathology and rehabilitation explored. In this discussion, I set them up as ideal types, simply as a way of clarifying the "entrapping–enabling" distinction. In actuality many niches will be mixed, with some entrapping and some enabling features, but the pure types—or close to them—do exist.

Entrapping Niches.   When working with disadvantaged populations, one is occasionally stymied by catch-22 situations. Some clients seem caught in circumstances from which no escape is possible.

> Having served time in the penitentiary, and being out on parole, client X needs to find a job. He feels he has little chance of being employed if he admits to his record, and if he lies about it and is caught in the lie he will be fired. His social world is made up largely of people who, like himself, have "done time," most of them repeat offenders.

> A 17-year-old high school dropout becomes pregnant out of wedlock and goes on welfare. She lives on the welfare check, plus help from a boyfriend at the local army base. Unskilled, with a baby to look after, without easy transportation, living in a housing project, and functionally illiterate, her immediate life prospects seem dim.

> A 40-year-old male lives mainly on the streets. In and out of the state hospital, he never seems to stick with community placement plans, and now subsists mainly on mission charity and panhandling. "Self-medicating" with alcohol and street drugs, he has come to be feared by his parents and relatives, who reluctantly keep him at arm's length.   .

These vignettes describe very different niches, yet all act as traps. The ex-prisoner on parole, the welfare mother, the "crazy"—all find it very hard to move to other niches. Niches of this sort we shall call "entrapping niches," and we will describe people who occupy these niches as experiencing "niche entrapment."

All entrapping niches appear to have certain qualities in common:

- Entrapping niches are highly stigmatized; people caught in them are commonly treated as outcasts by important others.
- People caught in an entrapping niche tend to turn only to "their own kind" for association, so that their social world becomes restricted and limited.
- People caught in an entrapping niche are totally defined by their social category. The possibility that they may have aspirations and attributes apart from their category is not ordinarily considered. To outsiders, the person is "just" a "bag lady," a "junkie," an "ex-con," a "crazy" . . . and nothing else.
- In the entrapping niche, there are no gradations of reward and status. One cannot be certified as a "Master Bag Lady," or work up to the position of "Head Parolee." Thus there are few expectations of personal progress within such niches.
- In the entrapping niche, there are few incentives to set realistic longer term goals or to work toward such goals.
- In the entrapping niche, there is little reality feedback; that is, there are few natural processes that lead people to recognize and correct their own unrealistic perceptions or interpretations.
- In the entrapping niche, there is little chance to learn the skills and expectations that would facilitate escape. This is especially true when the entrapping niche is free from the usual norms of work and self-discipline, and no demands arise for the clear structuring of time and effort.
- In the entrapping niche, economic resources are sparse. This in itself may lead to unproductive stress and cause some people to seek reinstitutionalization (in hospital or prison) for economic reasons.

The motto for the entrapping niche might well be, "Abandon all hope ye who enter here." This, it will be recalled, was the motto Dante read above the entrance to Hell.

Entrapment and Person.   It is usually no accident that people find themselves in entrapping niches, as our three case examples illustrate. Indeed, some might claim that the notion of niche is needless; and that our three cases simply illustrate the sad consequences of psychopathology and inadequate character formation. But something more is involved than individual pathology or deviant socialization. The life circumstances—the niches—available to people who have suffered major psychopathology will differ by culture and place. There is good reason to think that these niche differences may play a major role in recovery.

Consider a medical example. After any debilitating illness, a recovery period is needed. During recovery the patient regains lost capabilities, relearns lost skills, relinquishes old illness roles, and develops new life plans. This is as true of major mental illness as it is of some serious physical illnesses. Skill loss is shown in purest form with severe, protracted episodes of schizophrenia. Schizophrenia is a disease that disrupts information processing capabilities; its more florid symptoms are the result of such disruption. The disease typically interferes with social learning during important life periods. As with other debilitating illness, a recovery period is required for regaining capabilities, relearning old skills, relinquishing illness roles, and developing life plans that take into account altered abilities and circumstances. These recovery processes involve social learning and relearning, and hence are influenced in predictable ways by the social niches available after hospitalization. We do not have to assume that entrapping niches *cause* pathology in order to claim that they influence recovery from pathology. Much the same argument can be made for recovery from the effects of deviant or inadequate socialization or from the results of major life setbacks.

There is a sad irony here. Many—perhaps most—of the people suffering niche entrapment are returning to normal society from state hospitals, prisons, and mental retardation facilities. Such people often need to learn or relearn normal social skills, and need to incorporate reasonable social motives. In the entrapping niche, the chance of this occurring is very slim.

Enabling Niches

It might be thought that the provision of social services through the usual social agencies could make up for these niche inadequacies. If social skills need to be learned, why not teach them? In a limited way, this may indeed be possible. But the fact is that most complex social skills are best learned in niches, not in school. Often it happens that bright students take 3 years of, say, French, yet come out unable to converse with a native speaker. On the other hand, almost anyone can learn to speak French passably within a year if they are living in France and their niche demands it.

Indeed, for those with chronic mental illness or substance abuse problems, the truly successful programs appear to provide niches rather than discrete services. Examples are the Fairweather Lodges (Fairweather, 1964; Linn, Klett, & Caffey, 1980), and those rehabilitation centers that follow the Fountain House model (Foderaro, 1994). The niches in these settings are much like those found in normal social life; they provide graded incentives for learning social skills and for testing social reality. Such settings appear effective in reducing chronicity and rehospitalization rates (Finch, 1986).

If we look closely at the kinds of niches found at these and similar centers, they seem almost the mirror image of the entrapping niches. They are examples of "enabling niches." Such niches share the following characteristics:

- People in enabling niches are not stigmatized, not treated as outcasts.
- People in enabling niches will tend to turn to "their own kind" for association, support, and self-validation. But the enabling niche gives them access to others who bring different perspectives, so that their social world becomes less restricted.
- People in enabling niches are not totally defined by their social category; they are accepted as having valid aspirations and attributes apart from that category. The person is not "just" a "bag lady," a "junkie," an "ex-con," a "crazy." . . .
- In the enabling niche, there are clear, earned gradations of reward and status. People can work up to better positions. Thus there are strong expectations of change or personal progress within such niches.
- In the enabling niche, there are many incentives to set realistic longer term goals for oneself and to work toward such goals.
- In the enabling niche, there is good reality feedback; that is, there are many natural processes that lead people to recognize and correct unrealistic perceptions or interpretations.
- The enabling niche provides opportunities to learn the skills and expectations that would aid movement to other niches. This is especially true when the enabling niche pushes toward reasonable work habits and reasonable self-discipline and expects that the use of time will be clearly structured.
- In the enabling niche, economic resources are adequate, and competence and quality are rewarded. This reduces economic stress and creates strong motives for avoiding institutionalization.

Granted, there is always some slippage between the real and the ideal. Yet it is surprising how so many attempts at structural transformation—in psychiatric rehabilitation, community development, industry, classroom reform—have defined something like the "enabling niche." Indeed, if social work can take credit for one major social invention, it would be the planned construction of enabling niches. After all, this is what Jane Addams (1938) and her compatriots pioneered at Hull House. The neighborhood and settlement houses were set up to provide enabling niches. The phrase is new; the concept is new; but in social work the reality has a long and honorable history. In a very real sense, the definition of enabling niche is consonant with the more recent conceptions of community-building (see chapter 13). It is also the environmental analog of individual strength.

Of course, social work has no monopoly on the planned construction of enabling niches. The 1960s "therapeutic community" movement was an attempt to build enabling niches in mental hospitals (Jones, 1968). Many self-help movements have developed partial versions of the enabling niche. Sarason's (1972) book on the creation of settings was about the development of enabling niches in small places. Case management using the "strengths perspective" attempts to help clients find enabling niches.

Yet, as always, the devil lies in the details. Many well-meant attempts at social programming have gone badly awry because niche issues were disregarded. Examples are legion: the universal failure of high-rise public housing; the debacle of urban renewal; the mixed results of Aid to Families with Dependent Children; the deficiencies of the foster care system. There are clearly many reasons for these failures, but the clearest is also the simplest: The planners did not fully understand what they were doing. They thought they were "providing adequate housing to the poor," or "clearing away the slums," or "keeping kids from going homeless and hungry." In fact they were providing new habitats, new niches, new ecosystems. About the characteristics of these niches, or the adaptations necessary to survive in them, they often had not a clue. Good practice comes from good theory. There is as yet no form of program development, nor of macro practice, that draws on niche ideas. Perhaps there ought to be.

ESCAPING ENTRAPMENT: SUPPORT PODS

For persons in an entrapping niche, escape is problematic. Skills developed in the entrapping niche seldom help in other habitats, and new skills are not easily gained. Yet in fact some people do escape from such niches; resilience may be rewarded. How does this happen?

To this question there may be many answers, but one very common way of escape seems particularly important, because even the most entrapping niche has one potential, untapped resource. As we have seen in other chapters in this book, within any social niche, even an entrapping niche, people are themselves resources. They can come together as a group, cooperate, learn from the others' successes, and pool tangible resources. When this happens in a small and somewhat isolated group especially set up for the purpose, we refer to it as a "support group." Sometimes however larger reference groups may form; groups that cooperate, pool resources, provide support, and push for change and success. This kind of group may form within a church, a sect, an extended family, or an ideological social movement. The form does not matter so much as the results; for in the activities of the group, new skills may be forged, new strengths acquired, new opportunities shared. Within the solidarity of this large group people can, collectively, *augment their niche resources,* and even in the face of poverty and racism, this collective effort may sometimes provide escape from entrapment. When it happens in a large, cohesive group emerging spontaneously, we have no generic name. I would suggest that these groups and the environments they build be called "support pods."

An example:

In their study of Topeka High School, done 15 years after it was integrated by the Supreme Court, Petroni and Hirsch (1971) found internal *de facto* segregation: whites and blacks shared the same school but were concentrated in different classes and did not share the same associates. They were like two distinct species whose habitats partly overlapped—an arrangement the biological ecologist might call "resource partitioning." The larger group of black students devalued the education they received, some with good reason, and were hostile to those who took it seriously. Their grades were low, their dropout rate high, their life prospects poor. Studious blacks were despised and were called "oreos."

Within the same high school however was a smaller group of black adolescents—not differing much from the others in their family background or residence—who had somehow come to value education and upward mobility. They took classes in the college preparatory track and avoided their fellow blacks, treating them with scorn. Some in this group had taken their French teacher as a role model and mentor. They would meet for lunch in the high school cafeteria and talk together in French; clearly setting themselves apart from the others and erecting an impenetrable behavioral barrier. As a group, they reinforced each other's hopes and ambitions; as a group they studied together; and as a group they moved in time to the middle class. They had constructed their own support pod.

This is not perhaps uncommon. Support pods may develop around any affiliation. Collective action toward shared goals tends to build support pods. Thus Chapel Methodism provided a support pod for many of the laboring poor in Victorian England; the black church has played a similar role for some African-Americans; and Alcoholics Anonymous does the same for some recovering alcoholics. The micro-niches provided by such institutions have provided for many an escape from entrapment.

Some of these support pods are effective, some are not. In justifying them, people talk vaguely about the value of community, the need for social support, the virtues of empowerment. They often have trouble defining what they are doing in terms that make sense to legislators and managers. They lack any substantive theory with which to explain themselves to others or even to define their own intuitions. Perhaps the concept of "support pod" can prove useful in this regard.

SUMMARY

Building on Germain's ecological perspective, I have suggested that biological niche theory might offer some useful insights to the social work profession. The theory as it stands does not fit our needs, but it can be used as a framework for building new concepts and discovering new possibilities. This chapter represents a modest step in that direction: It presents a few ideas suggested by the biological concept of niche, and explores their use in thinking about disadvantaged people and how the ideas of niche and support pods might contribute to our thinking about employing the resources within a given environmental niche. The ideas introduced here have already been used to clarify the social conditions that promote recovery from schizophrenia (Sullivan, 1994) and may offer other leads for macro- and mezzo-level intervention.

Sometimes "new perspectives" in social work result in people saying the same old things in new and trendy ways. I do not believe that this is the case with the ecological perspective nor with niche theory. It seems likely that an extension of ecological and niche theoretic ideas can lead to new knowledge for social work, lead to useful research, and suggest new possibilities for intervention.

DISCUSSION QUESTIONS

1. What are the major differences between an enabling niche and an entrapping one?
2. Give and discuss examples of both kinds of niches in your practice.
3. What could a social worker do to facilitate the development of an enabling niche?
4. How might you use the idea of support pod in your practice?

REFERENCES

Addams, J. (1938). *Twenty years at Hull-House.* New York: Macmillan.

Barker, R. (1968). *Ecological psychology.* Stanford, CA: Stanford University Press.

Brower, A. M. (1988). Can the ecological model guide social work practice? *Social Service Review, 62*(3), 411–429.

Fairweather, G. (Ed.) (1964). *Social psychology in treating mental illness: An experimental approach.* New York: Wiley.

Finch, E. (1986). *Psychiatric rehabilitation outside the bureaucracy: A naturalistic study of the Fountain House model.* Doctoral dissertation, Lawrence, KS: University of Kansas.

Foderaro, L. W. (1994). "Clubhouse" helps mentally ill find the way back. *New York Times,* November, 8, 1994, p. B1.

Germain, C. B. (Ed.). (1979a). *Social work practice: People and environments, an ecological perspective.* New York: Columbia University Press

Germain, C. B. (1979b). General system theory and ego psychology, an ecological perspective. *Social Service Review, 52,* 535–550.

Germain, C. B. (1979c). Space, an ecological variable in social work practice. *Social Casework, 59,* 515–522.

Germain, C. B. (1981). The ecological approach to people environment transactions. *Social Casework, 62,* 323–331.

Germain, C. B. (1987). Ecological perspective. In *Encyclopedia of social work* (18th ed., Vol. 1). Silver Springs, MD: National Association of Social Workers.

Germain, C. B. (1991). *Human behavior in the social environment: An ecological view.* New York: Columbia University Press.

Hannan, M. T. (1989). *Organizational ecology.* Cambridge, MA: Harvard University Press.

Hannan, M. T., & Freeman, J. (1977). The population ecology of organizations. *American Journal of Sociology, 82,* 929–964.

Jones, M. (1968). *Social psychiatry in practice: The idea of the therapeutic community.* London: Penguin.

Linn, M., Klett, C., & Caffey, E. (1980). Foster home characteristics and psychiatric patient outcome. *Archives of General Psychiatry, 37,* 129–132.

Petroni, F., & Hirsch, E. (1971). *Two, four, six, eight, when you gonna integrate?*. New York: Behavioral Publications.

Sarason, S. B. (1972). *The creation of settings and the future societies*. San Francisco: Jossey-Bass.

Singh, J., & Lumsden, C. (1990). Theory and research in organizational ecology. *Annual Review of Sociology, 16,* 161–195.

Sosin, M. (1985). Social problems covered by private agencies: An application of niche theory. *Social Service Review, 59,* 75–94.

Strickberger, M. W. (1990). *Evolution.* Boston: Jones and Bartlett.

Sullivan, W. P. (1994). Recovery from schizophrenia: What we can learn from the developing nations. *Innovations & Research, 3*(2), 7–15.

part **V**

Conclusion

chapter **15**

The Strengths Perspective:
Possibilities and Problems[1]

Dennis Saleebey

$\mathbf{F}$ocusing and building on client strengths is not simply a counterweight to the prevalence of the deficit model. It is an imperative of the several values that govern our work and the operations of a democratic, just, and pluralistic society including distributive justice, equality, respect for the dignity of the individual, inclusiveness and diversity, and the search for maximum autonomy within maximum community.

In Walzer's (1983) view, justice and equality do not call for the elimination of differences, but the elimination of certain kinds of differences—those defined or created by people in power that are the bedrock of their domination of fellow citizens, whether the differences are couched in the language of race, class, gender, sexual orientation, or religious belief. As he says,

> It's not the fact that there are rich and poor that generates egalitarian struggle but the fact that the rich grind the faces of the poor. It's always what one group with power does to another group—whether in the name of health, safety or security—it makes no difference. The aim, ultimately, of the fight for equality is always the elimination of subordination . . . no more toadying, scraping and bowing, fearful trembling. (p. xiii)

For us, the message is that many models and institutions of helping have become pillars of a kind of inequality in Walzer's sense. They have evolved into means of domination through identity stripping, culture killing, status degradation, base rhetoric, and/or sequestering. We dominate, sometimes benignly with a velvet

---

[1] Part of this chapter is based on D. Saleebey, The strengths perspective in social work practice: Extensions and cautions. *Social Work, 41*(3), 1996, 295–305. With permission of the National Association of Social Workers.

glove, and we may do it in the name of good, welfare, service, helping, or therapy. What we have finally done, by emphasizing and assigning social status to a person's deficiencies, differences, and defects is to rob them of some of their inherent powers and motivations. Or at least we steal from them the opportunities, the courage, the presumption to use those powers. In a sense, we have impoverished, not empowered. All of our knowledge (theories, principles) and all of our technical orientations must be examined, "critiqued, challenged, or corroborated in the light of their relationships to power and interest" (Kondrat, 1995, p. 417). Whether we discover that we are serving corporate interests, malign political claims, or benighted professional frameworks, if they, in any way, obfuscate or distort local knowledge, ignore and suppress personal and communal strengths and powers (cognitive, moral, behavioral, political), then we, too, have committed a root act of oppression.

Whatever else it is, social justice is understood only in terms of domination; domination of the distribution of social goods—those resources essential for survival, growth and development, transformation, simple security and safety. Welfare, communal support and connection, commodities, goods, health, education, recreation, shelter, all underwrite identity, and personal resourcefulness and strength—the tools for becoming as human and competent as possible. A more just and equitable distribution system is at the heart of the development and expression of individual and collective powers and capacities. As social workers, we confront and promote the idea of strengths at two very different levels—policy (philosophy) and practice (principles)—but they always intersect in the lives of our clients.

In the 1960s, we talked of "power to the people." That apothegm had many different meanings. Not the least of these was that a government or social movement must dedicate itself to returning social, economic, material, and political goods to the people who had been systematically denied them. The idea of returning power to ordinary and oppressed citizens alike raised nettlesome questions. What, in fact, do people need? What are citizens entitled to? Whose claims to scarce social goods shall prevail? How shall these goods be distributed? When the ardor of the 1960s was stanched in the mid-1970s, these questions had not been answered. Today, in the debate over balanced budgets, the size of the federal government, welfare and health care reform, we seem no closer to answers.

In the 1980s, the New Federalism—Reaganomics, for some—made the idea that these social resources could be disbursed through the devices of the marketplace exceedingly attractive. But the marketplace, at best, can provide only limited resources, often on quite a selective and preemptive basis. And, it should be obvious to anyone who shops, trades, sells, invests, that the marketplace is no venue for the pursuit of justice, equity, or recompense. Unless it might sell beans, philosophic assertions about fertilizing the roots of democracy seem frightfully out of place in the private, for-profit sector of the economy. One would think, however, judging by all the books, talk shows, workshops, infomercials available that the marketplace distribution of social and psychological capital has been a tremendous success. I think, rather, that this procession of pop-psych, pop-soc nostrums indicates that we have failed through conventional socializing institutions to help many individuals develop a sense of autonomy, personal mastery, or communal connection; failed to assist neighborhoods, communities and cultures to retain their sense of value and distinctiveness.

We have argued in this book for a subtle change in the basic equation between equality, justice, community, and autonomy and asserted that there is power in the people and their environments. No matter how subordinated, marginalized, and oppressed individuals and communities may appear, people, individually and collectively, can find nourishment for their hopes and dreams, tools for their realization somewhere. These tools may be weak, distressed, or suppressed but, whatever their condition, they are there awaiting discovery and/or expression. When we talk of building on client strengths, of respecting people's accounts of their lives, of revering a people's culture, of hearing out an individual's stories, we are, in a sense, giving testimony that, in spite of injustice and inequity, people do have prospects. People do show a kind of resilience and vitality that, even though it may lie dormant or assume other guises, is inward. The quest for social resources and justice should never end, but we do not have to wait for the millennium in order to do this work well.

QUESTIONS AND CAUTIONS ABOUT
THE STRENGTHS PERSPECTIVE

Those of us who have been involved in practice, education, research and training using the strengths perspective have come up against a number of concerns expressed by practitioners and students. I will present these in the form of questions.

Isn't the strengths perspective just positive thinking in another guise? The United States has a long and honored tradition of positive thinking that even today is alive and well. From Mary Baker Eddy to Norman Vincent Peale to Anthony Robbins, our society has enjoyed an array of positive thinkers purveying their own nostrums and panaceas on television, in books, in workshops, and other media. The strengths perspective is not the mindless recitation of uplifting mantras or the idea that relief and surcease from pain and trauma is just a meditation or facile miracle away. Rather, it is the work of helping clients and communities build something of lasting value from the materials and capital within and around them. There is nothing else from which to create possibility and prospects where none may have existed before. Your expertise as a professional social worker is obviously one of the resources to be used. But by itself professional cunning and craft is not enough. We must help find, summon, and employ the resources of the client or community. This is hard work. People, especially people living against the onslaught of dire circumstance, are not prone to think of themselves and their world in terms of strengths or as having emerged from scarring events with something useful or redeeming. In addition, if they also happen to be or have been clients of the health, mental health, or welfare systems, they may have been indoctrinated in the ideology of weakness, problems, and deficiencies. As Holmes (chapter 10, this volume) argues, they are not easily dissuaded from using these ritual symbols to understand themselves and their situation. The strengths perspective requires us, as well, to fashion collaborative, appreciative client relationships that we have been taught are the basis for effective, principled work with clients. Establishing such relationships obliges us to a strict and accurate accounting of client assets. Finding these and utilizing them compels arduous and careful work.

Why is it that people do not look as though they have strengths? Why do they seem beaten, angry, depressed, rebellious? Dominated people are often alienated people; separated from their inner resources, external supports, their own history and traditions. People struggling with cruel circumstance, the betrayal of their bodies in disease, or foundering in the larger social world also find themselves isolated, separated from their own resources and sense of self and place. One of the key effects of alienation is identification with the oppressor. Such identification may assume many forms but it is, regrettably, common. One of its forms is the assumption of the self-identifying terms of a diagnostic label: Or, in other words, to be what the oppressor says I am (Freire, 1973). Joel Kovel (1981) reminds us that the mental health enterprise turns on the administration of people's minds and the bureaucratization of their health. Both depend on the power to define. The more specific the definition, as in DSM IV (American Psychiatric Association, 1994), the more the authenticity of inner experience and perception, the availability of capacities becomes lost. Consider, Kovel says, ADHD (Attention Deficit Hyperactive Disorder)— a disorder manifested by the fact that some kids, usually male, move around too much, that is, at least too much for school authorities (this is not to deny the reality that there is a *much smaller* group of youth who do seem to have complex neurobiological abnormalities underneath their hyperactivity). The child occupies the wrong kind of space in too little time and is thus considered to have a disease. Once the child is so defined, the system can control and administer. Once defined, the child also has the beginnings of a new identity so that some years down the road, he might define himself as a hyperactive adult.

Isn't it true that the strengths perspective simply reframes deficit and misery? Some people have claimed that what proponents of a strengths-based approach really do is simply reconceptualize the difficulties that clients have so that they are sanitized and less threatening to self and others. In this way, someone with paranoid schizophrenia is regarded as having an extraordinary and acute sensitivity to other's meanings and motives. Thus, clients and workers do not do the hard work of transformation, normalization, and amelioration, risking action and building bridges to a larger world. But the strengths approach does honor the painful reality of schizophrenia, for example. The approach's tenets and principles, its methods were forged in intense work with people with severe and persistent mental illness. In every case, to the extent that they apply, the authenticity of symptoms, delusions and hallucinations, the neurochemical and structural abnormalities, the necessity of medication are acknowledged and become part of the work of constructing a world of possibility and opportunity for the individual and family. We are not in the business of talking people out of painful realities. But there is reframing to be done. To help develop an attitude, a vocabulary, a story about prospects and expectation, and a picture of a genuine individual lurking beneath the diagnostic label. This is work: creating access to communal resources so that they become the ticket to expanded choices and routes to change.

How does practice from a strengths perspective change what social workers do? If we are to believe advertisements about ourselves, maybe not much. But both loudly and implicitly, the chapters herein have decried the medical model, the notion of the helper as sly and artful expert, as applied technologist, the idea that the professional social worker stands apart from clients. So, must we surrender our status as experts, our esoteric and practical knowledge and lore? While we might want to reexamine the notion of expert, especially the implicit paternalism nestled within it, we do have special knowledge and would be foolish to deny that. But, it might be very important to critically analyze and rethink the assumptions, the consequences of the use of our knowledge, as well as its cultural, racial, class, and gender distortions and biases. Many have commented on the attractive alternative to the usual construction of professional intervention developed by Donald Schön and Chris Argyris (Schön, 1983)—reflective practice (see discussion in chapter 1). Opting for relevance rather than rigor, Schön's description of the reflective practitioner not only highlights the considerable artistry, intuition, and extemporaneousness of practice, but also a radically different contract between client and professional, very much in keeping with the strengths perspective.

A reflective contract finds the practitioner with obvious knowledge and skills to offer for service but also recognizes that the professional is not the only one in the contractual relationship with the capacity for enlightenment. The professional defines the work as a mutual quest in which the client is joined in a search for solutions, surcease, and success. Both parties to the contract have control: In a sense, they are independent but bound together. The professional asks the client to continually judge the work that is done and to revise its content and course as necessary. In any case, the core of the contract is in the establishment of an authentic connection to the client. In Schön's (1983) words,

> the reflective practitioner's relation with his [sic] client takes the form of a literally reflective conversation. Here the professional recognizes that his technical expertise is embedded in a context of meanings. He attributes to clients, as well as to himself, a capacity to mean, know, and plan. . . . He recognizes the obligation to make his own understandings accessible to his clients, which means he often needs to reflect anew on what he knows. (p. 295)

The nature of the contractual relationship changes in the direction of power equalization, mutual assessment and evolving agreements. In a sense, the worker is the agent of the individual, family, or community. This may put the social worker in direct conflict with the agency, as discussed further below.

Perhaps the biggest change in practice will be a change in vision, the way in which we see and experience clients, even the most disreputable and frightening clients. Suspending skepticism, disbelief, and even our cynicism about clients and client groups will probably not be difficult for many social workers. We are of good heart, after all. But beyond that, to see in the internal and external environments of misery, pain, self-delusion, even self-destruction, the glimmer of potential, the glint of capacity, virtue, and hope asks of us a significant deepening of our consciousness of, and openness to, clients' worlds.

How can I work from a strengths orientation if my agency is shot through with the deficit model? We can hardly be about the business of empowering clients if we feel weak, powerless, defenseless, and alienated from our own work because of agency policies, philosophies, and attitudes toward clients. There is little doubt that in agencies in which social control supersedes socialization of clients, deep pessimism about client motives exists, negative expectations of clients hold thrall, work is defined in terms of controlling damage, and clients are defined in terms of degrees of manipulation and resistance, and the health of workers is compromised (Benard, 1994; Mills, 1995). Burnout, turnover, dissatisfaction, fatigue are too often the fruits of work conducted under these conditions.

If you work in such an agency, must you succumb to the blandishments and protective seductions of such a view of clients? We think not. There is always choice. For example, you can choose how you will regard your clients. You can take the time, make the effort to discover the resources within the client and in the environment. You can choose how you will interpret and use information about the client as well as deciding what information you will seek.

> Imagine learning that James, an adolescent of fourteen, has spastic cerebral palsy, frequently relates to his siblings and peers aggressively, is two years below grade level in reading and arithmetic, and has parents who are rarely present in the home. Without proceeding further you are asked to form an impression of James. Now consider the difference in impression when one also learns that James does an outstanding job on his paper route, likes to write poetry and fantasy stories, has a close relationship with his uncle and aunt who live nearby, and is making steady progress in physical therapy. (Wright & Fletcher, 1982, p. 233)

To discover the "rest" of James requires a lively commitment to and belief in the possibilities in him and his world.

How can I and why should I give up the disease or deficit model of the human condition when it is so acceptable and widespread in our culture, generally, and the culture of helping, in particular? Even though the devolution of health and mental health care toward managed care, the rise of third-party payments and vendorship, licensing, and the spread of private practice all play a part in the amplification of the disease model, it is, ultimately, an act of individual intention and purpose to renounce it. To do so you must examine it critically, examine the consequences of its employment in your work, and consider the advantages that the substitution of a strengths-based approach would confer on your professional work and on the welfare of your clients. The disease model has reigned in many fields, in some of them since the nineteenth century (psychiatry, for example), but it has produced very little in the way of positive results. By almost any measure, the problems we oppose with the disease model armamentarium remain rampant and poorly understood, except at the most general level (Peele, 1989). As Hillman and Ventura (1992) claim, in a different arena, *"We've had one hundred years of psychotherapy and the world is getting worse!"* The disease framework has reproduced itself over and over again in many different contexts so that, in spite of failures in treating common human frailties and conditions, more and more behavior patterns, habits, life transitions, life dilemmas, personal traits, are regarded as illnesses—from excessive shopping to extremist thought, from persistent sexual activity to adolescent turmoil.

Stanton Peele (1989), long an opponent of turning complex and often common human behaviors, relationships, and experiences into afflictions, maintains,

> The pseudomedical inventions and treatments of new diseases increasingly *determine* our feelings, our self-concepts, and our world-views. our emotional and behavioral diseases define our culture and who we are—this is the diseasing of America . . . the promotion of these new diseases—as well as being ungrounded scientifically and worse than useless therapeutically—holds out the possibility for a totalitarianism similar to but more insidious than the one George Orwell imagined would occur through political means in *1984.* (p. 28)

The fact that the DSM IV is not only twice the size (8 years later) of its predecessor but also a best-seller and the putative genre of the diagnostic enterprise says as much about our devotion to the disease model as anything else.

Yes, but . . . Many social workers and agencies claim that they already abide by a strengths regimen. A review of what their practices actually involve often reveals applications that stray from an orientation to client strengths. In many mental health agencies around the country, Individual Service Plans (ISPs) or the like are supposed to incorporate the strengths of the individual and the family in assessment and planning, along with the particulars of diagnosis. The author and other colleagues have examined many ISPs from around the country. More often than not they are rife with diagnostic elaborations, narratives of decompensation, and explorations of continuing symptomatic struggles and manifestations. Axes I (clinical disorders) and II (personality disorders or mental retardation) of the DSM IV are usually prominently featured. Often the strengths assessment is consigned a few lines at the end of the form. The accountings rendered on these forms are, for the most part, in the lexicon of the mental health system and not the language of the client.

Get real! There is evil in the world; people can do horrible things to each other and to innocent victims. Isn't that true? It would be naive and disingenuous to deny the reality of evil. Apart from any philosophical efforts to define what it is, there is little doubt that there are individuals (and groups) who commit acts that are beyond our capacity to understand, let alone accept. But the decision to write off such individuals and to circumscribe certain behaviors as irredeemable is an individual moral decision that you must make. Such a decision is not always rendered with clarity or certainty. For example, would you agree with George Bernard Shaw that "[t]he greatest of our evils and the worst of our crimes is poverty"? or would Sophocles' cry, "Anarchy, anarchy! Show me a greater evil!" be more compelling? Certainly the world has endured, on both small and large scales, horrendous destruction of both spirit and life itself. Everyday brings with it another disclosure of tyranny of the soul and body. But in terms of our work, there are at least three things to consider in answering this difficult question:

1. If there are genuinely evil people, beyond grace or hope, it is best not to make that assumption about any individual first, even if the person has beaten his spouse, or if she has sold crack to school-aged kids.
2. Even if we are to work with someone whose actions are beyond our capacity to understand or accept, we must ask ourselves if they have useful skills and behaviors, even motivations and aspirations that can be tapped in the service of change to a less-destructive way of life?
3. We also must ask if there are other more salubrious and humane ways for these individuals to meet their needs or resolve their conflicts. We cannot automatically discount people without making a serious professional and moral accounting of the possibility for change and redemption.

Finally, in my experience when the judgment of clients as being beyond hope is made, it often relates more to the rendering of them as manipulative, threatening, or resistant within the treatment process.

Doesn't the strengths perspective ignore or downplay real problems that people have? This is a very serious criticism. If practitioners using a strengths framework do disregard the real problems that afflict clients and those around them and, thus, end up contributing to the damage done to people's lives, that is capricious, perhaps even reckless. There is nothing, however, in the strengths approach that mandates the discounting of the problems of life that people bring to us. In each of the chapters of this book, authors call for a responsible, balanced assessment and treatment plan, seeking to undo the too-often imbalanced deficit or problem assessments. All helpers should evaluate and come to a reckoning of the sources and remnants of individual and family troubles, pains, difficulties, and disorders. Often, this is where people begin, this is what they are compelled to relate, these are matters of the greatest urgency. There may well be the need for catharsis, for grieving and mourning, for the expression of rage or anxiety. We may also need to understand the barriers, both presumed and real, to the realization of hopes, dreams, and expectations. As stated before, it is as wrong to deny the problem as it is to deny the possible. As Cousins (1989) suggested, we shouldn't deny the verdict (diagnosis/assessment) but *defy the sentence* (prognosis/outcome). Once having assessed the damage, the disappointment, we must ensure that the diagnosis, the assessment does not become the cornerstone of an emergent identity. To avoid that possibility, we want to calculate how people have managed to survive in spite of their troubles, what they have drawn on in the face of misfortune or their own mistakes. We want to understand what part of their struggle has been useful to them. We want to know what they know, what they can do, and where now they want to go. Whatever else that the symptoms that so bemuse us are, they are also a sign of the soul, of the struggle to be more fully alive, responsible, and involved (Moore, 1992). For social workers, the goal may not be the heroic cure, but the constancy of caring and connection, and working collaboratively toward the improvement of day-to-day living, in spite of, or because of, symptoms. So what is of interest to us is how people have taken steps, summoned up resources, and coped. People are always working on their situations, even if just deciding for the moment to be resigned. As helpers, we must tap into that work, elucidate it, find and build on its promise. In some contexts, even resignation about or acceptance of one's condition may be a sign of strength.

It is well, too, to keep in mind that labels always bespeak the reality of an outsider, they collectivize and abstract real experience, and make the client's own experience and stories seem alien and contrived. We must use labels judiciously if at all, and with a profound respect for their distortions and limitations, and also with an equally profound respect for their potential to "mortify" individuals, stripping them of their distinctive identity, and overwhelming them, through a variety of rituals and social processes, with their new and exotic identity (Goffman, 1961).

Does the strengths model work? We can argue about what constitutes evidence but given our usual methodological appetites, both quantitative and qualitative research shows that the strengths perspective has a degree of power that would suggest its use with a variety of clients. The most current research summary compiled by Rapp (in press) does imply that the strengths model, when evaluated on its own or compared to other approaches, is efficacious. If we examine various outcome measures—hospitalization rates, independence, health, symptoms, family burdens, achievement of goals, degree of social support among others—between and within studies, the strengths model consistently shows that it delivers results with populations that typically, over time, helped with more conventional methods, do not do as well on these measures.

It must be stated that modesty is appropriate here. The studies that Rapp (in press) cites include only two experimental studies, one quasi-experimental study, and three nonexperimental studies involving a total of 783 people. These results, however, do not include any of the studies reported in this volume. Much remains to be done. But if we add to these studies the reports of practitioners around the country, the testimony of clients, and the witness of our own experience, there is no compelling reason to shrink from the strengths approach to practice.

Whatever else it might be, however else it might be construed, the strengths perspective, like other perspectives, is a manner of thinking about the work you do. The test of it is between you and those with whom you work. Do they think the work has been relevant to their lives? Do they feel more adept and capable? Have they moved closer to the hopes, goals, and objectives that they set before you? Do they have more connections with people and organizations, formal and informal, where they find succor, a place, occupation, project, time well spent, or fun? Do they have more awareness and respect of the energy and aptitude that they have forged in the fires of anguish and trauma? Do they have the sense that you will be with them and for them as they try to construct a better life for themselves? Do they know that you trust them eventually to continue on a path without your help, guidance, and good will?

In the end, the disease model should be foresworn because it discourages two facets of good social work practice:

- searching the environment for forces that enhance or suppress human possibilities and life chances
- emphasizing client self-determination, responsibility, and possibility so cherished in the rhetoric of social work practice.

The disease model undercuts, in the broadest and deepest way, the possibility of personal autonomy and community responsibility by sparing no human behavior from the lash of disease, no group of human beings from the rack of illness. Even when we acknowledge the reality of an illness, we are not absolved from finding resources within that person, her environment and relationships, and assisting her in capitalizing on those in living beyond the disease and improving the quality of her life.

OF PARADIGMS AND PROSPECTS: CONVERGING LINES OF THOUGHT

In many different places and through many different means, it is claimed that Western culture, perhaps the world, is undergoing a fundamental paradigm shift. If we define a paradigm as a framework crafted of symbols, concepts, beliefs, cognitive structures, and cultural ethos so deeply embedded in our psyches that we hardly know of its presence, the crumbling of an existing paradigm and the rise of another can be a deeply disturbing phenomenon. While there is profound disagreement and even conflict about what the old paradigm is, and what it is being replaced with, some have seen the passing of the rational, linear, scientific world view to be replaced with a perspective that is more interpretive; one that claims that there are no singular, objectively wrought truths to be had. No perspective is final, maybe even no perspective is superior to another. All are deeply rooted in a particular social context and, thus, make sense therein, but might appear as sheer lunacy in another time and place. There is comfort here for voices that have struggled too long to be heard, for cultures and peoples whose understanding of the world has been thrust aside or debased, for all those who have something to bring to the intellectual, moral, and spiritual marketplace. There is also encouragement here for other paths of knowing and being in the world. Others would disagree with this perspectivalism. But, it does seem to many that "for better or worse, the world is in the midst of the torturous birth throes of a collective emergence of an entirely new structure of consciousness" (Wilber, 1995, p. 188). It may be that we are moving in the direction of some sort of integration of the spheres of life, seeing and expressing the intricate and still-evolving connections between the body, mind, and environment; the earth, cosmos, and spirit. None of this will occur without tremendous upheaval, resistance, and no one can be certain, if the older paradigm is shattering, what will appear in its place.

What has all this to do with the strengths perspective? In a very *small* way, the strengths perspective moves away from the "disease paradigm" that has dominated much of the professional world, the scientific and technological realms. That model, described in various ways throughout these chapters, assumes a different viewpoint on clients and our work with them than the strengths model does. So to begin to surrender it can be a wrenching experience—in a modest fashion, as disruptive as larger, more cosmic shifts in consciousness. But it is nonetheless a shift in consciousness, a change in the way that we see our clients and regard our work. Fortunately, we are not alone in this alteration of our professional consciousness. In other disciplines and professions, fault lines have appeared, and new conceptual and practical structures are becoming visible. Some of these have been alluded to in the previous chapters. There are three that I want to briefly emphasize in this concluding chapter.

Resilience

In the fields of developmental psychology, and developmental psychopathology in particular, it has become clear that children exposed to risk in their early years do not inevitably consummate their adult lives with psychopathology, or sink into a morass of failure, and disappointment. The field is not of one mind here, but after arising out of the presumption that there are specific and well-defined risks that children will face, and these will always end in some sort of developmental disaster, it now seems clear that most do not; most children surmount adversity and, while bearing scars, do better as adults than we might have predicted. Yes, some children do face trauma, institutional and interpersonal, so toxic that to emerge unscathed or relatively functional would be miraculous. But even here, there are miracles. We need to understand better what makes them happen.

Any environment is a welter of demands, stresses, challenges, and opportunities, and these become fateful, given a complex array of other factors—genetic, constitutional, neurobiological, familial, spiritual, communal—for the development of strength, resilience, hardiness, or diminution of capacity. We are only now learning what factors lead to more hopeful outcomes. Clearly in almost every environment, no matter how trying, there lurk not only elements of risk, but protective and generative factors as well. These are people, resources, institutions, and contingencies that enhance the likelihood of rebound and recovery, or may even exponentially accelerate learning, development, and capacity. To learn what these elements of the body/mind/environment equation are, we have to go to the community, the family, the individual and learn from them how transformation or resilience developed.

One of the more celebrated studies, mentioned previously, of the development of resilience in children as they grow into adulthood was the longitudinal research begun in Kauai, Hawaii in 1955 by Emmy Werner and Ruth Smith (1992). In their earlier report (1982), Werner and Smith reported that one out of every three children who were evaluated by several measures to be at risk for adolescent and adult problems developed, as it turned out, into competent and confident youth at age 18. In their follow up, Werner and Smith (1992) found that two out of three of the remaining two-thirds were caring and efficacious adults at age 32. One of their central conclusions is that most human beings have self-righting tendencies and are able to effect a change in life trajectory over time. One of the factors that contributes to that is the presence of a steadfast, caring adult (or peer in a few cases). It need not be a parent nor need the relationship be an everyday affair.

Over the past few years, elements of communities and neighborhoods have emerged as important in the balance among risk, protective, and generative factors. In those communities that seem to amplify individual and familial resilience, there is awareness, recognition, and use of the assets of most of the members of the community, through informal networks of individuals, families, and groups. Social networks of peers and intergenerational mentoring relationships provide succor, instruction, support, and engagement. These are "enabling niches" (Taylor, chapter 14, this volume), places where individuals become known for what they can do; where they are supported in becoming more adept and knowledgeable; where they can establish solid relationships within and outside the community; where they are, in fact, members and citizens in good standing. In communities that provide protection, generate growth, and minimize risk, there are many opportunities for participation in the moral and civic life of the community.

So resilience is dependent on the interaction of factors at all levels, from biological to personal, to interpersonal, and environmental. Not only do children and adults learn about themselves and develop strengths as they confront challenge and adversity, but, if they are lucky, they find and make connection with compatriots in the making of a better life.

Health and Wellness

Health and wellness are artifacts of a complex, reticulate relationship among body, mind, and environment. Generally speaking, the body is built for health maintenance. Much of Western medicine is predicated on fighting illness when it occurs, often with substances that are, even when carefully employed, toxic (for example, cortisone). Natural or spontaneous healing, on the other hand, depends on the resources that lie immanent in the body, as well as psychological readiness and environmental encouragement. To realize health, to experience regeneration after trauma or disease, to achieve levels of functioning unimagined earlier, some of the following factors are essential and understood.

- People do have the innate capacity and wisdom for health and healthy living. The possibility of soundness and wholeness lie within (Mills, 1995; Weil, 1995).

- Positive beliefs about oneself and one's condition seem indispensable for recovery and regeneration (Ornstein & Sobel, 1987).

- Health-promoting positive emotions probably support, or elevate, the functioning of elements of the immune system because whatever else they are, they are hormonal events (Pert et al., 1985).
- The community plays an important role in health sustenance. The connections between people, their common visions and hopes, important mutual projects, the mentoring and support that occur in vibrant and vital communities are important to health and recovery (Benard, 1994).

The resilience and health and wellness literature run parallel in many regards. Both assert that individuals and communities have native capacities for restoration, rebound, and the maintenance of a high level of functioning. Both suggest that individuals are best served, from a health and competence standpoint, by creating belief and thinking around possibility and values, around accomplishment and renewal, rather than focusing on risk and disease processes. Both indicate that health and resilience are, in the end, communal projects—an effect of social connection, the pooling of collective vision, the provision of guidance, and the joy of belonging to an organic whole, no matter how small.

Story and Narrative

The constructivist view, in its many guises (see perspectivalism above), urges us to respect the importance of making meaning in all human affairs. Human beings build themselves into the world, not with their meager supply of instinct, but with the capacity to construct and construe a world from symbols, images, icons, language, and ultimately stories and narratives. While culture provides these building blocks, we impart, receive, and revise meanings largely through the telling of stories, the fashioning of narratives, and the creation of myths. Many are given by culture, some are authored by families, individuals, and subcultures. And there is always some tension between the culture and the self in this regard. But individuals and groups do tell their own stories. Groups who suffer under the domination of the larger culture and social institutions, frequently do not have their stories told or heard in the wider world nor, regrettably, sometimes in their own world (Rosaldo, 1989). One of the characteristics of being oppressed is having one's stories buried beneath the landslide of stereotype and ignorance. This means, then, that one of the genuine strengths of people(s) lies in the fabric of narrative and story in the culture and in the family. These are generative themes (Friere, 1973), and they capture the hopes and visions, the trials and tribulations, the strengths and virtues of a people, of a family. It is part of the work of liberation, renewal, and rebuilding to collaborate in the discovery, projection, and elaboration of these stories and accounts. A story told and appreciated is a person, family, or culture affirmed. While we understand that there is an innate capacity or urge toward health in the human body, we may not understand as well that in a story or narrative may be the health of a culture.

CONCLUSION

The contributors to this volume—all of whom are practitioners as well as scholars and educators—hope that you find something of real value here that can be translated for use with the individuals, families, and communities that you serve. We all believe that the initiatory act in employing a strengths perspective is a commitment to its principles and underlying philosophy—a credo that, in many regards, is at serious odds with the approach we have variously labeled the deficit, problem, or pathology orientation. We firmly believe that once committed you will be surprised, even amazed, at the array of talents, skills, knowledge, and resources that you discover in your clients—even those whose prospects seem bleak. In a nutshell, that is, for us, the most convincing rationale for embracing a point of view that appreciates and fosters the powers within and around the individual. The authors also hope that you have found some tools to assist you in the promotion of the health, resilience, and narrative integrity of your clients. But, in the end, what will convince you to stay with this perspective is the "spark" that you see in people when they begin to discover, rediscover, and embellish their native endowments. That spark fuels the flame of hopeful and energetic, committed and competent social work.

REFERENCES

American Psychiatric Association (1994). *Diagnostic and statistical manual of mental disorders IV.* Washington, D.C.: American Psychiatric Association.

Benard, B. (1994, December). *Applications of Resilience.* Paper presented at a conference on the role of resilience in drug abuse, alcohol abuse, and mental illness, Washington, D.C.: National Institute on Drug Abuse.

Cousins, N. (1989). *Head first: The biology of hope.* New York: Dutton.

Freire, P. (1973). *Pedagogy of the oppressed.* New York: Seabury.

Goffman, E. (1961). *Asylums.* New York: Doubleday/Anchor.

Hillman, J., & Ventura, M. (1992). *We've had one hundred years of psychotherapy and the world is getting worse.* San Francisco: HarperSanFrancisco.

Kondrat, M. E. (1995). Concept, act, and interest in professional practice: Implications of an empowerment perspective. *Social Service Review, 69,* 405–428.

Kovel, J. (1981). *The age of desire: Reflections of a radical psychoanalyst.* New York: Pantheon.

Mills, R. (1995). *Realizing mental health.* New York: Sulzburger & Graham.

Moore, T. (1992). *Care of the soul.* New York: HarperCollins.

Ornstein, R., & Sobel, D. (1987). *The healing brain.* New York: Simon & Schuster/Touchstone.

Peele, S. (1989). *The diseasing of America: Addiction treatment out of control.* Lexington, MA: Lexington/DC Heath.

Pert, C., et al. (1985). Neuropeptides and their receptors: A psychosomatic network. *Journal of immunology, 135* , 820–826.

Rapp, C. A. (in press). The strengths model: Case management with people suffering from severe and persistent mental illness. New York: Oxford University Press.

Rosaldo, R. (1989). *Culture and truth: The remaking of social analysis.* Boston: Beacon Press.

Schön, D. A. (1983). *The reflective practitioner*. New York: Basic Books.

Taylor, J. (1993). *Poverty and niches: A systems view*. Chapter 14, this volume.

Walzer, M. (1983). *Spheres of justice*. New York: Basic Books.

Weil, A. (1995). *Spontaneous healing*. New York: Knopf.

Werner, E., & Smith, R. S. (1982). *Vulnerable but invincible*. New York: McGraw-Hill.

Werner, E., & Smith, R. S. (1992). *Overcoming the odds*. Ithaca, NY: Cornell University Press.

Wilber, K. (1995). *Sex, ecology, and spirituality: The spirit of evolution*. Boston: Shambhala.

Wright, B., & Fletcher, B. (1982). Uncovering hidden resources: A challenge in assessment. *Professional Psychology, 13*, 229–235.

Selected Bibliography on Strengths and Resilience

Anthony, E. J., & Cohler, B. J. (Eds.). (1987). *The invulnerable child*. New York: Guilford.

Benard, B. (1991). *Fostering resiliency in kids: Protective factors in the family, school, and community*. San Francisco: Western Regional Center for Drug-free Schools and Communities.

Clark, M. D. (1996). Brief solution-focused work: A strengths-based method for juvenile justice practice. *Juvenile and Family Court Journal, 47,* 57–65.

De Jong, P., & Miller, S. D. (1995). How to interview for client strengths. *Social Work, 40,* 729–736.

Gutierrez, L., & Nurius, P. (Eds.). (1994). *Education and research for empowerment practice*. Seattle, WA: Center for Policy and Practice Research, School of Social Work, University of Washington.

Journal of Emotional and Behavioral Problems: From Risk to Resilience, 3(1994, Summer).

Kagan, J. (1984). *The nature of the child*. New York: Basic Books.

Kaplan, L., & Girard, J. (1994). *Strengthening high-risk families: A handbook for practitioners*. New York: Lexington Books.

Kondrat, M. E. (1995). Concept, act, and interest in professional practice: Implications of an empowerment perspective. *Social Service Review, 69,* 405–428.

Kretzmann, J. P., & McKnight, J. L. (1993). *Building communities from the inside out*. Evanston, IL: Northwestern University, Center for Urban Affairs and Policy Research.

Masten, A. S. (1994). Resilience in individual development: Successful adaptation despite risk and adversity. In M. C. Wang & E. W. Gordon (Eds.), *Educational resilience in inner-city America* (pp. 3–25). Hillsdale, NJ: Erlbaum.

McLaughlin, M. W., Irby, M. A., & Langman, J. (1994). *Urban sanctuaries: Neighborhood organizations in the lives and futures of inner-city youth*. San Francisco: Jossey-Bass.

Miller, S. D., & Berg, I. K. (1995). *The miracle method: A radically new approach to problem drinking*. New York: Norton.

Mills, R. (1995). *Realizing mental health*. New York: Sulzberger & Graham.

Muller, W. (1992). *Legacy of the heart: The spiritual advantages of a painful childhood.* New York: Simon & Schuster.

Parsons, R. J., & Cox, E. O. (1994). *Empowerment-oriented social work practice with the elderly.* Pacific Grove, CA: Brooks/Cole.

Saleebey, D. (Ed.). (1992). *The strengths perspective in social work practice.* White Plains, NY: Longman.

Saleebey, D. (1996). The strengths perspective in social work practice: Extensions and cautions. *Social Work, 41,* 296–305.

Selekman, M. (1991). The solution-oriented parenting group: A treatment alternative that works. *Journal of Strategic and Systematic Therapies, 10,* 36–49.

Sullivan, W. P., & Rapp, C. A. (1994). Breaking away: The potential and promise of a strengths-based approach to social work practice. In R. G. Meinert, J. T. Pardeck, & W. P. Sullivan (Eds.), *Issues in social work: A critical analysis* (pp. 83–104). Westport, CT: Auburn House.

Weick, A., & Saleebey, D. (1995). Supporting family strengths: Orienting policy and practice toward the 21st century. *Families in Society, 76,* 141–149.

Weick, A., Rapp, C. A., Sullivan, W. P., & Kisthardt, W. (1989). A strengths perspective for social work practice. *Social Work, 344,* 350–354.

Werner, E., & Smith, R. S. (1992). *Overcoming the odds: High risk children from birth to adulthood.* Ithaca, NY: Cornell University Press.

Wolin, S. J., & Wolin, S. (1993). *The resilient self: How survivors of troubled families rise above adversity.* New York: Villard.

Index

Contributors

Bonnie Benard, M.S.W., has been a prevention specialist with the Western Center for Drug-Free Schools and Communities at WestEd in San Francisco since 1990. The research editor of the new journal, *Resiliency in Action*, and a consultant with Resiliency Associates in Berkeley, Calif., she has provided to practitioners and policy makers research support and conceptual frameworks for addressing and understanding prevention and youth development issues. In 1992, she received the Award of Excellence from the National Prevention Network and in 1995, the Paul Templin Award for Service from the Western Regional Center for Drug-Free Schools and Communities.

Mary Bricker-Jenkins is a mother, farmer, writer, and social worker in public practice. Born and bred in New England, educated on the streets of New York, she now makes her home in the hills of Tennessee at WIT'S End Farm. During the academic year, she teaches at Temple University in Philadelphia and does political work with people who are homeless.

Ronna Chamberlain, Ph.D., director of the office of Social Policy Analysis at the University of Kansas School of Social Welfare, first learned of the importance of a strengths perspective 20 years ago and has been a devotee since. One of the originators of the school's Strengths Model of Case Management, Dr. Chamberlain has continued to experiment with applications of the strengths model and is now particularly interested in its usefulness in developing social policy.

Rosemary Chapin, Ph.D., associate professor, University of Kansas School of Social Welfare, has extensive research, policy, and program development experience in the long-term care arena. For the past 12 years, she has been involved in research, training, and technical assistance to help craft more effective state long-term care systems. She teaches "social policy" and "social work and aging." The use of the strengths perspective in long-term care case management is an important component of both her teaching and research efforts.

Charles Cowger, Ph.D., is on the faculty at the University of Illinois School of Social Work where he has served in various administrative capacities during the past decade. He now teaches group work, community organization, and research. International social development occupies much of his time. He is the first vice-president of the Inter-University Consortium for International Social Development. Other interests include woodworking, canoe backpacking, and pottery.

Becky Fast, M.S.W., is the project coordinator of elder care research and training at the School of Social Welfare, University of Kansas. This position includes developing and providing training on strengths-based practice. She is the primary author of a strengths model curriculum and training program for case managers working with older adults. Prior to her current position, she evaluated long-term care policies and practices and provided technical assistance to administrative and field staff working in the public long-term care system in Kansas.

Howard Goldstein, D.S.W., is professor emeritus at the Mandell School for Applied Social Science at Case Western Reserve University. Professor Goldstein now lives in Maine and continues a most distinguished career as a scholar, educator, and practitioner. He has received the Richard Lodge Memorial Prize for his contributions to social work theory. Professor Goldstein's most recent book, *The Home on Gorham Street and the Voices of Its Children*, is a social history and ethnography giving voice to the elders—once wards of the home, an orphanage—who tell what it was like growing up there.

Gary E. Holmes, Ph.D., C.R.C., is a rehabilitation counselor and counselor educator. He has taught various counseling and rehabilitation courses in the past few years. He is interested in using the strengths perspective from social work as a philosophy of practice in other human service fields. He is also interested in approaches to practice that empower clients.

Walter Kisthardt, M.S.W., is an instructor and the director of Case Management Training and Technical Assistance at the University of Kansas School of Social Welfare. Mr. Kisthardt has been involved in the development, research, and dissemination of the strengths model of case management, now recognized by the National Institute of Mental Health as one of the prevailing approaches in the nation. He has provided training in the strengths model throughout Kansas, in 42 other states, and in England over the past 8 years. He has published numerous articles and book chapters on different aspects of the strengths model.

Richard C. Rapp, M.S.W., is a co-investigator and project director of the Continuing Studies of Case Management Enhancements Project and assistant professor in the Wright State University School of Medicine. He received his Master's from Indiana University and has extensive research, teaching, and clinical experience in the areas of substance abuse and mental health. Mr. Rapp has written and presented widely on topics of substance abuse, mental health, adolescent problems, and student/employee assistance programs.

Dennis Saleebey, D.S.W., is professor and chair of the Ph.D. program at the School of Social Welfare, University of Kansas. Much of his writing has critically reflected on the epistemology of the professions and of social work and explored alternative approaches to professional knowing and doing. He has also written on the necessity of incorporating biological knowledge into the biopsychosocial framework of social work practice. For the last 6 years, he has been project director of KU Outreach, a community development program in public housing.

W. Patrick Sullivan, Ph.D., is an associate professor at the Indiana University School of Social Work and has served as the director of the Indiana Division of Mental Health since September 1994. Previously, Dr. Sullivan was on the faculty at Southwest Missouri State University, where he received the S.M.S.U. award for outstanding scholarship. His research and writing is in the areas of severe, persistent mental illness, alcohol and substance abuse, and rural social work. He was case manager in the strengths model pilot project at the University of Kansas, and has since done training all over the country in the strengths approach.

James Taylor, Ph.D., is a professor at the School of Social Welfare, University of Kansas. A clinical and community psychologist by training, his current work and research is mainly concerned with crime, violence, and the criminal justice system. His publications (as senior author) include *Community Worker* (Aronson, 1975), *Tornado! A Community Responds to Disaster* (University of Washington Press, 1970), and *Using Computers in Social Agencies* (Sage, 1981).

Ann Weick, Ph.D., is dean and professor at the School of Social Welfare, University of Kansas. Her publications have focused on a variety of topics related to social work theory and practice. These have included essays and articles on human development theory, women's issues, health and healing, and the development of the strengths perspective.